THE FATE OF IDEAS

ROBERT BOYERS

THE FATE OF IDEAS

SEDUCTIONS

BETRAYALS

APPRAISALS

COLUMBIA UNIVERSITY PRESS

NEW YORK

Columbia University Press
Publishers Since 1893
New York   Chichester, West Sussex
cup.columbia.edu

Library of Congress Cataloging-in-Publication Data
Boyers, Robert.
  [Essays. Selections]
  The fate of ideas : seductions, betrayals, appraisals / Robert Boyers.
      pages cm
  Includes bibliographical references and index.
  ISBN 978-0-231-17380-3 (cloth : alk. paper) — ISBN 978-0-231-53989-0 (electronic)
  1. Philosophy, Modern—20th century. 2. Intellectual life—20th century.
3. Literature, Modern—Themes, motives. I. Title.
  B29.B69 2015
  810.9'0054—dc23

                                                               2014042956

Columbia University Press books are printed on permanent and durable
acid-free paper.
This book is printed on paper with recycled content.
Printed in the United States of America

c 10 9 8 7 6 5 4 3 2 1

Cover photograph: Edmund Kesting / © The Cleveland Museum of Art
© 2015 Artists Rights Society (ARS), New York/VG Bild-Kunst, Bonn.
Cover design: Lisa Hamm

References to websites (URLs) were accurate at the time of writing.
Neither the author nor Columbia University Press is responsible for URLs
that may have expired or changed since the manuscript was prepared.

FOR PEG BOYERS,

ALWAYS AND AGAIN,

AND FOR OUR DEAR FRIENDS

ORLANDO AND ANITA PATTERSON

CONTENTS

ACKNOWLEDGMENTS

Grateful acknowledgment is made to the following publications in which several chapters of this volume first appeared—though in most cases the earlier periodical versions have been substantially altered and enlarged for purposes of this book: *The New Republic, The Yale Review, Raritan, Virginia Quarterly Review, Agni, Salmagundi, Lapham's Quarterly, The Common Review, Twentieth Century Literature, The Normal School, Contemporary Psychoanalysis*.

Acknowledgment is also made to the following beloved former students at Skidmore College, who read and responded to chapters-in-progress of this book and inspired me to complete it: Hillary Reder, Catherine Pond, Hilary Reid, Daniel Kraines, Matthew Straus.

THE FATE OF IDEAS

INTRODUCTION

By its very nature, criticism is personal.

—GEORGE STEINER

What we possess . . . are the fragments of a conceptual
scheme, parts which now lack those contexts from which
their significance derived.

—ALASDAIR MACINTYRE

Ideas are the canned goods of intellectuals. So declared Saul
Bellow's character Moses Herzog fifty years ago. Back in those
days, in the 1960s, there were all sorts of new ideas in circulation, more than a few of the crackpot variety, though that didn't
stop them from winning hearts and minds. Lots of what Bellow
called "cant and rant." Alienation was then much in vogue, and
authenticity, and the new sensibility, and black power, and one-
dimensionality, and polymorphous perversity. Of course every
period has its catchwords and big ideas, and you can always smile,
in retrospect, a knowing and superior smile. But those of us who
came of age in the sixties were convinced that our seed time was
uniquely marked by ideas more thrilling and dangerous than
those of any other time. Of course we learned—in several cases
only decades later—to our mingled amusement and distress that
we had not properly understood many of those thrilling ideas,
and of course many of them rapidly became clichés, dead and

anesthetizing. Sticky and delectable, those apparently clever ideas, aimed especially at minds eager and willing to be violated.

No doubt everyone drawn to ideas has stories to tell about infatuation and remorse. The shelf-life of ideas tends often to be very short, and the experience of disinfatuation, however often repeated, rarely teaches the average buyer to beware and desist. Most of us wouldn't know what to do with ourselves without feeding on fresh supplies of ostensibly new and—so we tell ourselves—challenging ideas. For intellectuals especially self-respect seems to require what is called "the open mind," which usually turns out to be a mind defenseless against the claims of the new.

This is not to say that we care only for unfamiliar ideas. There are always, for those inclined to this sort of thing, variations on the venerable. Though Duchamp created a genuine revolution in the way we think about art and its relation to ordinary reality, legions of younger artists recycling what are by now tried and true ideas continue to believe that every extravagant or willfully provocative installation they contrive, no matter how inane, is a contribution to the ongoing "revolution," though it is now a hundred years old. Some ideas—think "revolution"—apparently never die. Or almost never. They go on, if only because they have become an essential aspect of someone's self-definition, transformed into attitudes or postures largely without significant content in spite of the meanings they had for those once capable of finding them disturbing or deranging.

Many of the ideas we have used to ask serious questions about ourselves or to tell the difference between one sort of thing or another come to seem out of reach, or change so drastically that they become unrecognizable. If you don't think that this is so, try saying the words "masscult" or "midcult" and you will confront the fate of ideas once thought—certainly by people of my generation—to be compelling and meaningful but now all but unthinkable. Or urge the merits of "disinterested" inquiry in a humanities classroom or graduate seminar and note that your students are puzzled, unable to understand why a teacher would urge on them an "objectivity" that can only be delusional. How is it, asks Jerome Neu, "that pride has gone from being one of the traditional seven deadly sins to becoming, in recent decades, the banner under which social movements [like Black Pride and Gay Pride] have declared their objectives?" Everywhere ideas whose meanings we thought we knew turn out to be more, or less, or other than we had supposed. When it comes to ideas, no center can hold. Changes in social structure, in the arts and sciences, in the way we think and argue and teach, in self-fashioning and concepts of identity, make it all but inevitable that even the most familiar and apparently durable ideas will come to seem unstable or will vanish more or less entirely from view.

Of course there is no single trajectory or pattern that will allow us to map the general rise and fall or transformation of ideas. Some die a natural death when they cease to answer to the concerns of the moment. Thus we no longer talk about the so-called domino theory, which dominated discussions of American intervention in Vietnam back in 1964. Many of the ideas that generated controversy at that time have passed away or survive only in name. Who can any longer think of "national liberation" in the way it was conceived by most progressive intellectuals in the sixties? Once a term that signified the optimism associated with the freeing of subject populations from colonial or neocolonial oppression, it is now more likely to be used—if at all—to signify the blasted hopes of people who believed that the winning of their own autonomous national identity would bring them the life they deserved. Though the idea of liberation remains attractive in selected contexts, and several countries—in Latin America, for example—have successfully slipped the yoke of imperial oppression or dictatorship, the idea of national liberation is now shadowed by a general awareness of disappointment and setback, of false hope and unacknowledged risk.

In some respects more puzzling and compelling than ideas that die or hang on in a sort of half-life are ideas that seem infinitely various and lend themselves to wildly disparate uses. Think, for example, of liberty, as employed by John Stuart Mill in 1859, and then as taken up by generations of thinkers of every conceivable political affiliation. Who is not an advocate of "liberty"? The devout fellow who takes an ostensibly principled stand against the right of gay people to marry insists that he is defending the liberty of decent heterosexual persons to preserve their long-standing conception of marriage as an institution available only to people like themselves. Or think of the contemporary French philosopher Alain Badiou, whose conception of liberty is the delirious "collective emancipation" represented by "Bolshevism in Russia, from 1902 to 1917," "the first sequence of the Iranian revolution," and "the great Cultural Revolution in China." Though Mill, and before him John Locke, believed that liberty was fully compatible with the right to private property and the existence of laws to protect against infringements on that right, others have argued, in the name of "equality," that private property is theft and inimical to any legitimate idea of liberty. Even Locke, who provided the foundation for our ideas of liberty in a democratic order, did not advocate toleration for atheists, who could not be counted on to honor the social contract that alone defends the liberty of all. Much the same sort of argument is heard at the present time from persons who support restrictions on the rights of Muslims in the interests of maintaining liberty for everyone else.

Perhaps no idea has attracted as many different interpretations as the idea of faith. Like liberty, it bears on many other ideas no less important— ideas associated with truth, and obligation, and authority, and the meaning of life. Of course, it is never possible to grasp with perfect assurance what we mean by "faith." Nietzsche set the direction for much contemporary discussion when he wrote that " 'Faith' means the will to avoid knowing what is true." But this was not, obviously, what the faithful had in mind when they avowed their belief in God, and even now Nietzsche's formulation will seem, to believers at least, unduly provocative and an expression of a radical misunderstanding.

There was a time, not so very long ago, when the death of God proclaimed by Nietzsche seemed all but a settled fact, and few prominent writers or intellectuals—the exceptions come readily to mind—outside of theological institutions professed to have much interest in matters of faith. When Freud published his little book on *The Future of an Illusion* in 1927, he could suppose that he was addressing an audience at least receptive to the idea that belief in God belonged principally to persons immature or underdeveloped, people who had not been properly analyzed, or who had been so thoroughly conditioned in childhood that they were unable to think, like adults, for themselves. But God has made a comeback in several Western countries, and the number of prominent Americans nowadays professing to varieties of religious belief is quite astonishing. The idea of faith has undergone some drastic revision, to be sure, but it remains, in signal respects, the very idea embraced by nineteenth-century thinkers like Cardinal John Henry Newman, who understood that faith was at risk in a climate of liberal ideas and needed somehow to be defended against the wild and unpredictable intellect of unbelievers. Recent thinkers, from Alasdair MacIntyre and Charles Taylor to Terry Eagleton and Marilynne Robinson, have sought to make a case for belief that would seem untenable to Newman but derives from an instinct to defend what must surely seem to nonbelievers indefensible. Eagleton in fact removes faith from any kind of doctrinal orthodoxy. He thinks of faith not as a belief in miracles or in godly intervention but as an experience of "commitment and allegiance." He and others like him insist that the idea of faith be associated with a "something" but not with a God who may be said to "'exist' as an entity in the world." And in this way an idea long held to entail at least a small number of certifiably stable convictions is changed, utterly, into another sort of idea—a better idea, it may be, but no longer what it was.

Often, where ideas seem to us opaque, out of reach, we look to our own intimate experience in the hope of getting to the bottom of our dilemma. We try, as it were, to construct a narrative that can potentially accommodate some version of the thing that seems, as a mere concept or principle, alien or forbidding. Is it possible, I want to ask, that a devout nonbeliever, who is intellectually cut off from thinking about faith as he would hope to do, might nevertheless, in his very bones, truly know what it means to be faithful? Am I, in fact—so I may wish to ask—a faithful person, one who believes in things—some things—even where he has no rational ground for believing in them? Are there, in my experience, objects of belief that seem to me sacred and that thereby unaccountably claim my allegiance? Are there mysteries to which I respond? If the idea of faith can be extended to "commitment" and "allegiance," as a new theist like Eagleton has it, with God and church nowhere in sight, why should not my own experience have brought me to faith in its most convulsive, nonsectarian sense? Or is this kind of self-interrogation, this opening to subjectivity and the "merely personal," a futile exercise?

Certainly the philosophers, for the most part, do not accept that mere experience or subjective intuition can conceivably furnish genuine access to things of the spirit, to the absolute and unconditional. And yet many of us are now inclined to honor the authority of experience and, more particularly, of witness. We avow that what we see, and deeply feel, and compulsively reflect on, as if it were a constitutive aspect of our very being, is all that we can reliably know. Of course theorists are around to remind us that passionate hearts are often misled by their intimate experience of ordinary life, that instances and examples and feelings are not proofs. And yet many of us insist on the potential uses, if not the authority, of personal, subjective impression. I may not believe that general laws of behavior may be drawn from what are essentially personal accounts of experience, including my own, but I do often rely on such accounts to check my own sometimes undue investment in ideas to which I am tempted. And I can't help thinking here of the many thinkers who have themselves resorted to confession, or the personal, and understood what benefit lay in that recourse.

The chapters of this book are essayistic. They are attempts to investigate, to find a path through selected ideas without pretending to anything remotely definitive or comprehensive. My objective here is to dramatize my encounter with ideas the better to identify what has made them difficult and elusive, sometimes dangerous. Dangerous to whom? To me, to others, for whom the ideas have sponsored attitudes whose consequences we have not always been willing to acknowledge. Because one purpose of this book is to examine how ideas change, or die, and come to be misunderstood, I have had to look carefully at what they have meant not only to me but to others. And so the chapters do in fact move between a reflection on ideas in their common, or prevalent, or traditional meanings and an inquiry into the present status of those ideas, their meaning for me and, I expect, for others as well.

But let me not bring this introduction to a close without briefly returning to my own quandaries where the idea of faith is concerned, and to the Victorian sages, however unfashionable, for a way through, or into, those quandaries. For I want, again, to bear witness to the difficulty of ideas, to the troubles we have when we attempt to ask what they amount to.

What do they say? In effect, that belief may be understood as a matter of disposition. If you are disposed, as it were, not to be talked out of a belief, then to some degree you are a believer. Newman, for example, writes the following: "I need not add what a cruel and despicable part a husband or a son would play, who readily listened to a charge against his wife or his father." Though he does not quite spell it out, he would appear to be thinking here, in the case of the wife, of a charge of infidelity. Bizarre, perhaps, to reach for words like "cruel and despicable" to describe the willingness of a husband to listen to such a charge, whoever brought it. And yet the proposition does compel at least some reflection. For what, in fact, would be a more suitable response? The implication here, and elsewhere in the Victorian framework of moral reflection, is that not only delicacy but faith would forbid the disposition to "readily" listen to such a charge. You would feel, would you not, that to do so would be to dishonor your wife and to concede that the ground of your loyalty and affection was paltry. To credit the charge would be to declare your own judgment in a sacred matter not only faulty but baseless. If, Newman suggests, we are to think the idea of faith applicable to us in our relations not only with God but with another human being, then the charge of infidelity would have to be repudiated at once with the full force of our conviction. Else nothing should be for us sacred.

Whenever I present this little thought experiment to my students, in a course in Victorian literature and culture, I find them shocked and appalled. Newman's reasoning seems to them willfully stupid. Would not an intelligent person, they ask, at once move to discover evidence to con- firm or disprove the charge? How can it be thought reasonable simply to dismiss it as if it could not conceivably be true?

Alright, I then propose. But how would you then go about amassing evidence? Would you confront your spouse with the charge? Hire a detec- tive to follow her about? Suspiciously study her every gesture and word so as to uncover clues? Would you be willing, in fact, on the basis of mere rumor or allegation, even on the basis of evidence promised if you would but "readily" listen to it, to renounce your faith in your spouse and thus proceed as if faith had nothing to do with your bond? Would you think it trivial to consider that your own breach of faith might well fatally pollute the relation most vital and dear to you?

No doubt we have, each of us, many ways of thinking about this, none of them, in themselves, adequate. For we are confronted once again—if we are willing to consider a view by no means restricted to a church- man like Newman—with the incommensurability of faith and reason. The demand for evidence is inimical to the idea of belief where belief is clearly not based on indisputable proof. To begin to come to terms, however provisionally, with the idea of faith is to try at least to imagine what it feels like to think oneself faithful and, in some fundamental way, to be possessed by one's faith. Yes, of course, we know that we want also, always, to be reasonable creatures and to be dispassionate about ideas, especially those that have a singular claim on us. But we do not want to pretend to an understanding of ideas whose several implications, whose singular force we have not grasped or felt. Newman's approach to the idea of faith—one of many tentative approaches he made in the course of his career—forces us, forces me, to imagine as I think I must if I am to get anywhere with an idea that remains for me tempting and forbidding in more or less equal measure.

And so the book I have written, sometimes personal, sometimes polemical, is not a history of ideas but a series of interrogations and probes in which imagination plays a central role. Its object is an opening onto ideas that cannot be neatly encompassed. The fate of ideas, as revealed to me in this book, is to lead me this way and that, while the ideas themselves seem now compelling and elsewhere inadequate, the product of minds sometimes fine and penetrating but too often foolish or willfully innocent of reality. Though at times in the writing of this book I have felt my own middling, sensible good nature an obstacle to the sort of relentless inquisition required of me, memory and imagination have reliably come to my rescue. Essential faculties, those. I think here of W. H. Auden, who said of Freud that all he did, really, was to remember like the old and to be honest like children.

Memory, honesty, imagination. Without those faculties where would we be? Without remembering how an idea has misled us, or caused an entire generation to embrace an illusion, how to get to the bottom of the instinct informing that idea? Without imagining the likely consequences of an idea too blithely or dogmatically embraced, how project its capacity to take hold of us, to provide us with a delusional or abject comfort? My old friend, the psychoanalyst Leslie H. Farber, used to say that anxiety was the result of willing what cannot be willed. In the domain of ideas, anxiety is most often the result of our willing that one idea or another be found sufficient to point our way through the world, to dispel uncertainty. It is the fate of ideas to be often tempting in this way, and of ordinary beings like ourselves to demand of them that they provide consolation, even on occasion a tolerable level of excitement, but that above all they protect us from confusion.

It is not faith alone that we cling to so as to hold off doubt or misgiving. Ideas, sometimes trivial, sometimes impressive, are typically embraced in the name of understanding when frequently they serve another purpose. Farber spoke, in one essay called "Lying on the Couch," of the "familiar psychoanalytic shore" that beckoned persons like himself, therapists or patients long accustomed to moving in an environment saturated with juicy ideas ostensibly ratified by generations of practitioners. He recalled a training session in which he, an aspiring student, consistently disappointed his training analyst Frieda Fromm-Reichmann, herself a legendary analyst. Reporting to her each week on his lack of progress in handling a schizophrenic patient, and finding therefore that he had nothing new to tell her and nothing much to say that would not disappoint her, he was thrilled when she suggested that the reason he had so little to say to her was that in some way she had all along reminded him of his own mother, with whom he had unresolved "issues" and therefore a reluctance to engage. This idea was the "familiar psychoanalytic shore" that would now allow young Farber and his eminent teacher to proceed as if they had discovered a key to their relationship. Though Farber knew that in fact Fromm-Reichmann did not in any way resemble his own mother, and that the "resistance" he had displayed was simply a reflection of his failure to achieve any sort of dialogue with his own mute patient, he seized his teacher's idea of the cause underlying their own failure of relation and bought into her misleading idea of "resistance." Only much later did he manage to recover from this episode and thus to convict himself of deception. Also self-deception. "Also known as lying."

Is this not often what becomes of ideas? That too often they deceive us and escape us in ways we are rarely equipped to understand or are determined not to understand? It is one important aspect of this book to ask that question and, where possible, to honor the ideas that do—or should—assist us to know who we are, what we have been, and what we rightly despise or admire.

[1]

AUTHORITY

KENT: You have in your countenance that which I would fain
        call master.
LEAR: What's that?
KENT: Authority.

An old teacher of mine once told me that you know authority when you see it. Know it the way you know things you don't have to understand to believe they're real. You hear it in the sound of a voice, familiar or unfamiliar, and when you hear it, it's impossible to mistake it for anything else. Lacking any gift for it yourself, you can't readily imagine how to get it or communicate it. Try, with all your might, to put it on, to assume a commanding accent and pretend you had it all along, and no one will fall for it. Forms or versions of authority may be contested or denied, but when authority claims you it can only seem indisputable.

In itself the deep, visceral acknowledgment of authority is neither good nor bad. It need not entail slavish or unthinking subordination. At its best, authority can empower and liberate. To dismiss it out of hand or instinctively subject it to ridicule is to cut yourself off from what may well be the most compelling or promising aspect of your experience. Though working through an unfortunate or neurotic relation to authority may be an essential developmental achievement for some of us, yielding to authority is not in general the sign of illness or disabling dependence. There is, there may be, in beauty a species of authority, or in understatement or scruple, or a willingness to speak truthfully when everywhere there are lies. And there is authority, too—there may be—in the example of suffering long borne, or in eloquence, or even in derangement where it is the expression of a refusal to compromise or to tolerate injustice. To bend or thrill to the authority of a superior example is, potentially at least, to aspire to do or to be better.

Of course authority is not at present much in favor. The educated tread with almost perfect indifference over a landscape littered with the remains of idols smashed and repudiated. Resentment has attained to what may well be termed the transcendent position. The standard tokens of authority provoke derision or laughter. The pronunciamentos of statesmen and leaders ring in our ears with an invariably hollow sound. The occasional inspiring exceptions, the Barack Obamas or Willy Brandts or Vaclav Havels, all rapidly disappoint and suffer our common condescension or disparagement. Little inclination anywhere to accord to authority the benefit of any doubt. Vigilance is our habit, for we are determined not to suffer the thick embrace of illusion, and authority—so we have trained ourselves to believe—is the name and the place of illusion.

There are advantages to be noted in the resistance to authority. Individuals committed to the ideals of self-reliance and self-actualization inevitably relish every opportunity to thumb their noses at the high and mighty and the conventions associated with a dominant regime. Nor is there a felt contradiction between the presumption of self-reliance and the demand for the easy accommodation of every appetite. The philosophers of self-reliance tend to expect from experience no significant obstacle to their fulfillments. Though authority is officially rejected as the recourse of the weak and unevolved, no one seriously objects to a little help now and then from the high and mighty. The adepts of self-realization are apt to spend at least a few hours each week deftly currying favor with whoever happens to be in charge of the relevant asylum.

In the history of the West it has often been noted that culture took the place of the church. Where once there was God and the faithful there came to be the exalted status of art and ideas. Among the educated classes, to be saved was to be cultivated—not, decidedly not, to know which fork to pick up at the well-laid table but which thinker or rare idea to invoke, which artist to collect or swoon over. Authority lay not in the Vatican but in the widely approved literary dictatorship of T. S. Eliot or the vanguard doctrines of Marcel Duchamp. On the way to unillusioned self-sufficiency, the detour into "culture," once the privileged domain of the few, was embraced by multitudes of the newly educated, eager for accreditation but fearful lest they seem susceptible to the exhausted spiritual goods and values peddled by church or establishment. Authority could seem compelling only in works, ideas, exemplars felt to be subversive or in some way difficult to reconcile with one's own quotidian habits or standards.

None of us can boast of any simple or single relation to authority, even where we have rejected it utterly. It is commonplace to observe that our experience of authority begins with infancy, where parental figures or surrogates loom over every aspect of our early lives and exact at least a measure of awe and obedience. But subsequent encounters with countless others cannot possibly inspire the same kind of respect or subordination. Though I can think of powerful teachers who seemed to me entirely admirable, there was never one from whom I expected or received what I got from my parents. So too does our resentment, or defiance, assume different intensities where we feel that other authority figures indulge in an abuse of power.

My wholesale disaffection from an intolerably dominating mother surely contributed to a lifelong mistrust of authority and authority figures. But I have never ceased to dream of incarnations that would seem to me legitimate and to give myself over to the sentiment of awe where I have felt moved to abandon caution. Though I can seem to myself credulous or ridiculous in the aftermath of an infatuation with one or another authority figure who has turned out to be unworthy, the appetite for masters and masterpieces seems to me a constitutive aspect of my very being. I wish to admire and, so far as possible, to be consumed with admiration. The flight from authority, however robust, seems to me often the mark of an incapacity even to imagine something higher, something out of reach, to which any one of us may, however hopelessly, aspire.

When I first wrote to Susan Sontag in 1966, she had only recently become famous in New York intellectual circles. She was in her mid-thirties, about ten years older than I, and I could think of her then not as a celebrity but as the author of essays and reviews published chiefly in a "little magazine" called *Partisan Review*. Though she did not give me what I wanted—an essay I might publish in my own, brand new little magazine called *Salmagundi*—she was willing at least to "associate herself" with our "project" and to promise "something" later on. Would she like to look at a piece I was writing on her idea of "the new sensibility"? She would read it, she told me, "when it came out" and would then, only then, let me know what she thought.

As it happened, it took a while for us to connect, really connect, but by 1974 Susan and I saw each other frequently. Though she was not thrilled with the early piece I had written about her work, she began rather quickly to distance herself a little from some of the views I had criticized, views she had seemed at least to sponsor in her early work, so that by 1974 we saw eye to eye on many matters and could build a friendship on our shared interests and our common aversion to aspects of mass culture. Though Susan had early promoted an openness to the counterculture and gave herself permission to write about science fiction and rock and roll, she was increasingly appalled at the way her early essays were embraced by people loath to make discriminations of any kind. When I interviewed her at length for *Salmagundi* in 1974, she had begun to cast a more than suspicious eye at ideas and enthusiasms she had embraced without misgiving only a few years before. Fiercely opposed to the American war in Vietnam and, forty years later, to America's war in Iraq, always a radical feminist and an enthusiast for the avant-garde, she was, at the same time, a critic of all movements and party lines and often went out of her way to pick a fight with those who shared her allegiances and inclinations.

Though my wife and I knew Susan well and occasionally saw her at her worst—peremptory, nasty, condescending, self-important—she remained for me a commanding presence, someone who inspired me often to think of how I might exceed, grow beyond, my own affinities and limitations. Her authority, for me, had as much to do with what she did as with what she was. Though I never thought her entirely lovable, I loved her, in my fashion, and had to agree with a mutual friend who said of her on one particularly tense night, when she had behaved very badly, that she could be a monster—but that she was "our" monster. An exaggeration, to be sure, but somehow right.

What this says, or may say, about authority in general is that you may find it and cling to it even where you have reason to turn away and learn to do without it. Susan was, for me, the embodiment of an authority that had everything to do with the tenor and substance of her work and the habit of intensity she could do nothing to ameliorate. At a time—the time of her time—when high seriousness had come for many of her friends to seem tedious and insupportable, she was committed to high seriousness. You saw this in almost everything she wrote. Of course she was, in her way, responsive to irony and, very occasionally, to lightness. She thought she wanted and deserved to have fun, and she wrote this down and repeated it so that no one, least of all herself, would forget it. And yet she was very much in earnest. She took things to heart and would not let them just be. A book she had just read had to be not only understood but placed. It was not only good but—trust her on this—entirely original in a significant way. That much one had to say. Or this other thing, she insisted, was the best of its kind. No one who failed to recognize this deserved to think herself discerning or intelligent. It was, to be sure, as she often repeated, tiresome to be forever rating things and ranking them, but really you couldn't just look at a film or a theater piece or dance performance and allow it to wash over you without that other labor of assessment and some sort of tallying up. Susan was a warrior of consciousness who had tried to believe it was okay to relax. Forever at odds with her own inveterate instinct to earnestness, wanting terribly not to be anything like those dour, forever judgmental Victorian sages she drove herself to disparage, she wrote and spoke as if everything she examined mattered a great deal, as if what she made of each new thing would surely matter to the rest of us about as much as it did to her. The enemy of verdicts and absolutes, she traded in them and gave no quarter to those who were easygoing or indifferent to questions of value or ambition.

Of course Susan's authority had for me also to do with a variety of related factors, only some of them associated with her unfashionable earnestness and sometimes withering, unbearable intensity. She was, after all, a writer who had made it her business to get inside things that others had found alien or unworthy. That instinct, to figure out what really was at stake in the new art of happenings, or what might be compelling in a film that seemed static or cerebral or obscure, allowed her to take us to places we had not visited before. Not seriously at any rate. We had read, perhaps, about pornography, put in our hours—happy or exasperated—with the thing itself. But Susan's essay on the subject had made a case for it, at its best, as something beyond utility and mere desecration. She had led us to the place where we might identify aspects of our very selves in our susceptibility to something loathsome or forbidding but, at the same time, exigent and powerful. She had made us feel, in much that she wrote, that there was nothing we might not examine to our profit, and that the great good gifts we would need were steadfastness of purpose and lucidity. No writer was ever more lucid than Susan, more insistent on saying exactly what she intended.

In the years since her death in December 2004, Susan has attracted a good deal of posthumous disparagement. Much of it has emerged in memoiristic pieces, most notably in a long, sometimes hilarious, sometimes petulant essay by Terry Castle in the *London Review of Books*. But these take-downs, whatever their literary merits, have served mainly to confirm Susan's status as a figure who meant a great deal to many of her contemporaries. Oddly, though, Susan's celebrity was more impressive to many of her detractors and admirers than her work as a writer. Much of the posthumous attention, after all, is focused on Susan's personality and on her efforts as a high-profile human rights activist in Sarajevo and other devastated war fronts. Those who praise her for these labors do not cite her "authority" but her bravery and persistence. Though she was, for many people, an inspiring figure, she was not—certainly not for Terry Castle and her fans—a presiding presence, one who would be felt to mark and uphold a standard of brilliance and intensity against which others in the culture might measure themselves.

In what sense, then, is it legitimate to think of Susan as a plausible embodiment of authority? Think, if you will, of the essays she devoted to intellectuals she admired. A number of these—on Walter Benjamin and Roland Barthes, on Elias Canetti and Paul Goodman, to name but a few—identified, unforgettably, what was most arresting and singular in the work of these writers. In fact, Susan's essays were especially memorable as studies in the dynamics of admiration. Her primary mission was to bear witness to her infatuation with her chosen masters. For she wished, clearly, to be ravished by the example of minds working at full throttle, and to think herself worthy of those she had singled out for her attention. Worthy, as in fit for the company of such writers. Devoted, but by no means slavishly so. Moved, but not moved to competitive envy or resentment. Fit as a colleague is fit who knows herself to have refused, like these others, to make things easy for herself, refused to aspire to merely attainable goals or popular acceptance. Refused, in effect, to relax or to aim at making a merely good or decent impression, refused to be practical or blithely forgiving or blandly tolerant. I remember thinking, on one particular evening when I had disappointed her—not for the first time—by making a lame excuse for a writer, known to both of us, who had just brought out a remarkably bad book, that she would not soon forgive me. I could read the certain verdict in her eyes: for those who make easy excuses for themselves or others, no forbearance or charity. Don't be nice, Robert, she would sometimes say to me. I like you least when you're nice.

Authority, then, a peculiar but telling species of authority. Not the more familiar cultural authority of a powerful book reviewer who confidently tells people what to think about new work, or the conventional authority of a seasoned talking head explaining the intricacies of the stock market or sagely walking us through a diplomatic conundrum. By no means the authority of an impeccably decent or lovely person who may be said to embody the wisdom of temperance, balance, unimpeachable good nature. Nor that other authority of the gifted classroom teacher impressive by dint of his mild but insistent manner, the one—as Helen Vendler said of I. A. Richards—with "the instinct of the bat, the soft inquiry of the mouse." Authority in Susan had always to do with her fierce concentration and the improbable, willing suspension of self in the approach to a powerful facing consciousness. No compulsory sweetness, nothing benign, no gentle will to exemplify the exemplary. No sense in anyone who revered her that she would inevitably be good for us, that she would make us better than we were. But a sense, nevertheless, that we would wish to be worthy of the interest—large or small—that she took in us and in the works of others. I cannot ever forget the times she offered her approval of something I had written—especially when the subject was an unjustly neglected or forgotten writer—or the time she told me that my lengthy review in *The New Republic* of a novel by Thomas Bernhard was "sour" and "withholding." Did I not think, she demanded, that such a piece deserved to be held back? Did it not occur to me that a piece so obviously unresponsive to Bernhard's goals as a writer might do actual damage by preventing readers in the United States from discovering a very great and unorthodox artist?

Again, when I think of the authority I was willing to grant to Susan I cannot but associate it with her own relationship to the masters she revered. In particular, her essays on thinkers are frankly devotional but strenuous negotiations with admired, alien, seductive others. They are marked by a disarming trust in the meaningfulness of work that could seem forbidding and in the seductiveness of men and women who could seem implacable. She is entirely honest in what she calls her "willingness to serve," for here she could be, she was, a writer who wished to identify with the ardor, the drive of those she had chosen, and she therefore appropriated the most bracing and difficult ideas with the hunger of someone who needed them to breathe. She was most alive when most possessed by other writers, thinkers, texts, works of art that seemed to her perfectly ravishing and altogether, indisputably, themselves. If I could not quite match her hunger, could not be implacable as she could be, I could tell myself with little misgiving that hers was an exalted and unreachable virtue, however linked in her with flaws of character and temperament. There were times, in her presence, when I felt small and supposed that it was the result of her desire to cast doubt on my ambitions and to belittle my inveterate habits of courtesy and moderation. But often she inspired only that other wish to be worthy and to aspire. Never to rely on mere charm to win support or assent.

For me, Susan's authority was palpable. Often I felt that she was witness to my thoughts and confusions. She was, unmistakably, in my head a good deal of the time, and often I found myself asking what exactly she wanted of me. Often I didn't know. Often I felt her urging me in a direction I didn't quite believe was mine to take. Could I be curious as she was about everything? Could I eliminate in myself the benign disposition she somewhat deplored? When I taught my students to love Stendhal I told them that she had once described him to me as a fire that consumed itself when it is not ablaze, and of course I knew that no less might be said of Susan. But my

soul was not such a fire. I valued in myself a feeling for loyalty and obligation and balance, for qualities not entirely consonant with Susan's primary
inclinations. When she wrote in her essay on Canetti that "the message
of the mind's passions is passion," I knew that she was speaking there of
herself, and of course there was a part of me that wanted to stand with her
and Canetti and those others whose work exemplified inexorability.

Thus, in a way that was fundamental to our relationship, I thought of
Susan as the unreachable not-me, and that is how I think of her still. The
fact of her death in December 2004 did not alter that relation. She had
always, in myriad ways, chastised and provoked me. She had driven me
to think against the grain of my own disposition. When I was young and
just starting out as a writer and editor in the mid-1960s, much of her early
work seemed to me indispensable and incisive and yet given to overstatement. It gave off an air of the haughty and peremptory, and I thought I
wanted some of that, little though I could actually take it unto myself or
stifle the misgivings it invariably inspired in me. The no-but and yes-but
of an essentially fair-minded, liberal temperament was deep in me, and
yet there was Susan in effect commanding that I be less circumspect, that
I go with my enthusiasms and aversions as if they were the unanswerable
sentiments and indisputable convictions I had been put on earth to tell.

I suppose my ambivalence in part explains why, in those same years
and ever since, I have also been responsive to the call and example of very
different critical voices. No need here to tell those other stories, though
there are other stories of another tenor to tell. In truth, the other voices—
particularly those of Lionel Trilling and Irving Howe—were no less deep
in me and belonged to writers no less admired. But they were not voices
that commanded me to obey. They were seductive, but they seemed to
me also to emanate from a place very near to my own sensibility. They
bespoke a desire for colleagues more than the will to power. To follow
them was to participate in a conversation, sometimes heated but never
remotely badgering or coercive. Though Howe was more tempted than
Trilling to polemic, less overtly circumspect, he was at one with Trilling in
mistrusting a consensus, even an advanced or ostensibly enlightened consensus. These were thinkers alert to complacencies and on guard against
their own pieties and habitual reflexes. I could wish, with all my heart, to
do the kind of work they did so well without ever feeling them breathing

down my neck or wanting me to stand in awe of their rectitude or discernment. They were ardent not on principle, and not exactly by disposition either, but because they had their eye on things that mattered and had, as Irving said, steady work to do. It never occurred to me, in my occasional times with Trilling or in my years of friendship with Irving, to think of them as authority figures. They were, in the best sense, a part of what I was and what I thought and felt, familiars.

Of course, as Leszek Kolakowski noted in an early essay, "Nobody has ever completely emancipated himself from authority, and nobody has ever given himself up to authority completely. These are ideal types, which are realized in reality only in varying degrees." Can the two tendencies, though—emancipation and loyal, willing, mature subordination—ever be "combined and balanced or 'synthesized,'" Kolakowski asks. Perhaps they are best regarded as "complementary," in which case they will not be thought to "neutralize" one another but to coexist in a kind of permanent tension. The effect of my long relations with the work of Trilling and Howe, and with the personal example of the critical spirit they embodied, was that I felt free always to be myself and to try to do the right thing according to my own lights and temperament. I could speak truthfully without climbing onto any high horse or assuming a posture.

At the same time, I struggled with the sense that the development of my own individual powers required an exertion not easy to make, that la Sontag—as one of her detractors called her—existed somehow as a standing affront to what felt right and natural and in keeping with my own disposition. To reconcile the tensions informing my sense of vocation would have required that I thoroughly dispense with, or yield to, the voice of authority—Sontag's voice—driving me on and, in several respects, blocking my way to self-approval. Yield to it how, exactly? By yielding to the summons it represented—as if that were ever entirely possible for a person like me—, for then the will to power, to the peremptory and authoritative would have become as natural to me as the other will—my own inveterate will—to balance, moderation and generosity.

Oddly, my thinking on the matter of authority was shaped by very close encounters with Susan's former husband, the sociologist Philip Rieff, who addressed an entire book called *Fellow Teachers* to me and to my colleague Robert Orrill in the early 1970s. When, in 1966, at age twenty-four, I read his book *The Triumph of the Therapeutic*, I knew at once that it would change me, change my thinking, in fundamental ways. Like other friends of mine on the political left—I think especially here of the historian Christopher Lasch—I was astonished to find that such a work could have so large an effect on a person like me. Rieff's was an essentially conservative mind. Sontag herself often referred to him as "Casaubon," the pathetic, failed intellectual at the center of George Eliot's *Middlemarch*, who inspires, as the critic F. R. Leavis put it, "a little amusement mingling with . . . piety." But Rieff was no failed intellectual, and his work had clearly affected in enduring ways many of the best minds in the country, from Alasdair MacIntyre to Norman O. Brown and Herbert Marcuse. Though *The Triumph of the Therapeutic* was by no means a narrow polemic reducible to a simple thesis, it did consistently ask searching questions about the nature of moral authority and about a culture "changing its definition of human perfection." How to think about authority and inspirational models, Rieff asked, when "the communal ideal" had shifted from "the Saint" to "the instinctual Everyman, twisting his neck uncomfortably inside the starched collar of culture"?

No need here to engage with the figure of the so-called instinctual Everyman, who always seemed to me something of an easy stereotype Rieff had gamely adapted for his own exalted purposes. But I was very much persuaded that, in signal respects, Rieff was right. Renunciation was not any longer an aspect of the communal ideal embraced by most persons of my acquaintance. Intellectuals especially had come around to thinking renunciation foolish, a form of neurosis, while reliance on authority of any sort seemed increasingly weak and pathetic. Sontag regarded Rieff's views as nothing short of preposterous, and she often wondered at my ability to move, as it were, between my friendship with her and my attraction to the work of Rieff, if not to the man himself.

Rieff only rarely thought of authority in the standard terms furnished by Freudian psychoanalysis. Throughout his work, to be sure, there are references to id and superego and transference. He was drawn to the Freudian ideal of analysis as a way of countering or loosening the infantile demand for security and illusion. But he was more insistently invested in the question, "How are we to be saved?" and thought of culture principally "as a system of moralizing demands" which imprinted itself on human beings so that they might be "guided in their conduct." He believed that we wished to be guided, in spite of protestations to the contrary. On those rare occasions when Sontag's name came up in my face-to-face meetings with Rieff, he contended that she had managed, to her great misfortune, to believe we could live without any recourse to such guidance. And in truth she smiled when I put to her one evening at a public symposium Rieff's notion of culture as "the higher learning." Though she operated very much within the terms of higher and lesser obligations, she disparaged "the higher learning" as a strategy deployed by people like Rieff for condescending to the pleasures enjoyed by the rabble. She had no feeling whatever for Rieff's ideal of faith as "the compulsive dynamic of culture, channeling obedience to, trust in, and dependence upon authority." Though she inscribed her last book to me and my wife "in fealty" and was, in her own eyes, an essentially faithful person, she was fierce in contending that she chose to be faithful selectively and could not be commanded to be so. Especially repugnant, she felt, was Rieff's view that the laws we obeyed were sunk so deep in us that we had no choice but to obey them. So too did she reject Rieff's notion that deeply imprinted moral demands would be associated with "personifications" from which we detached ourselves only "at the terrible cost of guilt that such figures of authority exact from those not yet so indifferent that they have ceased troubling to deny them."

And yet, as I have tried here to indicate, Susan was herself compulsively drawn to "personifications" from whom she was loath ever to detach herself. Did she worship her heroes? Though she was pleased to count herself an infatuate, felt herself very much to be in thrall to thinkers like Barthes and Benjamin and to artists like Godard and Sebald, she was never, she felt, obedient. She admired Elias Canetti for his devotion to his own chosen masters, but she would never have allowed her own heroes to prescribe for her what was to be read or venerated, as Canetti allowed Karl Kraus to determine his disciple's likes and dislikes. Not for Susan Canetti's utter, delirious dependence on Kraus, his willingness, over many years, to declare "He was my conviction. He was my strength." Not for her the sense of literal obligation entailed in Canetti's feeling that "every sentence [of Kraus] was a demand" and that the obedient disciple would therefore "not doubt a single word he said." Others might have a number of different, complementary, even competing personifications to fill them up and provide an unstable sort of guidance, but Canetti's was a rapture of obligation and willing discipleship that was absolute and exclusive in a degree nowhere to be found in Susan's passionate attachments.

Was there, in her relations with her chosen authority figures, an inherent demand system to which she felt inexorably summoned? Susan was, much of the time, in flight from the sense of obligation and from the guilt attendant on actual or imagined derelictions of duty. A moral demand system, she felt, was dangerous and unappetizing in the degree that it rested on what Rieff called interdicts, and on the enslavement to the authority figures who upheld and embodied them. For interdicts were the consensually agreed upon thou-shalt-nots without which, in Rieff's view, there could be no culture worth the having.

By contrast, Susan was often powerfully attracted to the transgressive, to waywardness and possibility. She marveled at those of her contemporaries who had little or no interest in the past, at artists and academics who had learned to be disdainful of the traditional canon, and yet she was unwilling to accord to tradition any binding authority over her or anyone else. She was as alert as Rieff to what he called "arrogant stupidities parading as originality," but she was, much more than he, a friend to the new and much less inclined than he to acknowledge the self-evident. She not only tolerated but craved, in the domains of art and thought, "the instabilities that are the modern condition," as Rieff termed them.

When I think of my long relation to Susan as an authority figure alternately feared and gratefully embraced, I cannot regret the difficulty that relation entailed. If therapy is, as Rieff had it, "the process by which a person is detached from devotion to an authority figure," I can only give thanks that I did not seek in therapy any definitive detachment from the species of devotion she inspired. Though I was frequently tempted to end relations with Susan, to escape the varieties of discomfort she caused me, I felt in her an odd dependence on me and on others whose loyalty she sought. When she phoned me at home one morning and asked if my wife and I might not come down "tomorrow" from Saratoga Springs to New York to "support" her at her "graduation" from a "smoke-enders" course, I thought yes, right: Susan will want us to bear witness to a protocol both meaningful and preposterous. She will want us to laugh about the strangeness of the thing and to remember always that she could stand and declare herself, in a room full of strangers and fellow sinners, one who had been a smoker and had managed to "cure" herself, and was—however improbably—proud to say so. In a degree that was not easy to fathom, Susan required some semblance of fellowship from the circle of people who found her not merely fascinating but by turns vulnerable and impossible. She was, for all her apparent conviviality and the access she had to the best and liveliest minds of her generation, a lonely person who needed loyal friends who could be counted on to love her in spite of what she routinely put them through. That sense of her neediness sustained me in times when she was at her imperious worst and never got in the way of that other sense of her as a commanding and exemplary presence.

Occasionally an authority figure—call this one benevolent—"prepares the disciple to be as his own master," Rieff writes. But then Susan was by no means invariably benevolent, and I was never in the orthodox sense her disciple. Susan was a charismatic figure of a peculiarly modern sort, one who did not overtly sponsor submission to established laws or obligations but seemed instead to operate outside of any conventional idea of submission. Rieff ridiculed contemporary "charismatics"—among whom he would surely have included Susan—who urged upon their followers openness and an experimental relationship to life itself, for their example would then inspire no particular loyalty to any lofty objective and summon the susceptible only to "feverish activity" designed "to demonstrate how alive they are." The best a Sontag might produce, in Rieff's sense, was a circle of the like-minded in which each would feel "free at last to be his or her own prophet without a message." Freedom, therefore, "in the name of nothing." Susan's attractiveness for persons like me was thus, in these terms, a function of "charisma as an amoral category of authority." Such affiliation could then only serve "to deal a critical blow to the very basis of authority." So Rieff believed.

Again and again Rieff railed against what he called "the therapeutic," which entailed, among other things, the communication of messages or examples that had "no claim to endure and set the direction of our conduct." He wanted genuine authority figures committed to "soul-making procedures" that would sink the laws within us so deep down that they would become "unconscious" and not subject to our volition. He deplored the "modern plenitude of orders, among which one can 'choose.'" Choices, he argued, that are not felt to be "sacred or final" can never be inspired by conceivably legitimate authorities. To have as authority figure an "anti-credal" charismatic like Susan was, by definition, to operate without a sense of laws felt to be higher than one's own instincts or desires.

But again, the situation was somewhat different from what Rieff supposed. For one thing, Susan was not "anti-credal" in the sense of believing that nothing was true, or that every assertion of value or morality was merely a matter of a Nietzschean will to power and therefore merely personal. She did, to be sure, acknowledge the force of Nietzsche's statement, in *The Gay Science*, that "we, however, want to become those we are—human beings who are new, unique, incomparable, who give themselves laws, who create themselves." But she did not suppose that we could manage this all by ourselves, or that success in feeling unique and powerful was all that we could desire. She was militant in the service of particular ends she took to be legitimate—not merely attractive—and worth fighting for. No empty militancy in Susan at all. She was always, to be sure, committed to struggle: the struggle for clarity in the face of everything lazy and ill-defined; for pleasure in the face of the felt sense of obligation to difficulty and work and self-overcoming; for masters when everywhere the very notion of masters and masterpieces was under assault, and those who had thought her simply an advocate of the new and adventurous were disappointed to find that she was ever in search of standards by which to judge herself and others. Rieff could not fathom the degree to which a person like Susan was ever responsive, not to law or orthodoxy but to an ideal of lawfulness, one to which she could be faithful, if not obedient. And he could no more fathom the mysterious hold she had on others who were moved by the combination of scruple and waywardness, fellow-feeling and intolerance, in her writing and in her personal deportment.

Rieff rejected the sociologist Max Weber's view that in the modern world authority might legitimately be embodied in "prophets" or "charismatics" who were "amoral." But Susan did not presume to be a "prophet," and she was not "amoral" in believing that all vindications of morality are necessarily irrational and personal. Of course she held that individuals are free to agree or to disagree on essential questions. But she did not hold that therefore, in the end, one view was like another, one judgment no

more or less tenable than any other. She never accepted that there were
no objectively defensible and binding standards of achievement or virtue.
Though she did not often refer to the virtues, she surely understood, in
Alasdair MacIntyre's terms, "that there is no way to possess the virtues
except as part of a tradition in which we inherit them and our understanding of them from a series of predecessors."

In other times and places that process of inheritance was more straightforward than it was for Susan. Her masters were diverse, far flung, her
hunger for worthy models ongoing. In her presence—in the presence of
her writing—one felt the intense, unsystematic drive to create a tradition worthy of her need to proclaim what was good. She could not rely
on "society" to provide for her what she needed. She did not, could not
regard the idols of the tribe as at all adequate. Though she thought it
necessary to know what was new and what passed for "advanced" among
those interested in the forward movement of art and ideas, she was often
out of step with the values and assessments of the professoriate and the
taste-makers. Susan acknowledged that she owed a great deal to the community of artists and intellectuals that had long found in her work so
much to admire. But she often, famously, rejected the established views
and practices of that community. Seated at a conference table with David
Ross, then just completing his tenure as head of the Whitney Museum,
she scorned his suggestion that "the satisfactions derived from art are
no different . . . from other kinds of satisfaction." She was, she said, "too
much of an American not to be amused" by all sorts of things, including
museums dedicated to exhibiting shoes or machine parts. But she was
unsparing in her criticism of those, like Ross, who were "driven by the
ideology of cultural democracy regnant in our corporations," museum
officials and academics who routinely reached for words like "snobbish"
or "elitist" when all they intended to say was that "no work should be
regarded as intrinsically superior." For her resistance to the dominant
views of many in her own community, this celebrant of Fassbinder and
Gombrowicz, Donald Judd and Mark Morris, Robert Mapplethorpe and
Marina Abramovic was often derided as a "cultural conservative."

In attracting that sort of derision, Susan was not so very different from
other intellectuals whose style and outlook could seem so alien to hers.
From Trilling, for example, who thought it his obligation to interrogate

the assumptions of the very liberalism to which he was, with however much ambivalence, committed. Or Irving Howe, whose long investment in varieties of political radicalism never prevented him from picking fights with his own constituency and arguing that people like himself had more to learn from the work of conservative or reactionary writers like Henry James and Dostoyevsky, or "bon vivants" like Stendhal, than from decent, well-meaning proponents of advanced, politically correct ideas.

Susan was distinctive in the sheer variety of her enthusiasms and the nearly missionary intensity she brought to her advocacy. She bore witness, in everything she did and wrote, to her belief in the significance of judgment, and she fully believed that those who did not read well, who did not apply themselves scrupulously to particular cases, were stupid or indifferent and thus incapable of either virtue or judgment. Susan's capacity for scorn, her sometimes fabulous impatience, was an expression of her fear that someone she wished to love or admire had been lax in reading a particular case or had failed to grasp the enormous importance of making a strenuous judgment, cultivating an enthusiasm, identifying a problem, being inexorable in the pursuit of the truth.

Authority, then, in her case, legitimate because derived from her sense of obligation, her allegiance to a common if also difficult good. In Western culture, Rieff argued, authority is justified as "the gift of an authority superior to the receiver of the gift." Thus Susan could be a legitimate, if limited, embodiment of authority only if those of us who received her gift took her to be also in thrall to "an authority" felt to be "superior" to her and her own instincts. That higher authority was, in one sense, the community of masters she routinely invoked, whose works she sought to get inside and possess and transmit to others. She could not be merely or principally a transgressive when she was obliged to take in and celebrate what was high or noble or beautiful or chastening in the work of others—her spiritual masters—whose authority was inscribed in the work they had granted to her as a gift of grace, bearing the ineffable spirit of their own mastery and striving and lucidity. Susan's authority—for me certainly—lay always in that sense she communicated that there was a "something higher" to which she was, in her own way, obedient and which she was obliged never to betray or cheapen.

[2]

PLEASURE

PART ONE: "THE FATE OF PLEASURE" REVISITED

> In a public Italian garden a Briton has all the things she loves
> about Italy—the sun, the food, the sky, the art, the sound of
> the language—without any of the inconvenient rules that
> attend their proper enjoyment.
>
> —ZADIE SMITH

Most of us will admit to a taste for simple pleasures. Tolstoy's
Stiva Oblonsky enjoys a good meal, a fashionable restaurant, an
unambivalent and willing governess. He has little taste for complication, and when it appears, he is unhappy and wishes to return
to the state in which simple pleasures may be simply enjoyed. If
you were to ask him about the meaning of happiness or the fate
of pleasure, he would wonder why anyone should concern himself with conceptual trifles. And in truth, even those of us with a
highly developed appetite for complexity understand all too well
Oblonsky's impatience with difficulty.

Very early in *Anna Karenina*, you will recall, Oblonsky digs
into a fabulous dinner while his companion, Konstantin Levin,
is "ill at ease and uncomfortable" in the elegant restaurant, and,
so we are told, "afraid of soiling that which filled his soul." Oblonsky tells him that "the aim of civilization is to enable us to get
enjoyment out of everything," but Levin characteristically replies,
"Well, if that is its aim, I'd rather be a savage."

Of course, there is much more to the contrast between Levin and Oblonsky, and the subject of pleasure is engaged in numerous different ways in the course of Tolstoy's novel. But there is a sense in which the scene in the restaurant nicely encapsulates the conflict over pleasure that has been an aspect of our culture over the centuries, a conflict never more sharply engaged than in the nineteenth century by writers as diverse as Keats and Browning, Flaubert and Stendhal, Tolstoy and Dostoevsky. What I take to be the classic twentieth-century essay on the subject, Lionel Trilling's "The Fate of Pleasure," ranges all the way from *The Confessions of St. Augustine* to Freud's *Beyond the Pleasure Principle,* but its chief examples are nineteenth-century poems and novels. By the time Trilling wrote his essay in 1963, the term pleasure had acquired a weight that made it seem ripe for inquiry, in a way that did not at all encompass the term happiness, which had come to seem almost quaint and archaic, no longer shimmering with any slightest prospect of revelation. Pleasure, by contrast, was again a big deal, as it had been for the Romantics and the Victorians, and though Trilling declared rather grandly, early in his essay, that "our present sense of life does not accommodate the idea of pleasure as something which constitutes the 'naked and native dignity of man,'" he is rather more ambivalent about the status of pleasure in his further reflections on the subject.

The debate over pleasure includes the obvious and the obscure. Trilling cites the standard "unfavorable" sense of the word, which emphasizes "sensuous enjoyment as a chief object of life, or end, in itself," or, even less favorable, "the indulgence of the appetite," which calls to mind "the primitiveness of the enjoyment" that will sometimes seem to us compelling or urgent. Just so, Trilling proposes, our "dignity" has often seemed, at different times in the evolution of culture, "to derive from the resistance which [we have offered] to the impulse to pleasure." What principally recommends Keats to us, therefore, is that his "intellect was brought into fullest play when the intensity of his affirmation of pleasure was met by the intensity of his skepticism about pleasure." For Keats, for Trilling, the inclination to resist pleasure principally derives from a sense that it is passing, unstable, doomed to be disillusioning. But the resistance to pleasure may have even more to do with a moral revulsion, or a spiritual reflex, inspired by the sense that the indulgence of appetite does not put us in touch with what is deepest and truest in our nature. When Levin is "afraid of soiling that which filled his soul," he is acknowledging his fear that the indulgence of appetite, the pursuit of pleasure, will diminish his sense of self and subvert his idea of what is true, genuine, and real.

Of course, the conflict between pleasure and truth (or reality) exists as well in the aesthetic realm. For a long time writers, academics, consumers of "high culture"—may I say simply "we"?—have condescended to the idea that poetry should be what Trilling calls "soothing, cheerful, healthful, [or] serene." Just so, we may add, few of us who think ourselves "sophisticated" (with however little claim on genuine sophistication) any longer uphold the view that works of art must embody positive ideas or that the pleasure we take in a painting has primarily to do with its faithfully reproducing the surfaces of ordinary reality. Pleasure, we feel, especially where works of art are concerned, has characteristically to do with the cultivation of tension, and if poets and artists have sometimes wished, as Keats had it, merely "to soothe the cares, and lift the thoughts of man," they have more frequently taught us the pleasure of resistance to the comfortable, the safe, the elementary. Trilling is at his very best in getting at the condition of our relation to pleasure in the domain of art, at least as that condition existed a half century ago. "Our typical experience of a work which will eventually have authority with us," Trilling writes, "is to begin our relation to it at a conscious disadvantage, and to wrestle with it until it consents to bless us. We express our high esteem for such a work by supposing that it judges us. . . . In short, our contemporary aesthetic culture does not set great store by the principle of pleasure in its simple and primitive meaning and it may even be said to maintain an antagonism to the principle of pleasure."

We understand Trilling entirely when we consult, with or without his assistance, the great works of nineteenth-century culture that mark a decisive break with the elementary appreciation of pleasure. Dostoevsky's underground man is, of course, one powerful embodiment of the resistance to pleasure, a figure who, as Trilling says, "has arranged his own misery . . . in the interests of his dignity, which is to say, his freedom." Instinctively, as it were, this man understands that "to want whatever it is, high or low, that is believed to yield pleasure . . . to use common sense and prudence to the end of gaining it" is to make himself "the puppet of whoever or whatever can offer him the means of pleasure." Though the objects of his disgust were not the speciously pleasing works of art that in his culture were available to soothe or flatter willing consumers, Dostoevsky's wretched figure was revolted by the reasonable and prudent, the apparently high-minded and high flown, as these qualities presented themselves to him in the rhetoric and posture of the decent people he encountered. Resistant to the beneficent, the plausible, above all to the "specious good" everywhere embraced by ostensibly decent people, the underground man exists, as it were, to challenge, or insult "the prevailing morality or habit of life." We now see, moreover, that Dostoyevsky's critique of easy or ordinary pleasures anticipated the larger modernist critique of utilitarianism, with its assumption that civilization can be efficiently organized to maximize human happiness.

The resistance to the prevailing morality, or, for that matter, to prevailing aesthetic decorums, is as evident in Tolstoy and Flaubert as in James and Melville. In *Anna Karenina,* the orchestration of the many parallel plots is such as to allow for full expression of competing insights, so that in the end no reader can feel that there is a fully satisfying resolution to any of the major problems set in motion. If a standard novelistic decorum would entail something closer to a pleasurable resolution, Tolstoy inclines instead to a permanent state of tension and misgiving. Even Levin, a figure who, we feel, by virtue of his faithful and beautiful nature, his disinclination ever to condescend, and his capacity to think well even of his enemies, clearly deserves to be happy, is permitted to thrash perpetually about, in doubt about himself and what he wants.

Just so, in *Bartleby the Scrivener,* Melville invites us to invest not in a reasonable man but in a man best understood as the embodiment of a negativity so radical as to say NO to everything: to tolerance, charity, compromise and every ordinary measure of moderate good will. And if there is some potential (if conventional) pleasure to be had in at least getting to the bottom of such a figure, Melville insists that any such pleasure be compromised by mocking all efforts at sympathetic explanation.

By contrast, the pleasure we take in so different a work as *The Charterhouse of Parma* has everything to do with Stendhal's playful handling even of the most serious matters. Murder, sexual betrayal, ecclesiastic corruption, love itself, are handled with the speed and impulsiveness of a spirit who, as Stendhal had it, "seeks to satisfy itself and not to give our neighbor a magnificent idea of our person." As readers who wish to think ourselves members of his happy few, we taste the pleasure Stendhal feels in doing as he likes and refusing to allow merely decent people to think well of him. Indifferent to the prevailing standards of novelistic construction and thoroughly unintimidated by dully predictable moral imperatives, he could write, in his preface to the novel, that his heroine is to be sure "blamable" and thus intend to say that the best of us would therefore find her irresistible. If there is tension in Stendhal, it is discernible in the persistent irony that reveals that laws and conventions are necessary principally so that men and women of spirit may subvert them. There is in Stendhal a clear antagonism toward pleasure in its elementary sense— the easy pleasure derived from abiding by prevailing standards—and a determination to fashion a work that will, in its own terms, judge us. In reading him we must decide, again and again, whether or not we are worthy to savor the frequently difficult transgressive tidbits he inexorably sets before us.

In *Madame Bovary*, of course, Emma is judged by the inferior quality of the pleasures she seeks, and we, as readers of the novel, are judged by our too ready investment in the condescension that Flaubert permits us to indulge in as he opens out for us the disappointing limits of Emma's consciousness. We are educated in our antagonism to the elementary pleasures—in this case the pleasures of easy condescension and unearned superiority—by a novel that is always in more than two minds about the very sentiments it ridicules, from exaltation to unbridled passion. Flaubert's irony is perfectly mobilized to undercut whatever elements of readerly superiority the novel permits. Our aesthetic delight thus derives from the sense that the novel is at least half in love with its pathetic infatuated heroine who displays a passionate nature we wish to admire and cannot help regarding—in this incarnation—as puerile and unfortunate.

In Trilling, the condition of aesthetic pleasure is associated, again and again, with what he calls "spiritual militancy." With confidence he asserts that nothing could be further from us than "the idea of 'peace' as the crown of spiritual struggle." A work of art conceived with the purpose of resolving conflicts or providing some unproblematic aesthetic "bliss" would "propose to us a state of virtually infantile passivity." So much is struggle the condition we insist on, Trilling argues, that those of us who belong to "the extruded high segment of our general culture" take themselves to be free from any "thralldom to pleasure," that is, to have moved beyond any desire for pleasure of a naïve or elementary kind. Not for us pretty pictures, untroubling harmonies, "positive heroes," or "affirmative" emotions. For us, the enlightened, the advanced, the aesthetic experience must release "psychic energies" that have nothing to do with "felicity." Trilling's extruded high segment of the general culture prefers unpleasure to pleasure—so he attests—and prides itself on going against the grain of the easy satisfactions embraced by other persons.

At the same time, Trilling notes, the populace, the numerous bourgeoisie, the unwashed and undereducated (hard, is it not, to deny the guilty thrill entailed in wielding these despised, thoroughly incorrect, derisory epithets) had by 1960 come to see the charm and attractiveness of the spiritual militancy that once seemed attractive only to the few. People who once scorned the difficult, the disordered, the fragmented, the radically experimental, seemed more and more to have come around to what Trilling calls the newly "accredited subversiveness" of modernist art and literature. "What was once a mode of experience of a few," Trilling writes, "has now become an ideal of experience of many," who wish to think themselves advanced, open, and brave in their attitudes toward life and art. Such a development, as we regard it from our own latter-day perspective, quite as Trilling says, "can scarcely be immune to irony." For, so we may say, we can hardly suppose that an "accredited subversiveness, an established moral [or aesthetic] radicalism," can long remain subversive or radical. As more and more people came to want their literature disturbing or difficult and the works of art they examined to be ugly or disorienting or incomprehensible, what was once genuinely challenging would inevitably come to seem commonplace, predictable, even gratifying, quite in the way that old-fashioned page turners or true-to-life portrait paintings once seemed easy and pleasurable. Perhaps not many among the so-called numerous bourgeoisie would be apt to have curled up with a volume of Pound's Cantos on a rainy weekend morning, but many surely did spend occasional Saturday or Sunday afternoons at the Museum of

Modern Art briskly moving past the Rothkos and the Barnett Newmans, delighted to abandon, briefly, the world of disreputable entertainment to which they were otherwise committed. Though modernist art and writing would continue for most of the new audience to seem more an obligation than a delicious self-indulgence, modernist works did nonetheless more and more assume the status of essential commodities.

Trilling's view of the fate of pleasure was, in fact, entirely prescient. He noted, precisely, the way that the radical and the subversive were already—by the time he wrote his great essay almost fifty years ago—changing into something else, "advancing," as he put it, "in the easy comprehension of increasing numbers of people." By the time he wrote his last book, *Sincerity and Authenticity*, a decade later, he had come to decry the lack of seriousness with which once advanced ideas were held and avant-gardism as an established principle was casually, routinely embraced even by people with no genuine feeling for art at all. It cost nothing for those "increasing numbers of people" to declare themselves enthusiasts for high modernist literature when the subversive ideas embodied in that literature were no longer regarded as dangerous or disturbing and could be embraced simply for their ability to confer on all who confronted them a delicious self-approval.

Matthew Arnold had much earlier noted, in *Culture and Anarchy*, the tendency of enlightened persons to be what he called (quoting Thomas Carlyle) "terribly at ease in Zion," that is, to be too comfortable in the precincts of advanced, unconstrained thought and to find nothing dangerous or unthinkable, nothing, that is, they could not handle, so far removed had they become from any deep sense of a sacred whose violation might actually offend them or an aesthetic decorum that might seem worth upholding and whose casual violation might arouse disgust or unease. Though Arnold did not observe exactly the tendency cited by Trilling, he was, as he might have said, on the same line a hundred years earlier.

And there we might leave matters were it not tempting to ask what—if anything—has changed in the years since Trilling published his essay on "The Fate of Pleasure." Is the condition of pleasure, in the domain of the arts at the present time, something other than it seemed to Trilling in 1963? Most of Trilling's original readership has by now disappeared along with the old *Partisan Review*. The distinctions—as between high and low, popular and avant-garde, serious and unserious—that seemed important fifty years ago are rarely invoked in what passes for contemporary cultural criticism. Nor would it be accurate to say that the disappearance of those distinctions from the discourse of contemporary criticism has largely to do with semantic preferences. Writers and intellectuals are today reluctant to invoke such distinctions because they believe them to be misleading and to promote attitudes they would prefer not to encourage. The militancy required to dismiss a certain kind of work as "popular" or "pandering" or "obvious" is rarely in evidence in our culture, where trash may be solemnly studied in the academy and accorded respect for its political content, and professors of literature no longer think it a part of their function to educate taste or to rescue their students from escapist fantasy.

Is this development worth noting? As a recent former president would say, it depends on what you mean by "worth noting." If pleasure was, not long ago, associated with the capacity—on the part of most writers, artists, and intellectuals—to maintain a certain spiritual militancy that would allow them to savor works uncommonly rigorous or demanding, works that withheld from their audience an easy or immediate gratification, and that militancy is no longer felt to have anything to do with the pleasure most of us seek, then a momentous change has surely occurred. The reluctance to invoke certain distinctions brings in its wake a progressively developing inability to make them. Thus do we see the blurring of boundaries as between one sort of thing and another, the debasement of the language of value and description into meaningless labels or the borrowing of terms that once had a particular meaning for entirely alien purposes.

Consider that the word "kitsch" may now be used to describe something banal and simply wonderful because undisguised and perhaps even boldly aware of its own banality. Likewise, consider the use of the word "evil" to mean spirited or thrilling, or "materialist" to mean bravely innocent of metaphysical pretension, or "popular" to mean honest or true because free of difficulty or large ambition. In such instances we observe not the creative deployment of language for purposes of vital expression but the emptying out of meaning from terms that actually described something real and around which serious reflections on value might actually still be freshly inaugurated.

What we get, then, is not a systematic, centrally organized cultural formation but a tendency in culture to deny the meaningfulness of terms and distinctions that enable, in the Victorian sense of the term, discrimination. We all know and accept that language is unstable, that significations and valuations inevitably change, that standards of beauty vary from one generation to another. But the tendency identified here points not simply to the inherent instability of language or the fickleness of taste but to a flight from a language geared to differentiate and evaluate and make essential choices possible. There is, undoubtedly, pleasure conceivably to be had in the contemplation of the sporadically amusing work turned out by contemporary artists like Jeff Koons, Damien Hirst, and Takashi Murakami. As Jed Perl notes, we are not, most of us, "angered by their work" but by "the significance that arts professionals are attaching to [their] work." Why be enraged by work that is occasionally "ingenious and charming" but that clearly has virtually nothing to do with art? The scandal is that the several establishments that educate students and shape the discourse on contemporary art have determined that the work most worth promoting—most apt to find favor with a broad public—will be remarkable principally for the brashness of its assertions and its instinct for what will play well with consumers primed to approve of the next new thing. Such a development can come to pass only in a climate dominated by what Perl calls "laissez-faire aesthetics." This aesthetics, Perl argues, has it that "any experience that anyone can have with a work of art is equal to any other," and that belief, in turn, is enabled by a carefully nurtured sense that meaning is entirely in the eye of the beholder, whoever he or she is, and that words and concepts can be made to signify whatever anyone wishes to make of them.

Thus Jeff Koons's stainless-steel balloon animals—"masterpieces," according to a *New York Times* critic—can be regarded, simultaneously, as insouciant (because so playfully and unsolemnly invested in the imagery of popular culture), brave (because so disdainful of old-fashioned high-art decorums and restrictions), outrageous (because so clearly an extension of the Duchampian assertion that art can be anything an artist or museum says it is), and honest (because so frankly and unapologetically pitched to an audience with an appetite for what is already commercially accredited). To study the literature generated by the Koons industry is to note how the language of value and discrimination is progressively emptied of meaning, and thus what is said to be "fresh" or "original" is actually what is calculated, and what is said to be outrageous or brash is actually audience-tested, obvious in its appeal, and entirely safe for consumption.

The pleasure associated with much of modernist art was often associated with the delectation of irony. To be sure, there were major exceptions. Mid-twentieth-century abstract art was not, for the most part, ironic, and the quality principally valued in that precinct had to do with the enactment of tension and the refusal of closure. So-called action painting "judges itself morally," wrote Harold Rosenberg, "in declaring that picture to be worthless which is not the incorporation of a genuine struggle, one which could at any point have been lost." But if irony was not at issue in the paintings of Jackson Pollock or Willem de Kooning, the evoked expression of risk and struggle in their best work pointed the way to what was essential in modernist irony. It was not an easy irony, and it afforded pleasure by virtue of its affirming difficulty and a permanent state of tension. When Thomas Mann sought in his fiction to achieve some semblance of equilibrium, he found himself confronted by irresolvable ambiguity and contradiction. Listen to the improbable words he places in the mouth of his Pharoah in one resonant passage of his Joseph tetralogy: "All your speaking," he declares to the riddling Joseph, "turns on the Yes and at the same time on the No. . . . The wrong right one, you say, and the wrong one that was the right one? That is not bad; it is so crazy that it is witty." Such words express a delight in paradox and irresolution that perfectly mirrors the pleasure a reader trained in modernism will take in the ongoing difficulty represented by works of art inhabited by contradictoriness and a will to sufficiency they yet know to be out of reach. Irony is the mark of the gap between what is willed and what is actual, between apparent adequacy of expression and a content or purpose that cannot be fully expressed. Pleasure, in the modernist sense, is typically felt when a reader or viewer is moved, or forced, to acknowledge the irony inherent in the artist's failure—however brave or genuine the enterprise—to be equal to his ambition, whether the cause has much or little to do with the recalcitrance of the artist's medium or has solely to do with the sense conveyed long ago by Browning's Andrea del Sarto: "Ah, but a man's reach should exceed his grasp, / Or what's a heaven for?"

In the domain of "laissez-faire aesthetics," however, the tension is no more and the irony, such as it is, betrays no genuine anxiety or fear of insufficiency. Pleasure, in these terms, may be had only by blithely and resistlessly giving oneself over to the spirit of a work that in itself embodies nothing in the way of struggle. Consider, in this regard, the work of the late Felix Gonzalez-Torres, featured artist at the American pavilion of the 2007 Venice Biennale and by now an iconic figure on the international art scene. Gonzalez-Torres is sometimes described as a "relational artist" whose work reaches out to viewers and invites them to participate in the "creation" of the event that is, in effect, the artwork, properly understood. The best known of the works is probably "Untitled" (Portrait of Ross), a work not unlike others that followed, featuring piles of candy, individually wrapped, which museum- or gallery-goers at various sites have been invited to take, consume, and reflect on. A friendly gesture, to be sure, and one made poignant by the carefully provided information that the installation memorializes the artist's lover, who died of AIDS, as the artist himself was to do in 1996. Thus, as the critic Jonathan Fardy had it, the work is to be understood as "a direct and very personal response to the AIDS crisis," in terms of which the innocent act of eating candy "comes to symbolize the eating of the artist's body of work. Benign eye-candy suddenly becomes food for thought. . . . Gonzalez-Torres dares his audience to take candy from a stranger with AIDS, to trust the Other and to reach out across sexual and political divides."

Presumably there is something genuine in the impulse informing such a work, and what one fan called its "succinct conceptual clarity" does pass in this domain for achievement. But what, exactly, is the pleasure entailed in the engagement with such a work? What genuine pleasure does it legitimately afford? A viewer who can be contented with the neat, formulaic transition from "benign eye-candy" to "food for thought" will not need to puzzle over such questions. Such a viewer will not register the degradation of the word "dares" in the notion that there is daring and breakthrough in the spectator's reading of an explanatory placard and consumption of a candy. Even the suggestion that the installation represents an encounter with a "stranger" or an "Other" is misleading, for the "Other" here is an all-too-familiar, thoroughly trivialized emblem of difference served up in such a way as to seem anything but menacing or unassimilable. The pleasure on offer in the Gonzalez-Torres work has everything to do with an inoffensive, uncomplicated availability. Such a work knows perfectly what it is and what it wants from its audience, and it has no reason to be in doubt about its adequacy as a vehicle for the elementary feelings it wishes to share. There is no tension at all in its sense of what matters, and it is smugly self-satisfied about the cleverness of its self-presentation. If it is ironic about the apparent disparity between the commonplaceness of candies and the loaded context of young men dying of AIDS, its handling of the irony is such as to instantly relieve any viewer of misgiving or discomfort. To give oneself to such a work is to feel, with bland self-assurance, that one has indeed, unproblematically, "reached across sexual and political divides." The so-called thought that is said to be an aspect of a viewer's experience here costs nothing, involves no exertion, and yields, at best, a pleasure that has entirely to do with self-approval.

Of course we readily acknowledge that pleasure is one of those broad terms that lend themselves to diverse uses, and not many of us would wish to deny that it can include common or coarse and unreflective delectation. But in the realm of art and thought, to arrive at the point at which most of us no longer take pleasure in resisting what is specious, or what is merely politically correct, is to arrive at a peculiar place. It may well be, in fact, that the vocabulary of aesthetic valuation has more and more come to seem, to most of us, inoperative, dead. When, late in her life, Susan Sontag described the work of the artist Matthew Barney as "coarse," she knew that she was in effect saying something that would seem to most of her audience quaint and largely meaningless. But of course Sontag intended by the word "coarse" to signify a quality in Barney's work that would necessarily limit the pleasure she might take in it, however she might be impressed by its ingenuity or scale. She was exercising her aesthetic judgment in a way that would bear on her actual experience of pleasure.

Just so, when Sontag used the term "chic" to describe a work, she meant not simply that it was fashionable but that its appeal to its audience was spurious and therefore to be resisted. She did not use the term in a narrowly denotative sense but actively welcomed its judgmental force as a term of derogation. There was pleasure for Sontag in resisting what was merely chic or obvious, and she was unimpressed by the claims of artists who argued that their work was only incidentally chic, or obvious, or coarse. Sontag's spiritual militancy did not prevent her from encouraging her readers to lighten up and have fun and embrace now and then what was elementary, delightful, or undemanding, but she insisted that we acknowledge essential distinctions and not confuse the difficult, intense pleasure we take in a Balanchine ballet or an Ingmar Bergman film with the very different, more ephemeral pleasures we permit ourselves as casual film-goers, or as revelers at a dance club, or as readers caught up in an intricate, deftly plotted mystery novel.

PART TWO: SIMPLE PLEASURE, SEXUAL PLEASURE: MYSTERIES OF THE ORGANISM

How was it that he had never taken due note of this—the beauty, power, wisdom, and justice of women's thighs?

—MARTIN AMIS, *THE PREGNANT WIDOW*

Of course I know as well as the next fellow how to say "hold on" or "not quite" to the story I have told about the fate of pleasure. It is, as I read over it, terribly high-minded. It makes perhaps too little allowance for the possibility that the so-called pleasures it describes—aesthetic pleasures, in the main—are by no means superior to the much more available and familiar pleasures I myself routinely enjoy. Why such insistent emphasis on tension and difficulty? What, after all, is the tension or difficulty I experience in the daily walks I take with my wife during a sabbatical leave in Italy? What obstructs or complicates my innocent pleasure as I take in the turning autumn leaves of the trees arched above the Tiber, the occasional domes and spires on the near or far Roman horizons an uninsistent promise of other pleasures, easily available and consumable? Why turn my nose up at the homely self-portrait we enjoyed (and almost purchased) in a tiny gallery off Piazza Santo Stefano during our most recent month in Venice—a painting by no means ambitious or original or especially expert but touching in its naïve self-assurance and straightforwardness? Why not just admit that for me there is no pleasure so intense as the one I experience when my wife and I are welcomed into the homes of our adult children and offered a bed for the night, and a home-cooked meal, and lively, sometimes contentious conversation? What has this intensity of pleasure to do with "the fate of pleasure" as I have been moved to describe it?

Perhaps I should say—if only to see what it looks like—that I am, in reality, rather a simple man. That (o the shame of it!) in many ways I have more in common with Tolstoy's Stiva Oblonsky than with the more brooding and complex and admirable Levin, for whom we named one of our sons. Perhaps I should go further and say that we are, all of us, so far as I am concerned, whatever our pretensions to the contrary, somewhat simpler than we sometimes suppose. And that we take our pleasures where we find them and, insofar as they are truly pleasurable, enjoy them precisely because they do *not*—whatever Lionel Trilling said to the contrary— "judge us." I am *not* judged by my experience of the trees along the Tiber in the course of my innocent walk, and I do *not* dispute or anguish over the innocence of my enjoyment. Neither do I regard the pleasure I take as a spectator at a Yankee game as somehow unworthy of me.

I recall, when I had lectured on "the fate of pleasure" to an audience of academics at a Nineteenth-Century Studies Conference some years ago, that a young colleague of mine came up and asked why I had not so much as mentioned sexual pleasure. Surely it had occurred to me, as a man, she said, that the very word "pleasure" would immediately call to mind passion and the body. Not much about the body, she said, in your lecture, which seemed odd, a deliberate omission.

Right, I replied. Deliberate, if by that you mean calculated. So as to make a certain point, build my case.

I felt that, she went on. And so far as it goes, I get it. The point you wanted to make. And still I don't see how you can leave out something so central to the idea of pleasure.

And is that the sort of pleasure that comes most immediately to your mind, I asked her. Absolutely, she said. But not, apparently, to yours. Strange, I thought, that we should be speaking to one another in this way, standing there in the brightly lit corridor of a hideous academic building, apparently companionable and confiding but awkward and separate. Not at all intimate, each of us careful not to draw too close, not to overstep some line neither of us would have known quite how to identify.

The probing mutual, now she had opened up the subject in this other way, but as yet academic, safe. To her I was a man, which is to say someone with a "point of view" that might be securely differentiated from the likely "point of view" of a woman like her. And more than that, an "older man," a great deal senior to her in the college, and on that score too likely to be cautious when it came to saying certain things about pleasure to a younger woman. Even if she had, as it were, provoked this particular encounter and did not seem at all reluctant to press me for a candor she had missed in the lecture she had heard.

In the event I didn't quite give my colleague what she wanted. Suggested that the sex thing was, as an aspect of pleasure, already too familiar to seem tempting, at least to me. Which of us, I asked, had not heard, and read, and spoken, more than enough, of the pleasure associated with sexual transport and libidinal transgression? Which of us had not paid some considerable attention to Casanova's witty line, "the best moment of love is when one is climbing the stairs," or to Foucault's equally witty correction, "the best moment of love is when the lover is leaving in the taxi"? Who has not had occasion to think of pleasure in its carnal dimension? Of rise and fall, consummation and tristesse?

And yet I did think, when my young colleague had left the building— pleased, I supposed, that she had had the courage to point out to me my astounding omission—that my own experience of pleasure had been only very partially disclosed in the lecture I had prepared for what was, after all, an academic occasion. But then who can identify all the many aspects of pleasure? How to account for the pleasure I take—a pleasure largely indistinguishable from an associated pain and distress, almost unto the point of tears—in visiting a Roman synagogue and reading, by no means for the first time, about the appalling fate of the Italian Jews during the Hitler-Mussolini years? Nothing in the way of a fresh revelation there, not for me. Nothing edifying. No tales of brave resistance, such as might have been mounted in that same modest basement room, had those in charge of the display placards chosen to emphasize resistance rather than the more familiar story of destruction. But pleasure, for me, simply in remembering, again, even on a subject I have read about and written about and debated over many years. A complex, unfathomable pleasure, down in that humble basement space, as in other such spaces, in Berlin, or Prague, or Paris, a sensation unmistakably of a distinctive, peculiar pleasure, which I do, on each such occasion, interrogate, though to what end I cannot say.

No more than I can name the end or objective in interrogating other varieties of pleasure to which I am susceptible. So that I ask what purpose there can be in affirming, as if there were any question about it, that I am as susceptible to the elementary pleasures as anyone else? That often sex is the name of my desire. Simply that. Why deny it? And yet what revelation is there in stating what is for most of us most obvious?

Michel Foucault notes, in an interview called "Sexual Choice, Sexual Act," that for many centuries sexual pleasure had much to do with people wondering whether or not the object of their attention would "surrender," or "give in." All "the interest and curiosity, the cunning and manipulation" revolved around that question, with the pleasure entailed in the "seduction" and, finally, in having the "uncertainty" satisfactorily resolved. Inevitably, Foucault argued, once "sexual encounters" became "extremely easy and numerous," everything would change. This was the case most especially, he claimed, in the domain of homosexual relations, where typically "complications are introduced only after the fact." In "this type of casual encounter," he goes on, "it is only after making love that one becomes curious about the other person" and asks, for example, " 'By the way, what was your name?' " In a culture where sex is easy to come by and sexual encounters are more and more numerous and casual, Foucault concludes, "all the energy and imagination, which . . . were channeled into courtship, now become devoted to intensifying the act of sex itself." And thus do we have greater and greater attention paid to a "whole new art of sexual practice," designed to forestall or prevent "boredom" and to "innovate and create variations that will enhance the pleasure of the act."

Not surprising, of course, that Foucault should name the goal involved in certain sexual practices as "introducing perpetual novelty," with S and M variants compared to "a chess game in the sense that one can lose and the other can win."

I won't pretend not to know what such references, to winning and losing, can and sometimes do entail. Even the most banal experience of sexual encounter—whether homosexual or heterosexual—will include its share of wins and losses, with intensity and duration of sensation the primary measure of success or failure.

But then this whole way of thinking about pleasure does largely eliminate, or ignore, the species of sexual satisfaction centrally involved with relationship and mutuality. The novelty sought in Foucault's scenario has, as its objective, the intensification of a sensation that is, in its very nature, "casual." To speak of "love-making" in such a context seems to me a category error. And pleasure? No doubt about it. Though the pleasure on offer in this precinct is far removed from the combination of lust, inwardness, sympathy, and charity that mark—may mark—other kinds of sexual pleasure more conventionally associated with relationship, and with love.

It is perhaps unnecessary to concede that these varieties of sexual encounter and sexual pleasure are, all of them, human, all too human, and that we are, all of us, apt to be drawn to different varieties and intensities of pleasure in accordance with who we are. I freely confess that the idea of "perpetual novelty" in the domain of sexual practice has never seemed to me especially compelling. That I regard the idea as somewhat ridiculous, in fact, given the limits assigned to us by our bodies and our capacities for experimentation. And that the pleasures afforded by frequent sexual encounter with one singular other person have long seemed to me not merely sufficient and consoling but surprising in their intensity. Reading of a long-married character named Henry Perowne in a novel called *Saturday* by Ian McEwan, I was startled to find a passage that perfectly captured my own experience of sexual pleasure. "If the world were configured precisely to his needs," Perowne thinks, "he would be making love to [his wife] Rosalind now." How can that be, that there, only there and not elsewhere, would be the object and the source of the precise pleasure he craves? "By contemporary standards," he thinks, "by any standards, it's perverse that he's never tired of making love to Rosalind, never been seriously tempted by the opportunities that have drifted his way. . . . When he thinks of sex, he thinks of her. . . . In one lifetime," he goes on, "it wouldn't be possible to find another woman with whom he can learn to be so free, whom he can please with such abandon and expertise. By some accident of character, it's familiarity that excites him more than sexual novelty."

Of course, like Perowne, I can then allow myself to think that perhaps the so-called accident of character includes some deficiency, or timidity, some absence in me of curiosity or "masculine life force." So that the pleasures I allow myself to taste and savor—in what is quaintly called "real life," though not in art, or literature—are merely the pleasures suited to a tame creature averse to novelty and risk.

But then, again like Perowne, at least where pleasure is concerned, I must conclude that there's nothing I can do about myself. I am what I am, and I find in myself no deficiency of pleasure, and regard in my one and only wife of forty years someone who would surely let me know if she felt deprived. If, to remain monogamously tied to me, she needed perpetually to curb her own healthy appetites. So at least I tell myself, perhaps deluded, but content to leave it at that.

In truth, then—contrary perhaps to what I have suggested in writing about "the fate of pleasure"—pleasure is not for me, or not entirely, the product of lowly or puerile instincts resisted, or challenges met. This I freely accept. Not inevitably or everywhere the consequence or the byproduct of difficulty mastered. To differentiate, as between greater or lesser pleasures, pleasures in which we are fully invested—as it were, with all our hearts—and pleasures merely casual, however momentarily intense, is not to dismiss the one in favor of the other. It is, rather, to say that one sort of pleasure is not the same as another, and that our capacity to experience different kinds of pleasure is in signal respects a mark of who and what we are.

And yet still I wonder if I have begun to answer the charge leveled by my young colleague, who felt that, in purporting to speak of pleasure, I had managed to avoid the aspect of pleasure most obviously mysterious and compelling. Perhaps—I say it again—I don't really know how to go beyond the bland, hardly illuminating statement that pleasure will come to each of us in the several ways we are suited to accommodate. If, in the domain of art and ideas, I am judged—want and need to be judged—by the quality of my own pleasures, I must also feel, like Perowne, that where my own sexual pleasure is concerned, I exercise "no real choice." I have what I have to have, and I am under no obligation to account for myself in any other terms. And this may well be true of a wide range of other pleasures I routinely taste and allow myself to enjoy.

As always in such matters, where I don't quite feel that I have answered a charge or a complaint, I turn to any source I can think of to assist me, even at the risk of sowing further unease or confusion. And so I turn to an improbable, more or less incidental encounter in what seems to me the single most gripping book I have read in the last decade or so, which is Coetzee's *Elizabeth Costello*. The encounter—one of many in a book of many different parts and narrative stratagems—involves Costello's visit to a very elderly man named Mr. Phillips, once a painter, now nearing death, enfeebled, unable to speak. For a while she holds his hand, cold and blue, and notes that "there is nothing pleasant in any of this." She notes as well the humiliations to which Mr. Phillips is by now inured, his inability to help himself, to hold a cup, to say what he makes of her visits. And she decides, for no reason, surely, that would involve pleasure, certainly not her own, suddenly, "to drop a hand casually on to the bedcover and begin to stroke, ever so gently, the place where the penis, if the penis were alive and awake, ought to be; and then, when there is no response, to put the covers aside and loosen the cord of Mr. Phillips's pyjamas . . . and open up the front and plant a kiss on the entirely flaccid little thing, and take it in her mouth and mumble it until it stirs faintly with life. . . . Nor is the smell pleasant either," she goes on, "the smell of an old man's nether parts, cursorily washed."

Of course Costello herself wonders what it is possible to "make of episodes like this," and, somewhat like her, I can claim only that it tells me something indispensable without quite allowing me to sum it up or penetrate to the core of its mystery. It is not, surely, an erotic episode: "too grotesque for that," Costello rightly concludes. It is not even what may be called, not in any ordinary sense, a pleasurable encounter, some-thing any of us would yearn to experience again and yet again. Perhaps, Costello thinks, only "the Christians" have "the right word" for such a thing, the word "caritas." And how would Costello know that this was in fact the right word? "From the [utter, illimitable] swelling of her heart she knows it," she thinks. Though a few lines later she seems, again, not at all certain and speculates finally that episodes like this are "just holes, holes in the heart, into which one steps and falls and then goes on falling."

And is that, I wonder, what I myself want in the end to say about pleasure? That it is something into which, like it or not, I fall and go on falling? That the episodes in my own life that give pleasure, however singular or often repeated, are never to be fully understood, no more than the impulses and affiliations that incline each one of us to this rather than to that form or exercise of pleasure? That pleasure is for me, perhaps even more often than I know, more a matter of tender mutuality and gift-giving than of mastery? Again, hard to be certain about this. But certain all the same that, however absurd or impossibly tender or otherwise improbable the occasions of my own pleasure, I am bound to consider, if only after the fact, that often—though not invariably—my own pleasures remain somewhat mysterious to me.

Is there, in my own experience, anything that accords with the peculiar episode I have cited in Coetzee's book? Suppose I say that there is, in Costello's encounter, the record of a peculiar kind of pleasure, evoked, registered, in part denied, but unmistakable. I have no sweeping epithet at hand to identify the kind, but there is, I insist, a species of pleasure that we find in the image Coetzee provides of the woman, no longer young, "crouched over the old bag of bones with her breasts dangling, working away on his nearly extinct organ of generation." My own pleasure here a matter of amusement at Coetzee's way of pressing things beyond what any reader would have imagined. Or amusement at Costello's sense of the thing as loaded with meaning and, at the same time, merely absurd, the record of a falling into the sort of conceptual and human hole you dare not hope to emerge from, however much you reach for terms like "caritas" to help you out.

In a way, though, the peculiar pleasure involved in the act performed on the limp Mr. Phillips has to do, I think, with the very difficulty it presents to Costello herself. For she is a woman very much given to analyzing and comparing. She has a fondness for analogies and theories. Though she is, like her creator, a novelist, an artist, she is drawn to ideas and likes to think herself at the least adequate when it comes to working things out and tracking their implications. But the encounter with Mr. Phillips does not satisfactorily accord with any theory. Not so far as Costello herself is concerned, and not, surely, so far as her reader is concerned. Caritas is not centrally at issue in Coetzee's book. Neither is there any attempt made to argue the notion that what is done for, or to, Mr. Phillips is a genuine act of charity. The swelling of Costello's heart is a sign that she is moved by what she has done as if it were a charitable act. But she knows very well—and tells us so—that what chiefly moves her, what is "uppermost"—"is what she will make of it." The encounter with Mr. Phillips matters because it provides the pleasure Costello derives from engaging with something strange and unexplainable and even, in its way, perverse, insofar as its foundation—the central act itself—is intrinsically unpleasurable.

I have known this sort of pleasure. The pleasure of engaging with something not immediately gratifying, or appealing, or beneficial, but in some way promising. Is this not the pleasure we derive from our encounter with works of art difficult or unlovely or so unfamiliar as to seem forbidding? Is it not at least somewhat akin to the pleasure we take in performing an act that has little discernible or immediate impact but has called up all our intelligence and resources on behalf of nothing certain? The pleasure I take—an absurd pleasure, I may rightly think—in patiently explaining to a somewhat recalcitrant student the nature of the shoddiness apparent in the lousy term paper he has handed in, alert all the while to how hopeless a business this is, how inadequate my charms in the face of so indifferent a student?

My late father-in-law was a man of the political right, and a devout Catholic who had opinions on everything under the sun. People who believed that women had a right to abortions condoned "murder." People who wanted to raise taxes on the rich were "socialists" or "Communists." Liberals were the kinds of people who routinely, for their own nefarious ends, "exaggerated" the abuses committed by priests and other church officials. People who shunned FOX News had been "brainwashed" by the "Liberal Media."

In truth, though he had forgiven me for being born Jewish and marrying his daughter, even for being what he called "an unrepentant leftist," I had no reasonable hope whatsoever of converting my father-in-law to my own view of anything. But there was pleasure for me in the many hours we spent together just talking, particularly during the last decade of his life, when he was past eighty and spending most of his time puttering around his Miami Beach apartment, finding small ways to get through each long day. When, in a telephone conversation, I asked him how he was doing, he would say, breathing out, breathing in. Not much else to report. Pleasure for both of us, on long visits several times each year, in simply engaging in more or less strenuous conversation—not quite debate—with no prospect of altering a thing. Attempting, somehow, to meet one another half way. Agreeing that racists, for example, were idiots. That, however you felt about "choice," abortion was a serious matter not to be taken lightly. The pleasure involved in these exchanges no doubt modest but pleasure nonetheless, in overcoming reluctance, in charitably reaching out to someone you had reason either to mistrust or to fear, someone you might well have shunned or driven away, someone whose exertions you might find, in the moment, touching, your own efforts to overcome distaste or aversion likewise for you, as also for the other, pleasurable to behold, to savor. Nothing in this of the sensation you associate with the transports enjoyed, again and again, with your wife or partner. But, no question, pleasure. Mild, unmistakable, real. One of the holes, perhaps, I have often fallen into, not quite able fully to say how deep and sustaining the pleasure. But an aspect of what I take to be, indisputably, the thing itself.

When I was young, a decade or so before I met my father-in-law, a number of radical thinkers argued that permissive societies organized to maximize pleasure and to make the widest possible variety of pleasures easily available to everyone were, in the end, more efficient than traditionally repressive societies in controlling their citizens. A paradox. For these permissive arrangements denied people the very autonomy they thought they were buying by embracing "liberation." How so? In promising them a multitude of sensations and immediate gratifications in return for their loyalty and obedience. In making them feel grateful for the absence of sensory deprivation and thereby binding them to the standard renunciations required of citizens by any established social order. In encouraging them to feel "naughty" and "liberated" while remaining reliably well-behaved. In creating what Harold Rosenberg called a contented "herd of independent minds."

This view of things accorded very well with my own disposition. I always thought of people who demanded perpetual novelty and perpetual emotional breakthrough as in fundamental ways underdeveloped. Exciting, perhaps, even sometimes exemplary in their determination to press forward, to repudiate everything familiar and, so far as they were concerned, stale and enervating. But lacking, I felt, in other crucial areas of human experience. In understanding that the exercise of the individual will rarely yields what is promised by enthusiasts of untrammeled self-assertion. Trilling got it exactly right, I felt, in *Sincerity and Authenticity*, where, in describing the "character structure" prized by Herbert Marcuse, he wrote the following: "He *likes* people to have 'character.' . . . He holds fast to the belief that the right quality of human life, its intensity, its creativity, its felt actuality, its weightiness, requires the stimulus of exigence." For such a man, "necessity," the domain of that which is and cannot be other than it is, contains what may be called "a perverse beneficence," for "upon its harsh imperative depends the authenticity of the individual and his experience."

And so back, once more, to pleasure, the highest pleasure, as an experience—even where habitual and comfortable—of persons who are aware that some things have weight and others not, that when the "wins" and "losses" in view are matters of the moment, to be taken casually, as of no enduring consequence, the pleasure is commensurately meager, even if sharp and, in the short term, bracing. Not an impression I want, not here, to insist on, as if I thought no other impression at all compelling or legitimate. But again, pleasure, under "the stimulus of exigence." An idea, or ideal, of pleasure fit at least to set beside and compare with the multitude of casual, indifferent, fleeting pleasures we crave and, if we are very fortunate, permit ourselves to enjoy.

[3]

READING FROM THE LIFE

You keep taking note of whatever confirms your ideas—better
to write down what refutes and weakens them!

—ELIAS CANETTI

I spent a day with V. S. Naipaul in the fall of 1980. He was teaching undergraduates that semester at Wesleyan University in Middletown, Connecticut, and he'd agreed to be interviewed for a projected special issue of *Salmagundi* magazine. My companions on this visit were the novelist Bharati Mukherjee and my wife Peg Boyers. From the first, in our preliminary phone conversations, Naipaul had expressed objections about my friend Bharati. "Why bring an Indian with you?" he asked. "It's not as if I were an Indian writer. I wouldn't want to be questioned by a person who thought of me in that way." Of course I was tempted then to remind Naipaul that there was in fact some reason to think of him as a writer with roots in India, though I knew what he meant and disliked ethnic labels as much as he did. All I said then was that Mukherjee was a colleague and a friend who had introduced me to his work, and that he would find her eminently suitable. That word, suitable, struck me at once as perfectly suitable for the moment, and as Naipaul took it in he decided, for his own reasons, to let the matter drop.

But at the interview Naipaul's hostility to Bharati surfaced at once, from the very moment we shook hands. Pleasant enough to me and to Peg, he was visibly uncomfortable and sour with our friend, who had put on for the occasion a gorgeous sari. Of course Naipaul could not have known, as we did, that Bharati rarely wore such clothing and was more apt to show up for her classes at Skidmore College wearing American sports clothes, khakis or jeans. She had also, on this occasion, painted in the middle of her forehead a bright red dot, knowing that a short time before our visit Naipaul had been asked by Elizabeth Hardwick for a brief *New York Times* interview about the significance of that mark or sign on the heads of Indian women. It is a statement, Naipaul had replied. "It says, my head is empty."

Before we set up our portable tape recorder in Naipaul's amply spacious office we exchanged what were intended to be the standard pleasantries. But Naipaul went on the attack the moment we seated ourselves across from him. "So you've driven from somewhere nearby in New York State?" he asked. "A few hours," I said. "Not much of a drive." "And you?" he asked Bharati. "Where are you from?" "Calcutta originally," she said. "But more recently a decade in Toronto."

"Oh Toronto makes sense for you," he said. "As a city of lower-class immigrants."

"You know Toronto well?" she asked him.

"Well enough," he said. "By repute mainly. And here I'm confirmed."

There was a bit more of the same before we turned on the tape recorder. Did he not enjoy teaching at a place like Wesleyan, which enrolled exceptionally gifted students? "Not terribly gifted, in fact," Naipaul replied. "And the fact of it is, it's diminishing, you know, to spend one's time in the company of inferior minds. But you would not have felt that, I think, that diminishment," he said, "or perhaps not." And then: "To give you some sense of the conditions here, you might visit the bookstore, which has really no books to speak of, and doesn't carry even the issues of the *New York Review of Books*, so that I have to be driven somewhere to find a copy of my own latest article. It's a trial, really, to be at such a place."

No doubt it was, had been, a trial, and no doubt the words were, all of them, a reflection of what Naipaul actually felt, of what he was. Genuine too was our sense that he was more than a bit of a prick. Not a bore. Never that. But a man for whom a habit of contempt was deeply ingrained. Hard not to think, on the spot, in that light-filled, sparsely furnished office, of Hazlitt: "If a person has no delicacy, he has you in his power." But then Naipaul had his moments of delicacy. In the course of the taped interview he rose to the occasion, as it were, and betrayed what seemed, in its way, a genuine sensitivity to the condition of servitude and bleak or uncertain prospects he described in the sometimes wretched places he had visited and written about—in Jamaica and India and the Congo. And yet the contempt was ever at the ready, the impulse to mock directed especially at the practiced sensitivities of the officially liberal professoriate in the American university, at the "bleeding hearts" trained never to find fault with the wretched of the earth, unable, in Naipaul's view, even to consider the complicity of those unfortunates in what had been—and would continue to be—done to them.

And so we came away from our day with Naipaul—the interview itself stretching over several hours, followed by a lunch in the college cafeteria and a leisurely stroll on campus—with a vivid sense of the man we had come to meet. Bad manners was the least of our impression. Our sense was of a man wounded and trying hard not to be defined by his wounds. A man who had much to say about postcolonial politics and ressentiment and racial privilege but who seemed oddly not to understand a great deal, even on subjects powerfully brought forth in his novels. There was something peculiarly abstract and almost comically superior about his reflections on issues he had obviously thought about before, a fastidious, even formal manner he had of engaging with something as if it had nothing much to do with him. Though he proposed, when we were saying our farewells, that perhaps he might be invited to lecture "some time" at "your little college," I thought no, this would be it, felt that I'd had my fill of this really very little man. Proust may well have been right, that though snobbery—and the contempt that comes with it—are "grave," they are not "utterly" or inevitably "soul-destroying." But this was not a proposition I was willing to test. My distaste for Naipaul was such as to make him seem the last person I would ever again hope to meet.

An elaborate anecdote—too elaborate perhaps—for a series of reflections on the uses of personal knowledge for readers of what was once called "serious literature." But I have wanted, from the first, to establish that many of us have grounds for believing that we know something about a writer whose work we admire. I arranged the interview with Naipaul because I had begun to teach his work and wanted to devote an issue of *Salmagundi* to him. I thought that his work opened up questions about the world that had nowhere else been raised so vividly, questions about the so-called advanced and underdeveloped nations, about the struggle between modernity and tradition, about the legacy of colonialism and the efforts to create what Naipaul called "new men" in places like the Congo and even "among the believers" in Pakistan and other Islamic societies. I had also begun to write about him for a book I was planning on politics and the novel. Though I hated much that he had to say in his political journalism and essays, I was chastened by his account of places I thought I knew something about. I was also astonished that he knew so well how adept were liberal intellectuals like myself at concealing from ourselves things we did not wish to acknowledge. He was a man it was easy to dislike on the basis of his writing alone. He had made his recent novels vehicles for expressing hard truths that my friends and I often felt honor-bound to resist. Though we had found his earlier works hilarious or—in the case of *A House for Mr. Biswas*—unforgettably beautiful and moving, there was nothing remotely beautiful or consoling in *The Mimic Men*, or *Guerrillas*, or *A Bend in the River*. Because Naipaul had made himself a writer who was assiduous not to present anything that would seem to a reader attractive or congenial, he had made a claim that was not to be ignored. So I felt.

And so I had to ask what my impressions of the man himself might count for in my estimation of his work. For the work was, as I say, compelling and also troubling. If you had read only *Guerrillas*, or *The Mimic Men*, you might well have supposed that Naipaul had nothing like a sense of humor, and surely no capacity for generosity, no slightest inclination to accord to most persons even a trace of dignity. With *Mr. Biswas* in mind, you would suppose that the vision informing the later, unrelentingly bitter novels was dark not as the expression of a settled disposition but as the mark of an intelligence that had once known benevolence but had been overwhelmed by horror and disgust. Uncertain about such readerly impressions, anyone convinced of Naipaul's large gifts would rightly want to know more about him, even to know something about his intentions.

Was *Biswas* intended as an homage to the author's father, pure and simple? Was *Guerrillas* merely a transcription into fiction of the material Naipaul had shaped for his journalistic essays on Jamaica? Did the author himself regard his fictional account of political unrest and violence in the former Belgian Congo—entitled *A Bend in the River*—as a reliably accurate report of what had gone on at that bloody place?

Often we feel that the more we hear from a writer or artist about his intentions the more we know whether or not to trust our impressions of his work. If the painter Frank Stella tells us that there is nothing in his stripe paintings but paint, that he is not interested in "expression" or "sensitivity" or "symbols," that his stripes are simply "the paths of brush on canvas," we are inclined to try at least to think of his work in those terms. A contradictory impression of the work, to be sustained, would have to seem irresistible. Often we go to interviews with writers and artists in order to check on or to shape our impressions. That is why we often feel, when we have gotten to know a writer, that we are in possession of a more or less useful way of assessing our sometimes inchoate responses to his books. My own feelings about Naipaul himself, though based on a single extended encounter, were so strong that only my deep and considered admiration for his best work allowed me to withstand the impulse to abandon admiration and simply, forever more, to regard even the novels as a reflection of the intolerable fellow who wrote them.

That has often been the way with such matters. Routinely, even among writers themselves, impressions of persons, deep personal antagonisms, are permitted to color responses to works of literature. A poet will say, casually, that she had never felt the poems of another leading contemporary poet to be "repellent" until she met her and took in her cold, unforgiving demeanor. A writer-friend reports that, when a famous contemporary poet—a woman—arrived at her university to deliver a reading, she shook hands with the assembled creative writing faculty, all six of them men, then turned to my friend, the one woman present, and wordlessly held out her coat. That cool peremptory gesture has ever since, over several years, colored my friend's sense of the poet's work, which seems to her bookish, remote, humanly indifferent, "academic."

Even brief encounters are typically enough to shape not merely a sense of a person but a disposition toward that person's work. Those who record that trajectory are rarely apologetic about their susceptibility to so scant a foundation for a long-term judgment. E. M. Cioran wrote that "one can no more refute [a fashionable] idea than a sauce," and this would seem often to be the case with a powerful impression, especially a first impression that has not been decisively contradicted and overturned. Nothing seems so self-evident as a powerful sentiment that can be used to certify the authenticity of whatever we think we feel about a writer's work.

The case of V. S. Naipaul seems to me especially compelling here. My own vivid experience of him, however limited, had been accredited not only by the two companions who were with me at the time of our single meeting but by many others who knew him. Naipaul is, he can be, an unkind and abusive man. There is something like a consensus to support or sponsor that view of him. On top of that, we have lately had an authorized biography that depicts Naipaul as an unsavory fellow, one, moreover, who did not object to the publication of a book that would speak of wife beating and other facts of a long life. He is, has been, a man determined to put well behind him any traces of his humble origins, a man determined to be a British writer, not an "Indian" or "Commonwealth" or "Trinidadian" writer. The figure portrayed in the biography is, in many respects, the man I thought I saw on that memorable day in Middletown, though of course there is much more to him than I could have surmised on my own.

But the question—it seems to me an essential question—is what we think we can do with the knowledge we have of a writer or an artist. We understand that a fellow we dislike may also live with doubts and vulnerabilities, that Naipaul may be quick to condemn in others what he fears to reveal or discover in himself. While exhibiting a flamboyant disregard for the standard niceties, he may well be sensitive to slights and even miserable about his own inability to seem genial. Drawn to the exposure of cant and political correctness, he may wish he were better able to identify moments of grace that have made his own life tolerable. The man we think we know is bound to be, as we like to say, complicated. Our simple impressions may seem close to caricature in the eyes of a biographer who has conducted interviews with family members, former wives, friends. In the round Naipaul may remain, to a considerable degree, a sour, embittered little man seething with contempt and,

Nobel Prize firmly gripped in his avid fist, unsatisfied ambition. But he will, inevitably, also inspire admiration for his occasional willingness to go against the grain of his own least admirable propensities, and in the end he will elude perfect summation.

You would suppose that most critics and teachers, and even most "general" readers, would be reluctant to presume too much in their efforts to read a novel armed with incomplete information and fragmentary impressions. But knowledge can be, often is, a dangerous thing, as we have often heard before. Our predisposition often determines what we find and what we confirm. It is easy for a reader convinced that Naipaul is a distasteful fellow to find confirming "evidence" in his novels. Does he not relentlessly pillory characters who strive to better themselves in ways that must seem hopeless, pathetic, comical to a superior fellow like Naipaul? Does he not ridicule the speech patterns of the natives in places like Trinidad, Antigua, and Jamaica, the better to emphasize the futility of persons in "backward" countries who aspire to a sophistication that does not, so far as Naipaul is concerned, belong to them? Does he not hold up to ridicule the intellectual pretensions of students and professors in African and Middle Eastern universities who routinely speak of "revolution" and "progress" when their societies are mired in ethnic or tribal conflict and their "new men" are preoccupied with lining their pockets and transferring their wealth to secure havens in more stable countries? Does he not take obvious pleasure in depicting backward societies as places whose inhabitants are bound to remain ignorant, held back by superstition, susceptible to the tricks and corruptions that will always be practiced on them by their own leaders?

Of course there is a kind of delight some of us are bound to take when a writer brazenly goes against the grain of accredited liberal opinion. In a literary universe where most writers are intent on presenting an enlightened face, it may well seem refreshing to find in a Naipaul someone robustly unconcerned about striking an appealing posture. Perhaps more to the point, the style in much Anglo-American criticism over the past few decades has tended to be prosecutorial, works of literature combed for signs of incorrectness and, wherever possible, dismissed for being insufficiently sensitive or likable. Satire has thus seemed acceptable only where the targets are the approved targets—the powerful, the patriarchs, the neocolonialists, the tyrants, the hypocritical. Off-limits, for the most part, are those who have any claim to subordinate status. "Never blame the victim" is a rule, an unofficial edict, that Naipaul has violated again and again in his work, and he is thus, for many readers, a writer one simply loves to hate. Ignore the many-voiced music of a novel like *Biswas* or the gentle dignity of a later novel like *The Enigma of Arrival* and it is not hard to summon the sort of visceral distaste that informs much of the criticism devoted to the man and his work. In part this has to do with Naipaul's "reactionary" views, but much of the distaste he inspires has to do with tone and temperament. He has seemed to take too much pleasure in deriding the soothing narratives offered up by generations of the credulous who believe in progress and compassion, and he has seemed, as well, in making his case, to assemble mainly the data that will be loyal to him and his agenda.

Again, much that has been said against Naipaul has relied on what must be called "personal" impressions. He has operated, it is felt, from an apparently fixed disposition, very much in the way that he seemed to be when I met him years ago. The late Edward Said, a brilliant and knowledgeable critic, thought Naipaul an "imperialist" writer, one who designed his work to appeal to the prejudices of "Western" readers, to confirm their view of the "third world" as hopelessly backward and uncivilized. So secure was Said in promoting this view of Naipaul that it did not occur to him that Naipaul's Western readers would be as quick to disparage the novelist's depiction of the non-Western world as he was. When, in the course of a panel discussion at Skidmore College, I suggested to Said that Western liberals were not at all inclined to accept Naipaul's view of Africa and Africans, he insisted that the largely favorable reception accorded to Naipaul's books flatly contradicted my view of the matter. Naipaul was, Said insisted, an apologist for Western imperialism who had an instinct for expressing and justifying the deep, often unconscious prejudices of his audience. This was obvious, he felt, and no recitation of the hostility that often greeted Naipaul's books—even from critics who admired his artistry—would at all dissuade him. Had Said read the novels themselves? Of course he had. But his antipathy had much to do with his impression of the man and what he felt to be his purposes. And did he agree, I asked him, that his own disposition significantly shaped his impression of Naipaul's work and purposes? Was Said's reading of Naipaul not very largely a reflection of Said's own demand for fictions that were unambiguously "correct" in their depiction of the "true" relation between oppressors and the oppressed? Disposition had nothing to do with it, Said insisted. He was in no way disposed to find what he found or to feel what he felt, and his impressions were derived from what he called his own "scrupulous" encounter with Naipaul's writing.

Of course there is no way to settle this sort of dispute, but I will say, simply, that my own exchanges with Said, over many years, only very occasionally in face-to-face meetings, followed a pattern all too familiar to those who have labored in these precincts. I think here of a 1961 essay by the poet-critic Randall Jarrell, which begins: "Mark Twain said that it isn't what they don't know that hurts people, it's what they do know that isn't so. This is true [for example] of Kipling. If people don't know about Kipling they can read Kipling, and then they'll know about Kipling: it's ideal. But most people already do know about Kipling—not very much, but too much. . . . They know that, just as Calvin Coolidge's preacher was against sin and the snake was for it, Kipling was for imperialism." Now Jarrell did not wish to argue about Kipling's view of British imperialism. He wished simply to argue that Kipling was "one of the most skillful writers who have ever existed. . . . You can argue about the judgment he makes of something, but the thing is there." To come to such a writer armed and defended against him with impressions of his bad, bad outlook and ideas was for most right-thinking readers sufficient reason to dismiss him with the standard disdainful epithets.

Said, I believe, came to Naipaul armed with such impressions. He despised Naipaul's ironic severity, hated its deployment on behalf of what he took to be unworthy objectives. He refused, moreover, to take seriously the fact—it is a fact—that in the novels and essays he derided as "imperialist" texts, Naipaul is by no means a defender of "the white man's burden" nor of any ideology that may be said to sponsor a confident imperialist posture. Neither would Said accept as in any way significant the fact—also clearly a fact—that no character, white or black, who represents privilege or power is permitted to come off well in Naipaul's work. To be sure, Naipaul's novels are rarely hopeful, but they do take seriously, in ways Said was unwilling to acknowledge, the most extravagant ambitions of characters who are, much of the time, deluded about what may be accomplished in places whose inhabitants have been long inured to misery and violence. Though Said did not approve of what he took to be the purposes informing Naipaul's writing, he should have been able to see that his works treated politics not merely as the pathetic pursuit of chimeras on the part of hopelessly backward people but as the necessary, often heartbreaking effort of persons in despair to change their lives. Did Naipaul sometimes go out of his way to point up the awfulness of something that might have been portrayed with greater charity? No doubt. But there is nothing in Naipaul's mature work that would seem to be borne of sheer perversity or unalloyed nastiness. Alas, the works themselves will never entirely banish the willfully dismissive, one-dimensional readings that grow from too resolute a "knowledge" of what Naipaul presumably intended, given his professed views and famously sour disposition.

The wrong kind of knowledge, the kind that incapacitates a reader in significant ways, may be traced to many different sources. Martin Amis once noted that "the literary interview won't tell you what a writer *is like*. Far more compellingly, to some, it will tell you what a writer is *like to interview*." Interview John Updike, Amis says, or read around in the accumulated gossip culled from diverse sources, and you may come away with "a garrulous adulterer who lives near the sea." But, Amis goes on, "as for what Updike is like—in his head, in his private culture—I knew all that already." Knew it how? Obviously, by reading his books. Which tell us what? That "he is almost dementedly sensual." That he "cowers under a cataract of sense impressions" and has a "fascination with the observable world [that] is utterly promiscuous." That his brain is "horrendously encyclopedic," and that "the unblinkingness of his eye is opposed to the mighty wooziness of his heart." That he is possessed by "an invigorating and majestic cynicism." Read Updike and these qualities will seem unmistakably to define what he is like. Read him disposed to think of him principally as a suburban grandee, however rooted your disposition or "knowledge" in ostensibly legitimate journalistic sources, and it is likely that you will largely miss what this writer was "in his head, in his private culture."

In 1997, not long before his death, I visited the novelist Gregor von Rezzori at his townhouse on the upper west side of Manhattan. I'd been commissioned to interview the author of *Memoirs of an Anti-Semite* for the Canadian quarterly *Brick*. There are few recent novels I admired—still admire—as much as von Rezzori's book, a work of fiction that reads like a sly, only slightly fictionalized autobiography. Mischievous, crafty, vulnerable, haughty, the book had troubled my imagination for more than twenty years. I had taught it to students who thought it appalling and to others who liked in it nothing so much as the opportunity it presented to test their own tolerance for the outré. By the time I went to interview von Rezzori I had made up my mind about the novel and about other books by this author. I believed him to be at once whimsical and earnest, a man intermittently thoughtful but not at all a thinker. Now and then he seemed to me an innocent in search of lost dreams, but there was also something feral about him. If he could seem, more than occasionally, adolescent, he was the sort of adolescent who had never quite stopped looking for an advantage.

Von Rezzori and his wife, Beatrice Monti, could not have been more welcoming and genial. Rapidly my wife and I established that we had in common with them a love of most things Italian. We agreed that my interview with the writer would range over his works in general and that I would feel free to inquire about periods and aspects of his life, including the World War II years when he worked in Germany as an employee of Radio Hamburg. Would he like me to send him the edited manuscript of our interview for approval? That would not be necessary, he said, for he had "no misgivings" about the document I would produce.

In many ways the session, which went on for several hours, was all that I might have imagined. Von Rezzori spoke freely of his likes and dislikes, of his aversion to "stupidity" and his own susceptibility to varieties of "hatred" which, as a rule, he deplored. He noted, in his work, a tendency to poeticism and beautiful writing which he labored mightily to control. The "character" of his writing, its flavor, he believed, had more to do with an inveterate cynicism. Refusing the soft, the tender, he relied on a tested instinct to "move against the good rising up in me." When I offered that there was, in his work, "a relentless, sometimes cruel and self-assured irony," he agreed, though when I compared it to the ironies of Thomas Mann he balked: Mann, he said, "has the irony of a German sophomore," a "low irony." Amused at my resistance to this, at my incredulity at the word "sophomore," von Rezzori went on to associate his own peculiar brand of irony with what he called "Jewish wit": "I was schooled by Jews," he added, the trace of a malicious smile discernible in his broad, handsome, robustly elderly features.

And in fact it was the turn to things Jewish that precipitated in our interview a rather more strenuous exchange, only a part of which made it into the published transcript. Von Rezzori had been going on about his sense that there was much in his own nature he had learned to check. When he felt himself writing "too beautifully," he had learned to "step on the devil's tail," so as to "squash something in myself." This rapidly became a leit-motif in our conversation, so that the habit of stepping, as it were, on the devil's tail could be easily applied to a whole range of things: "Look," he said, "as a writer—I've said this before—I have to work against myself as a human being. Against the good, against my hatred, against my particular sense of the ridiculous. . . . I can't be always hating and mocking, you know, so I'm working against my hatred, though I also have to allow it expression." The habit, moreover, had most especially to be mobilized where Jews and Jewishness were concerned, given von Rezzori's flirtation with crackpot racialist theories, his easy references to "typically Jewish attitudes" and "Jewish qualities," to New York City as "a kind of shtetl environment," to the idea that anti-Semitism is not only "addictive" but "an inherited disposition." No reader of *Memoirs of an Anti-Semite* would be surprised at von Rezzori's interest in such ideas, though I felt—perhaps foolishly—disappointed that he himself continued to take seriously ideas that he had used to such brilliant and satiric effect in his fiction.

But the most poignant and disturbing moments in our session came when the doorbell rang in the townhouse and, noting that his wife had gone out for a while, von Rezzori asked us to turn off the tape recorder as he rose to attend to his uninvited guest. The guest, however, was a repairman who had been phoned earlier by Beatrice Monti and summoned to fix a kitchen appliance. Clearly angry, apologetic, hesitant, von Rezzori led the intruder to the kitchen, where he was forced to spend ten or fifteen exasperated minutes, after which, when he returned to us, somewhat undone, asking us to join him in a drink, he recalled what he had been saying earlier and went on, intimately, gamely attempting to clarify. "You know," he tried,

> with the Jews it's a strange thing. It's not something you can just put aside. You saw that man a minute ago? I can't even now remember what he looks like. I don't know his name. But he angered me. I don't like to be interrupted and I can't help feeling somehow that the man was responsible. From the moment I opened the door and he set foot in the house I was irritated and I thought to myself "that dirty little Jew." The man who rang that bell more than once and forced himself in here had to be a dirty little Jew. And I held on to that thought, or it held on to me, the entire time we were there together in the kitchen. And when I prepared myself to come out here and resume the interview I looked back over my shoulder and I saw, behind me, the devil's tail, and I thought it's time now to step on it, which I tried to do, though you can see it still, I suppose, there behind me. You can hear it in my telling you how hard it is not to be taken over by that hatred. It's an old habit, and I try to suppress it.

Coming from the author of the *Memoirs*, such remarks could hardly astonish. What is more, they emerged, under the circumstances, with an almost winning air of candor and vulnerability. Was not this von Rezzori fellow open and confiding beyond anything his ardent interlocutor might have expected? Was he not exposing himself to ridicule or derision? And was he not, moreover, the unfortunate victim of a tendency, an obsession, for which he could not have been entirely to blame, given his central European background and "Aryan" conditioning? As he shared with us his disgusting susceptibility, we might almost have been moved to offer commiseration and to congratulate the man on his determination, however futile, to step on the devil's tail.

And yet the thought of that confiding outburst did not leave me. As I walked along Madison Avenue with my wife a few hours later, soon after we had been cordially invited to meet again with the von Rezzoris that summer in Italy, I declared that any further meeting was, so far as I was concerned, out of the question. Perhaps if the novelist had not shared other related confidences in the course of our session, the indelibly ugly accent of the one singular outburst would not have sounded quite so insistently in my memory. For he had assured me that of course, during his time working for Radio Hamburg in the 1940s, no one ever spoke of what was being done to the Jews at the time. There were, he insisted, so many other things to discuss, and no inclination on his part or anyone else's to think about something that did not really concern them. If he had been, as he had often put it, tutored by Jews in the course of a long and not always unpleasant acquaintance, that did not imply any particular solicitude about the fate of the Jews as a people. And it seemed to him—on this he was clear—a bit surprising that I should have assumed that "this business of the Jews" would have interested a man who worked at a major news outlet at a time when the Hitler regime was carrying out "The Final Solution." And what then did he think about back in those days? "Nothing much," he replied. "Hardly anything, in fact."

To turn back to the *Memoirs* in the aftermath of our memorable afternoon, as I prepared once more to teach the book, was to hear the familiar passages in a new way. What had seemed to me the anti-Semitism of a character suddenly seemed to me noxious in a degree I found surprising. When, in the past, I had come upon the narrator's derisory references to Jews who seemed distasteful as a result of their "embarrassing self-confidence" or their "repulsive social climbing," I had felt only admiration for an author so adept at exposing the empty condescension and blustery rage of a narrator—a "Gregor"—he knew well enough to despise. I admired not only the relentless effrontery of the narrative but its insidious charm, its way of making the narrator's racism seem almost quaint and forgivable, like an affliction indulged but never sanitized. Was it possible, I now wondered, that I had invited students to laugh at a passage like the following?

> Salzburg in the summer of 1937 was just awful. It was overrun with Jews. The worst of them had come from Germany as refugees and, in spite of their luggage-laden Mercedes cars, behaved as if they were the victims of a cruel persecution and therefore had the right to hang around in hundreds at the Café Mozart.

So preposterous were passages like these that it was hard not to think them satiric, the wit obviously directed against anyone who could turn up his perfect Aryan nose at the idea of "a cruel persecution." But von Rezzori himself had taught me to think that perhaps my own literary conditioning had somewhat blinded me to the more obvious charge of such a passage. Was I not now positioned to appreciate the true awfulness of von Rezzori's playful, occasionally over-the-top, even boastful racism? Was his narrator's complacent aplomb in the face of his sometimes murderous hostility to all things Jewish not in fact grotesque rather than merely symptomatic and candidly revealing?

In the introduction to a 2008 edition of the novel, Deborah Eisenberg argues that "it is precisely [the] tone of levity that is the very substance of the book's gravity." How can this be? We hear in that levity a persistent "self-mockery," Eisenberg writes, and that, more than anything else, "prevents us from being able to dismiss [the narrator] outright as nothing more than an amazingly frivolous lout." The "highly unwelcome insights" he shares with us must then "steadily dismantle his equanimity." Our belief, our informed sense, that the outlines of the narrator's life resemble von Rezzori's disposes us to believe that the mockery directed at the narrator extends as well to the author.

In truth, I am drawn still to this reading of the novel and share, with some reluctance, Eisenberg's appreciation of the "levity" that underwrites the entire work. My experience of the author himself is nothing I would wish to correct, and yet I continue to teach the novel very much in the way I did before our interview in New York. The novel has not seemed to me fatally compromised by my vivid sense of the man who wrote it.

What is more, von Rezzori's novel is not marked by the impenitent and hysterical ardor that so befouls the tracts and novels of a very different thoroughbred anti-Semite like Louis-Ferdinand Céline. The epithets insistently strewn about the pages of Céline's more hysterical works impart to them a quality of crude obsession very rarely discernible in von Rezzori's work. Overstatement and rant are the marks of Céline's style, which can only remind us that, by contrast, von Rezzori's prose is marked by an esprit de finesse nowhere present in the pages of the Frenchman. Céline's writing has a defiant, even principled lack of proportion and a commitment to abjection. Whatever his manias and resentments, von Rezzori was ambivalent about most things and capable of expressing, in a single breath, both affinity and detachment, tenderness and revulsion. To think of him principally as the man complaining about "the dirty little Jew" in his kitchen is to miss him—to miss the true voice of his fiction—more or less entirely.

There is no need to look very far to identify prominent instances of the misreading to which we are all, in varying degrees, susceptible, misreading inspired by knowing what we know about a writer or an artist. In a recent review of a biography of Arthur Koestler, the author of *Darkness at Noon* is referred to as "yesterday's man, unfashionable and obsolete." His work, another writer declares, cannot be properly understood without the "reconstruction of some modes of thought nearly vanished from the earth." Readers today, Anne Applebaum argues, will have no appreciation of "concepts like 'belief' and 'faith,'" concepts central to Koestler's political fiction and commentary. What is more, Applebaum goes on, many who might today read Koestler have heard about "the extravagance of his sexual and personal transgressions." They will know him to have been notorious for the way he treated women. "Blatantly unfaithful" to his wives, an unabashed "sexual predator," an "alcoholic" and a man "consumed by violent hatreds," he behaved in a way that is said to be more fitting for "Hollywood starlets and pseudo-celebrities" than for "serious people." No wonder—so Applebaum has it—hardly any reader will any longer wish to make his acquaintance. And if all these defects of character are not enough, consider that Koestler "understood the term 'intellectual' in a much broader sense than we do today, and felt comfortable ranging over a huge number of fields in which he had no professional expertise whatsoever. This approach to the life of the mind," Applebaum concludes, "perfectly acceptable in the Vienna of Koestler's youth, simply looks amateurish from the perspective of the present."

But of course the so-called approach to the life of the mind exemplified by Koestler does not in the least look amateurish to anyone still inclined to take seriously the work of other "amateurs" like Walter Benjamin, Elias Canetti, and—nearer to home—Edmund Wilson or George Steiner. In fact, Koestler wrote what may well have been the single most influential account of the Communist mind in *Darkness at Noon*, though he was not a scholar with "professional expertise to his credit" nor a trained psychologist armed with the standard tools of the discipline. For that matter, much of the work that seemed "perfectly acceptable in the Vienna of Koestler's youth," produced by other so-called amateurs, mere free-floating intellectuals, continues to seem central to our understanding of modernity, whatever our quarrels with particular formulations or opinions.

Beyond this, the notorious defects of character reported by Koestler's biographers are surely less responsible for the decline in Koestler's posthumous reputation than the other fact dutifully cited by Applebaum: "To put it bluntly," she writes, "the deadly struggle between Communism and anti-Communism—the central moral issue of Koestler's lifetime—not only no longer exists, it no longer evokes much interest." If Koestler's work is too little read and taught nowadays, that is not the consequence of his having been a sexual predator or an all-around son of a bitch. But Applebaum's "distaste" for the man looms very large in her estimation of his achievement, largely because, as she concedes, she had read almost none of his books before coming to write her review on assignment from the *New York Review of Books*. To her credit, though, when she picks up *Scum of the Earth*, one of Koestler's autobiographical and journalistic volumes, she finds it "a revelation: astonishingly fresh, clear and relevant." Just so—if she picked it up—would Applebaum find astonishingly relevant and gripping *Arrow in the Blue* and other recklessly brilliant, insinuating works by Koestler.

Again, the tendency to read, or to ignore, works of literature based on gossip, bad vibes, or secondhand "personal" information is a troubling aspect of our customary relation to writers and their work. Consider a final, perhaps decisive instance, among many others I might cite, which is the case of the English poet Philip Larkin. When he died in 1985, Larkin was a beloved figure in England and a poet with a large following in the United States as well. Though the attitudes contained in the poetry could be rather harsh (religion was "that vast moth-eaten musical brocade / Created to pretend we never die"), and the lines could ring with acerbities ("They fuck you up, your mum and dad"), Larkin had what one critic called "a genius for making his readers feel vicariously brave as they entered a life of such enforced solitude, such unfulfillment, such concentrated horror at age and death." He was, in fact, a poet whose words all sorts of people committed to memory and shared with one another, a poet admired by his peers for his craftsmanship and adored by the common reader.

And yet all that changed with the publication of Larkin's letters and the appearance of Andrew Motion's superb biography. At once a reassessment of the poetry began, prompted by the discovery that Larkin was really a bad chap. Hard now to suppose that anyone at any time had thought Larkin an agreeable sort of fellow or had managed not to find the poems themselves some of the time mean-spirited and even repellant. But then Larkin was also funny and clever. He could be mournful and eloquent. For all the "fucking" and "pissing" and "groping" in the language of the poems, there was, much of the time, a compensatory rue, a genuine-sounding note of wry self-deprecation or irremediable sorrow. Nothing, really, even in the nastiest bits, to quite prepare a reader for letters deploring again and again the "wop," the "coon," the "too many fucking niggers," the ever bound-to-be-disappointing sexual partners, the never-ending "ree-lay-shun-ship between men and women."

Of course the best critics, responding to the letters and to the Motion biography, were moved to ask—as William Pritchard asked—"Why . . . one [would] want to read all this when the matchless poems are there, still fresh and glittering as creation itself." And they naturally answered, with Pritchard, simply, that of course "we want to know everything, even too much, about the man who wrote them." But then, for many other readers, the letters and the biography were an enormous, not to be gotten over trial. "Attitudes that read as irony in the lyrics," wrote Phoebe Pettingell, "turn[ed] out to be for real in the man," and thus the poems had inevitably to be read, or reread, in light of revelations as to what they must have intended or not quite made explicit. The poet Tom Paulin wrote in the *TLS* of the "sewer under the national monument Larkin became," and an English professor named Lisa Jardine wrote in the *Guardian* that it would no longer be possible for her and other academics to teach Larkin's work to students as they had in the past. His work, after all, could no longer be presented as "self-evidently 'humane.'" For professors who customarily encouraged students, as Jardine described it, "to 'read around' their key literary texts," the poems of Larkin would now be revealed as the work of "a casual, habitual racist, and an easy misogynist. Not to mention a malicious gossip who relished savagely caricaturing fellow authors," and so on. Obviously Larkin's poems served merely to conceal "implications" and left "familiar prejudices intact." And so the task of educating students "to see through" the poetry would fall to persons like Jardine herself, adept at exposing "patriarchal beliefs" and all-around incorrect prejudices. Though Tom Paulin and many other writers declared, as Jardine had it, that "we are no longer allowed Larkin (or Virginia Woolf), because their writings are structured by key beliefs to which we can no longer subscribe," others would make appropriate use of such "texts" and would thus alert the world to their sinister implications.

To all this we might best respond by remembering what writers like Larkin do to us when they are operating with the benefit of their finest powers. Did Larkin write, some of the time, what John Banville termed "heartbreakingly tender" poems? He did. Was the nastiness in the poems often undercut, complicated, by "an impish and highly ironical smile" that made the performance by no means a straightforward exercise in bigotry? It was. And would we ever really want to read poems to be confirmed in our niceness and our impeccably sound views of society and human "re-lay-shuns"? Probably not.

And yet we may want, all the same, to acknowledge that this business of reading and responding is perhaps not so very easy to manage. Banville rightly declares, in the piece on Larkin, that "all this, of course, is incidental to what matters, which is the poetry." Of course. But then the poetry matters in several different ways, and those may well include consideration of the spirit inhabiting a body of work. "There was much ugliness in Philip Larkin's character," Banville writes, "but what mattered most to him was beauty, and the making of beautiful objects. In this lay his greatness." And thus we are not, in Banville's view, to judge Larkin on the basis of the ugliness, any more than we are to "judge Shakespeare's plays because he willed to Anne Hathaway his second-best bed." To which we can only say, alright, fair enough, and then follow up with something like: but what if the ugliness in the character, the provincial prejudice, the murderous ressentiment—defects we associate with writers as various as Larkin, Ezra Pound, Céline, Naipaul, von Rezzori, and others—can be shown to infect the poems and novels and plays? What if the infection is not incidental to the work but an essential aspect of its character and tone?

In short, we may not wish too readily to dismiss questions about the spirit of a work, though we will want to affirm our allegiance to an idea of literature that sharply differentiates the poem or the novel from what appears to be its "message" or its "views" or the character of its author. "The only true thoughts," T. W. Adorno once wrote, "are those which do not grasp their own meaning." In which case, insofar as a Larkin poem or a von Rezzori novel is an expression of "true thoughts," the thoughts must not be reducible to an elementary message or unequivocal meaning. If that is what we take to be the case with such writers, then what will matter most to us when we read them will not be their reprehensible sentiments but something else that insistently arouses and incites without our quite knowing what it is. I want, with however much reluctance, to know everything I can find out about writers whose work I admire. But I want also to trust in the elusiveness of works that must remain, in the end, resistant to me and to my purposes.

[4]

FIDELITY

And, as in life, so in art, both are necessary, husbands and lovers. It's a great pity when one is forced to choose between them.

—SUSAN SONTAG

Even now, sin is all but incomprehensible to him inasmuch as the moral demand system no longer generates powerful inclinations toward obedience or faith, nor feelings of guilt.

—PHILIP RIEFF

I

For a long time fidelity meant nothing to me, and infidelity did not exist. Not one kid I met in my working-class, mainly Jewish neighborhood in 1940s Brooklyn was the child of what used to be called "a broken home." Until my teen years in the 1950s no one ever mentioned to me the word divorce. Married people might quarrel or even hate each other, but they had no choice apparently but to stay together. That is why I was shocked one day, a year or two after my own bar mitzvah, when my rabbinical grandfather pronounced my own father "a saint" for remaining with my difficult, sometimes hysterical mother. What did he mean? How could my father not have stayed with his wife?

Like most persons—so I suppose—I came to think about fidelity in a sustained way only when I began to think myself unfaithful. Having committed myself, at age sixteen, to love, honor, and cherish a high school girl I married four years later when I graduated from college, I was soon troubled by what I had done and tempted to escape the confines of an arrangement that felt, in several respects, all wrong. Never did I believe that I was unsuited for marriage, or feel that my young wife was to blame for my distress. But I did find, more or less at once, that we didn't much like or trust one another, that I was attracted to other young women, and that my wife was also entertaining other options, even as we were producing a first child and doing what we could to convince ourselves that we wished to remain together.

These unfoldings took place in the 1960s, at a time when the educated classes in the United States were conducting an assault on the nuclear family and learning how to talk about liberation and the virtues of excess and experimentation. Though even then I had little patience for what often seemed to me the delusions of the radical culture critics whose books I nonetheless devoured, I was swept up in an atmosphere that made it difficult, even for someone like me, to think fidelity an important virtue.

Fidelity, after all, seems to most young people in ostensibly long-term relationships a good idea only if they are more or less content with one another. Once I began to examine the idea of fidelity, I couldn't but feel that it asked of me more than I was then prepared to give. And how, I wondered, could it be otherwise? Of course I knew that anyone might work out a modus vivendi in terms of which a couple might carry on as if they were faithful and thereby sustain their marriage. Among my own friends were couples who behaved as if the vows they had made were sufficient to get them through the standard temptations and occasional dalliances. But I was disdainful of the compromises this arrangement entailed. The modus vivendi seemed to me a form of lying. Why be faithful in the absence of a fully compelling reason? To tell yourself to do the right thing was worthless if you didn't trust yourself or anyone else to know what was right. Nor did it help to be confronting these issues when you had ample reason to mistrust anything merely practical or convenient.

Of course fidelity and monogamy must always have seemed at least somewhat problematic, even during periods when there was an accredited consensus about virtue and character and the unimpeachable merits of the straight and narrow. In the nineteenth century, defenders of the nuclear family saw it as a defense against what John Ruskin called "the hostile society of the outer world." Husbands and wives were routinely reminded that theirs was a "sacred place," and that they were to be on guard against crossings of the "threshold" established to prevent "terror, doubt, and division." But such language has a decidedly Victorian accent, and it was bound to seem unpromising to a young person like myself, at a time when even devout upholders of home and fidelity were loath to resort to terms like "sacred space" or to suppose that anything might effectively banish doubt or division. Nor was doubt likely to seem the enemy, even for those wracked (as I was) by misgivings about "liberation" and struggling against the impulse to be unfaithful. Doubt was a good thing, and misgiving, and division. To want to be faithful was not to want to be stupid.

The obvious objection to fidelity in the sphere of love and marriage was not merely that it left us wanting more than we had but that it decreed an impoverishment of our faculties. Many writers in the 1950s and 1960s worried less about doubt than about the deadening effects of habit and stability. Faithfulness required a commitment to what was and had to be. Infidelity, by contrast, "believed in elsewhere," as Adam Phillips puts it in his book *Monogamy*. Infidelity shakes us up, Phillips says, and "gets all the action." No wonder we are drawn—some of us, at any rate—to the heretic and the outlaw and those who are forever imagining "the possibility of a double life." Monogamy and fidelity are for those determined to be satisfied with the unified life in which two are content to be as one and to entertain no forbidden alternatives. To be nothing but faithful would seem, by this standard, to be always operating in terms of what is not to be done, and thus to live with the looming specter of impoverishment. "The incontinent," Phillips writes, "are our negative ideals," and those who are faithful deny themselves such ideals only out of fear that they will be led away from their frail if tender allegiances.

And yet it does seem rather a mistake to pose the alternatives in so starkly antithetical a way. A mistake even for those of us apt to be charmed by Phillips's wry, closing formulation: "Monogamy and infidelity: the difference between making a promise and being promising." Delicious, to be sure, and playfully mischievous, the antithesis on offer by now almost a cliché. Think Emma Bovary, think Anna Karenina, and you get at once the drift of such starkly drawn alternatives. Again and again we find, in the classic fictions devoted to the subject, that fidelity is almost invariably associated with timidity and reluctance while infidelity is associated with daring and courage. Even where excess and promiscuity are evoked as terrifying and destructive, fidelity must be made to seem tame. Though readers of novels may hope that characters they love will eventually make happy marriages, they too are thrillingly invested in the exploits of rogues and courtesans and those who throw caution to the proverbial wind. Like the faithful wife Marketa in Kundera's *Book of Laughter and Forgetting*, we often feel that to be true is for most souls a depressing option. "The only reason she was better," Kundera writes, "better" in this case meaning simply faithful, "was for want of anything better." Once "spirited" and "indomitable," the hopelessly loyal Marketa is sadly diminished, reduced to being steadfast, good, pathetic. So her creator, with however much ambivalence, decrees. And in this he takes his place in a long line of writers with a predictable take on these matters.

Of course I was not alone in refusing to acknowledge, for a long time at any rate, how easy it was to disparage fidelity as the recourse of the weak and unimaginative. When in the early 1960s I read Denis de Rougemont's classic *Love in the Western World*, I was thrilled by its erudition and by what seemed to me its unanswerable attack on fidelity. Obvious, was it not, that only "an acquired respect for the [existing] social order" could uphold the idea of fidelity? And was it not obvious as well that most people were now committed to "the revelatory value of both spontaneity and manifold experiences," so that persons faithful and monogamous were bound to seem disappointing to a spirited partner and uninteresting even to themselves?

Of course I was aware, even then, that instinct and spontaneity often provided no more than the illusion of a more vital experience. Who hadn't noticed that the intensity on offer in a life consigned to sharp if temporary pleasures might soon seem paltry? Who hadn't wondered at the spectacle of desire ceaselessly indulged and relentlessly depleted? And yet there was little in my own as yet negligible experience that would allow me to resist the proposition that intensity belonged principally to those suddenly, spontaneously, deliriously "in love" or otherwise in a state of "possession." With fidelity again the tame wager on a decent future and the inevitable renunciation of instinct and spontaneity. *Civilization and Its Discontents*. Fidelity a second best. No apparent opening here for the thought—largely forbidden in the precincts of the advanced—that there is no necessary opposition between affection and desire, freedom and continuity, love and sex.

II

But then thinking of these issues exclusively in terms of love and marriage and sex and relationship unduly limits what we want to say, and to discover, about fidelity. Promises and transgressions, after all, have much to do with other aspects of our lives as well. J. M. Coetzee's alter ego, Elizabeth Costello, declares "fidelities" the primary word "on which all hinges," but she is not remotely thinking about marriage and adultery, and the plural, "fidelities," proposes that there are many kinds and degrees of faithfulness. Nothing in this, to be sure, of Cole Porter's playful sense of the thing when he has me singing that it is possible for me to be true, "darling, in my fashion," for there, in the spirit of the song, to be true is a provisional thing, which I may intend while holding wide open the possibility that I will soon change my mind and move on to other provisional commitments. The Porter lines speak to a jaunty, teasingly naughty attitude toward conventionally serious matters. Costello, on the other hand, takes fidelities to be, at least potentially, matters of life and death. Confronting them, she can think that she would rather have been another sort of person, one who knew how to "have more fun" and would thus not be so earnest about promises and betrayals. But there it is. You do with an idea like fidelity, and a temperament, only what you can, and if "fidelities" seem to you not merely an opportunity for wit but the word on which everything hinges, well, there you are.

And so I ask myself, for starters, what seems, outside of marriage, a suitably telling instance of fidelity, or infidelity. And what comes to mind, at the moment of this writing, is the imbroglio that has kept me awake through several recent nights. Trivial maybe, or ridiculous, as the cause of sleepless nights. Too much inclination to moral exquisiteness in solemnly playing it over, too much opportunity for arriving at the conviction of my own perfect rectitude. And yet, to be sure, an imbroglio—this no one will dispute—bearing on the question of fidelity. Not to be lightly passed over. The friend, or colleague, involved not to be forgotten—not by me—or absolved.

A quite famous writer, this friend, or colleague. My employee, actually, teaching for me over several years at the New York State Summer Writers Institute, which I have directed for more than twenty-five years. A person I like and admire, had admired, easy to like, never warm or affectionate, not with me, but reliably genial, by no means a favorite with students but, so far as I knew, conscientious, more than adequate. A seasoned instructor, with no trail of troubles in her record. None that had reached me. Excellent recommendations from the few senior people I had consulted. A safe bet who had turned out to be quite alright. So I had concluded.

Until, one day, at the close of a two-week institute session, a student asked me for an appointment, arrived, and informed me that her instructor had been dismissing her students at each scheduled three-hour workshop after only one hour. No explanation given. No apparent reason. Nothing to suggest illness or a pressing outside concern, the teacher as usual bright and more or less attentive to the student works slated for discussion, the conversation perhaps more briskly driven than seemed quite usual, and with little opening for student comments, but useful.

No big deal, obviously, though the student in my office thought it disturbing enough to want to report it. A student new to me, studying in our summer program for the first time. Not, I repeat, a very big deal, but troubling enough so that all day I couldn't get the thing out of my mind and wished that the teacher hadn't already finished her time with us and driven off to wherever it was she would spend the remainder of her summer. And of course I wondered whether the report I'd received was entirely reliable, and whether the thing alleged constituted something grave, the violation not merely of a contract but of a promise to be faithful. Faithful in a way that so worldly and intelligent and imaginative a person as this brilliant writer might have been expected to understand in precisely these terms.

And so—no need here to rehearse the steps in detail—I moved to speak with several other students from the same workshop, who had moved into session two of our summer program, and I ascertained that indeed they too had noted the incredibly early dismissal of their fiction workshop and had thought to report this later on in the written evaluations they would send in. No one expressed anger, only puzzlement and disappointment. Not, again, a very big deal, so far as they were concerned. They were to study with other teachers now, and they were optimistic.

I then fired off a lengthy email letter to my writer-colleague, friendly, as I thought, but wanting to know whether the reports I had now received from several students were accurate, and what could possibly have caused her to cut short each of her class meetings. Difficult, I found it, to suppress my irritation and unhappiness. And difficult also not to enjoy too much the pleasing sensation of being in the right and asking someone else to accept that she was in the wrong. But with a clear sense, nonetheless, that at issue was basically something quite simple, a promise violated, a shocking dereliction on the part of someone who could not claim—how could she?—to be in any sense of the term "innocent." A successful, widely read novelist who had written, after all, with considerable sophistication, about transgression and responsibility.

But more shocking by far, or so I found it, than the deed itself was the explanation offered, so casually set out in a letter notable for its brevity and its complacent presumption of, yes, no doubt about it, innocent good intentions. Of course our instructor had, as reported, dismissed her class two hours early on each class day. And why not do so, she asked, when the work submitted by the assorted graduate students in her class was so clearly without genuine interest, so "unambitious"? If I had been there in the workshop I would have seen for myself that fifteen or twenty minutes with each thirty-page manuscript, three per class day, was as much as they deserved. Why waste their time and hers in such a situation?

When I wrote back to my colleague I could not quite believe that she would disagree with what I said. Did she not feel, I asked, that there was any other way she might have been useful to students enrolled in an advanced class whose work seemed to her elementary? Did she not feel some responsibility, if not to the terms of the actual contract she had signed, then to the students, who might profit by her further instruction? Did it not occur to her that she might bring with her to class sixteen copies of stories by William Trevor or Alice Munro to assist her students to contrast the ambition informing such works with the impoverishment of range and idiom displayed in the student manuscripts? Were there not exercises she might have had her students do right there in class? Was she not, I asked, a teacher, which is to say, one who devises ways to instruct? It did seem to me—so I wrote to her—that what she had done, and failed to do, was really quite appalling. She had not kept faith. Had not tried to take seriously what in effect she had sworn to do. She had betrayed her students and—far less important but not to be overlooked—she had betrayed me, the one who had recruited her and shown her my own faithful attachment by hiring her back over several summers.

In the end I was not surprised—surprise was now out of the question—when my colleague wrote back very briefly to say that she would "consider" what I had said, but that I should also "consider" that there was "more than one way of looking at these issues." That brief reply sealed things for me, brought, so far as I was concerned, our exchange, our relations, to a definitive close. No, I told myself, there were not several different ways of looking at this issue. There were different kinds and degrees of faithfulness, different kinds of promises, understood by different people in sometimes incompatible ways. But my colleague had been flagrantly, blithely unfaithful, and she had then pretended that there was not one single conclusion to which her conduct should invariably have led her.

III

Some will say—I have said it myself—that there is a significant difference between a merely implicit promise and a formal promise deliberately avowed. Not all of us, or not at all times, will understand that, in entering into a relationship or a course of action, we have agreed to keep a promise. But we do, most of us, accept that promises, even when implicit, are so far as possible to be kept. Occasionally, in private conferences with my own students, I suggest that they have in effect not kept faith with their own important promise or promises. That, in not turning in an ambitious, carefully researched paper, or in failing to rise to the challenge of questions I have put to them in class, they have been disappointing in a way that might best be understood in terms of a concept like fidelity. One recent student took offense at my introduction of that term and asked, reasonably, why I did not just say instead that she had been lazy, or that perhaps she had not liked my question or thought she had anything intelligent to say in response. What had this to do with fidelity, she wanted to know, and didn't I think that it was a mistake to use a word that had a clear meaning in one context for purposes that were apt to seem obscure in a very different context.

An excellent student, this young woman, who had been with me in three previous courses and whose work, and abilities, I knew well. Someone I admired so much that I was not at all reluctant to say to her that I wanted her to have a properly exalted idea of herself and to be faithful to that idea. Why not, I asked her, fidelity to me, your teacher, who wants to think as well of you as he has in previous years? Too high-minded, I asked her? Maybe, she said. Pompous maybe, I suggested? That too, she answered. And worse than that, do you think? I can't think of anything worse, she said. Presumptuous, I pressed. At which point we agreed to let it go and just get down to talking about particular aspects of the paper she had come to the office to discuss.

And so yes, presumptuous, perhaps, and too exalted for a transaction as mundane as the passing encounter between student and professor. But where then would that leave it, if we yielded to that verdict? Elizabeth Costello again: "While she has less and less idea what it could mean to believe in God, about the devil she has no doubt." A good thought, that one, which I am tempted to try in this way: I have less and less idea what it means to be perfectly faithful, or why even on some mundane occasion I am required to give that solemn obligation any thought. But I have no doubt that it is possible to violate a promise and that this is a thing not—not lightly—to be done. The devil is in the place where nothing has weight. To take seriously what you do and fail to do is in essence what this is all about. "Because you are after all not a child," Costello says to the fellow, the novelist Paul West, whom she has chosen to chastise for a dereliction of writerly duty. Had she been dealing with a child, she suggests, she would not have thought to remind him that as a writer he has made certain promises that are his to keep.

With my student, of course, I must ascertain that she is capable of hearing what I say to her, that she can consider—because she is "after all not a child"—what it means to be faithful, to keep her promise as a student. That she can take in the idea of what is not to be done, not especially by her as an unusually gifted young person. That to be faithful here entails simply taking seriously her own gift, her promise.

IV

Once, in an extended conversation I had with Saul Bellow, in front of a large and sometimes combative audience, Bellow remarked that it was not always easy to distinguish between high and low seriousness. A cautionary remark, perhaps directed at something he disliked in what I had said, which perhaps reminded him of an accent he occasionally detected in his own utterances. Perhaps some trace of that very will to moral exquisiteness Bellow sometimes indulged, always hated, and successfully put to route in his best work by a practiced resort to humor and witty self-disparagement. He wanted—so I felt in his company—to bear witness to what he thought fundamentally important without wearing his will-to-virtue on his well-worn sleeve. Not easy, not for Bellow, not certainly for me, to think fidelity without fearing that fall into low seriousness, the banality of a platinum-plated idea too good not to inspire misgiving and irony.

Irony in what sense exactly? Irony as the laughter of the gods directed at the solemnities of earnest hand-wringing and high-flown phrases expended on what looks, certainly from afar, like trifles. Fidelity and betrayal thus as ideas susceptible to satire and even contempt. The stubborn insistence on such ideas a tribute, it may be, to something no longer alive or meaningful.

As with another friend, also a writer, decidedly not a god, who wrote me recently to say that he didn't think the words "fidelity" or "infidelity" had any longer a meaning worth disputing. "Too late," he wrote. "Fidelity too much a matter of faith and hope and because." Which got me to thinking that maybe he was right, that every sentence dealing with these subjects will necessarily assume some capacity for belief largely vanished among us and, more crucially, given what we have become, will hinge on a "because" and therefore be. . . . But here I had trouble formulating the objection. Objection to what? So what if I say: I choose to be faithful *because*. Or: I regard as betrayal this rather than that *because*. Or: Those who do not know what fidelity is will lead impoverished lives *because*. Do these formulations somehow invalidate the force of the central terms, simply because they entail an explanatory element? If I decide that it is irrelevant to invoke a *because* and instead simply declare, with entire confidence, what I know to be true about fidelity and betrayal, will I stand somehow on firmer ground, making my stand on truths I apparently take to be self-evident?

I am not sure how to fight my way out of these questions, though I am convinced that the sentiment of fidelity, and the corresponding experience of betrayal, are best grasped when explanation is felt to be largely (or entirely) beside the point. Of course we are good at assigning causes. We can say that a fellow is "true" only because he has never found anyone who could attract him the way his wife does, or because no one he has flirted with has ever returned the favor. We can account for an infidelity by citing diminished sexual avidity in a marriage, or by tracing the course of a sudden, fatal attraction. We can cite "philosophical differences." Different "career trajectories." Plausible, all of these "explanations." And yet we know that they fail, in many ways, to get at what we want. That we are disappointed, too, by more sophisticated-sounding accounts, as when we hear that men are "addicted" to sex, or that they are "biologically programmed" to want sex with as many women as they can get. Evolutionary biology thus made accessible, routinely tempting, and hopeless.

Hopeless especially where fidelity is at issue. As we know when we are confronted with an account that refuses to rely on any of the readily available formulas and seems, precisely for that reason, compelling and modest and true. As in the case of Joseph O'Neill's 2008 novel *Netherland*, often described in rapturously enthusiastic reviews as "exacting" and "desolate," and thus improbable as an instance of the very thing that will seem so rare in contemporary accounts of fidelity. For O'Neill's central character Hans is by no means what will pass for an inspiring figure. In fact, he is, as more than one reviewer noted, "an ordinary European everyman" whose wife leaves him at a critical moment in his life and soon takes up with another man. And yet this Hans, desolate as his prospects can seem, is also an unmistakable instance of a decidedly unspectacular and uncommon faithfulness. Not merely because he deals rather well with his marital problems and eventually wins back his wife, but because he operates more or less consistently from a modest sense of the way things are "supposed" to be. If this is an everyman, he is also a more than promising instance of a fidelity with no need of a because.

Most telling, for our purposes, are Hans's relations with a character named Chuck Ramkissoon, a man only briefly a friend and, in several respects, something of a mystery. A man, moreover, likely involved in corruption and extortion, and possibly worse. A man central to the feel of a book in which he is not the primary character but somehow implicated in all its primary concerns. There is no way to think this fellow Chuck faithful, in spite of his many qualities of warmth and enthusiasm. But clearly he is a person who brings out in his friend Hans an uncommon affection, however laced with misgiving and suspicion. Tempting to think of that affection as underwritten by some moral conviction, but there is little or no sign of that here. Here the affection is the effect of a simple, steadfast loyalty. Hans van den Broek is faithful to his friend not because he has reason to be. He is faithful in the absence of compelling reasons. The "fidelity," such as it is, exists in spite of what Hans knows and suspects.

Thus two men are friends, and that is that. No principles are involved. No formal promise or contract. When, two years after Chuck has disappeared from his life, Hans learns that his remains have been found in a canal, "handcuffs around his wrists" and "evidently . . . the victim of a murder," he realizes at once that he is "angry" at the way the death is casually described by a reporter obviously sniffing around for a story. And then, shortly after, angry again at his wife's way of speaking about the dead man with "a detached note I don't like." Later in the novel, in a remembered exchange with Chuck, he bristles at what he takes to be his friend's inflated optimism, the "excess of [his] peroration," and he cautions him to note "the difference between grandiosity and thinking big." Everywhere we find in Hans a resistance to grandiosity, a habitual way of bringing things down to size, a refusal even to think big if that entails even a hint of exaggeration. So that the attachments, the loyalties must themselves be modest in scale and feeling. Fidelity an instinct, not the effect of a principled exertion. But an instinct, all the same, however indisputably felt, rooted in something larger than an ephemeral whim or passing fancy.

Toward the end of the novel Hans's wife says of Chuck, "he must have valued you," but then immediately adjusts that to "I mean, you were valuable to him. He wasn't interested in you. . . . Not really." Hans takes this in and is, he reflects, "too tired to explain that I don't agree—to say that, however much of a disappointment Chuck may have been at the end, there were many earlier moments when this was not the case and that I see no good reason why his best self-manifestations should not be the basis of one's final judgment." Spoken, is it not, in the voice of a friend not besotted or delusional but faithful and with no need to rely on reasons or to make a perfectly balanced assessment. Fidelity with no need to be right.

And with no need, moreover, to reverse itself when it becomes anxious. O'Neill's Hans, after all, must engage not only with his wife's dislike of Chuck but with her cunning observation that her husband's faithfulness has everything to do with the fact that the object of his fidelity is a Trinidadian black man. "She has accused me of exoticizing Chuck Ramkissoon," Hans notes, "of giving him a pass, of failing to grant him a respectful measure of distrust, of perpetrating a white man's infantilizing elevation of a black man." Zadie Smith contends that "this conversation signals the end of Chuck's privileged position (gifted to him by identity politics, the only authenticity to survive the twentieth century)." But in truth Chuck never had, for Hans or for the reader of the novel, the kind of privileged position that exempts a character from suspicion or mistrust. What he had, again, was a friend's faithful and sustained affection, maintained even in the face of suspicion and disappointment. And if Hans does surely take in the suggestion that "identity politics" played some part in his willingness to give Chuck "a pass," he does come also to deny the charge, and we are given no reason at all to doubt him.

Hans, after all, routinely makes the familiar civilized noises, invokes the usual "manifestations" and the "basis" for a judgment. He speaks as a man who has been trained, like the rest of us, to respect evidence and to acknowledge the difference between one interpretation and another. He would not, if challenged, deny this, would not speak of fidelity as entirely an affair of heart or instinct with no connection to mind or reasons. And yet the man does stake his claim to affiliation without building up anything like a full or decisive foundation to support him.

Is this what we mean, ought to mean, when we say "fidelity"? That it is a sentiment utterly unconditioned by reasons? Adam Phillips seems not to agree. He says that "most people would never have engaged in monogamy if they had never heard monogamy spoken of." Which suggests, unless I misread him, that marital fidelity will seem compelling only if it is authorized by an established consensus based on what seems to most people unimpeachably good reasons. Fidelity *because*. Fidelity as "a good idea." And thus by no means mainly the expression of instinct and generous disposition, as embodied in Joseph O'Neill's remarkable "everyman."

V

When I knew myself, as a very young man, to be unable, or unwilling, to think seriously about the prospect of my own infidelity, I might well have said then what the deceived husband in Ford's *The Good Soldier* says, when asked how it felt: "It is all a darkness." For infidelity, I felt, would say nothing important about me except perhaps that, like others, I was susceptible to powerful desires. This entailed some considerable dishonesty, as I allowed myself then to suppose that I didn't or wouldn't care about the betrayals to which my wife or I might be susceptible with our partner's example to provoke or inspire us. And of course I was also willfully blind in failing to imagine what might be the consequence of giving myself over to a kind of existence whose implications, even then, I should have understood quite well.

I tried, back then, to believe that fidelity had principally to do with some "agreement" you had made, some understanding you had reached with yourself. If you had agreed not to ask very much of yourself, then there was no reason to be disappointed in your behavior or attitudes. If you had agreed to be careless about your marriage, and your spouse knew that you had reached that agreement, then both of you would know what was and was not to be expected, and no possible complaint would be in order. You would be "faithful" only to your own more or less clear understanding. Honest, then, about your limitations, and unwilling to pretend to a capacity for loyalty that you didn't want or have.

But in the 1960s this was a hard position to defend. Though it could seem compelling, at least in the sphere of intimate relations, it could hardly seem defensible where the responsibilities of citizenship were at issue. You might want to say that you were not the sort of person to be constantly worrying about the state of the union or the war in Vietnam, that you exempted yourself from the obligation to stay abreast of current affairs or to participate in any sort of political action. Again, you would be honest about your limitations and not pretend to civic virtues to which you never aspired. And yet you would seem, in staking out such a position, certainly to people like me, a sort of an idiot, or worse. When I read a writer like Sartre at this time, I was persuaded that there could be no private life worth having that was not alert also to the lives of others. Writers who thought of what they did simply as self-expression and thought themselves beholden to no one were deluded and irresponsible. It was, as Sartre had argued many years earlier, a scandal that Pierre Bonnard continued to paint, throughout the years of the Nazi occupation of France, as if nothing momentous had occurred to affect his work. Bonnard, no doubt, had concluded—if he ever gave it a thought—that the public world was not for him, and that he would be faithful—he had no other choice—only to his own private vision. A nude woman and the ritual of the bath and the tub were more than sufficient to exercise his imagination.

Though I now accept entirely Bonnard's view and believe that artists have no responsibility other than to their own sense of what matters, I do not extend this exemption to others. I routinely ask—sometimes demand—of others that they keep their promises, even where they argue that they have not themselves agreed to acknowledge that those promises exist. Of course, like other educated persons, I am reluctant to divide the world into us and them, the saved and the sinners, the faithful and the faithless. To believe that the matter of fidelity, or fidelities, is the issue on which everything hinges is not to move through life with an assurance of one's own perfect rightness. I know that I feel as I do because certain images, or facts, or narratives, have an overpowering claim on my imagination. I know that what I feel about fidelity also has something to do with the time when I knew myself to be casual and thoughtless about infidelity and hated that sense of myself. But I know too that this picture of my own evolution has nothing to do with the standard story of guilt and redemption and can by no means be made into an edifying discourse useful to others.

When I say that I hated the sense of myself I say, in effect, that my "condition" seemed to me an ugly thing. I hated having to regard myself in this way. Ugly, in particular, was the easy indifference to the meaning of my own compulsive flirtations, the growing sense that I came on to potential targets mainly to discover what would sell.

Detestable, too, was the dishonesty entailed in the adoption of this posture, for I was not at all an adequate representative of the species *hip young man*. Nothing I could do would make me seem, to myself or anyone else, genuinely cool or careless. The flirtatious, insouciantly promiscuous young man I sought to project was transparently misleading, even to me. I knew myself, even then, to be a fraud, though of course I hoped that some of those I selected for my performance would be taken in, if only enough to be mildly impressed. Having much earlier discovered that I did not know how to play with conviction the role of faithful married husband, I now discovered that I had a growing fear of being found out as another kind of fraud, a man without a center, a character in search of a genuine self.

In almost every other way—as a political activist, a polemicist, and an editor of my own quarterly magazine—I was and had been an unusually committed, often comically earnest person. So that my casual yet compulsive habit of flirtation was perhaps more puzzling and troubling to me than would have been the case with someone else in my cohort. In fact, my habits and compulsions seemed to me to belong to the arsenal of an essentially promiscuous person, though nothing I had done quite seemed to me the mark of a successful predator, and I found myself recoiling, as from something unclean. What I feared, really feared, was not that I would somehow get better at seduction than I had been and then find myself disgusted at the hollowness of my many triumphs. In truth I couldn't quite imagine that level of success and consequent disappointment. No, I feared simply that I didn't quite know what I was and that my habits bespoke a way of evading the questions I would need somehow to confront, sooner or later.

This was, after all, the early 1970s, and I was still impressed by those who were, as I was, willing to put their bodies on the line in opposition to the Vietnam War. Many of the thinkers I read were pessimistic about our common prospects, and yet there was something hopeful in feeling that you could not be seduced by the usual enticements offered by the usual institutions of the society to those who did what was asked of them. People who were casual about everything, from politics to sexuality, seemed to me contemptible. Promiscuity was the word that best described those who at most pretended to convictions they didn't have, and at worst moved through life with the sense that everything was permissible, nothing more sacred or important than anything else. In my own case, the fear I felt had much to do with the sense that, whatever the commitments I had made, there was something in me that wanted too much to be wanted. An inclination to make the seductive noises and accommodations that win lovers or followers, that cover over differences and help you to feel beautiful and irresistible.

Though a number of my friends have been—and remained—promiscuously unfaithful husbands or wives, I have never felt that their behavior was fatal to our friendship. But I have not found a way to like or respect persons promiscuous in other, more comprehensive ways. Certainly I have no love for public figures who say different things to different audiences and operate as if their sole purpose is to sell themselves and their "message." And I have no patience at all for writers—especially famous writers—who are perpetually currying favor with one or another constituency by contriving to say politically correct things or by carefully avoiding anything that might give offense. Writers who are nothing but strategic. And no love either for faculty members at my own college who wish to be all things to all students and all colleagues and stand for nothing but the will to niceness. Or for therapists whose prime ambition is efficiency and whose only "truth" is that really everything is permitted as long as it doesn't make you feel bad about yourself.

VI

In my late twenties, at a time when I could see no hope for a marriage that had already featured several protracted separations, I met a young woman to whom I have now been married for forty years. Though she was, when very young, unmistakably a child of her time, she possessed what seemed to me an unfamiliar, highly developed sense of sin. Odd word, sin, for someone decidedly unreligious, secular through and through. But sin nonetheless. A lapsed Catholic, a graduate of Marymount High School in Rome before her college years, my wife early introduced me to expressions I had not heard before. Most striking was, "to put yourself in the occasion of sin," an expression that made both of us laugh when she first said it, and has—so far as I can tell—nothing that would recommend it to anyone else in our present cohort. An expression clearly unpromising and yet strangely attractive, in that it so entirely contradicts the dogma—our advanced dogma—of complete toleration and openness.

To put yourself in the occasion of sin is to open yourself to temptation. In the erotic realm it is to expose yourself to the possibility of an attraction, or consummation, you might wish (would wish) to resist. The implication entailed in the use of the word "sin" is that you are determined—would be determined—to say NO to what, given the chance, you might find that you want. In learning how not to put yourself in the occasion of sin, you deny yourself the opportunity to discover how much you want what is forbidden—forbidden at least to you, given who you are and your active sense that there really are things that ought not to be done.

The most unsavory aspect of this formulation is its underlying assumption that people can be trusted—can trust themselves—only if they are not confronted by temptation. This takes us all the way back to the cloister and the veil and regimes of confinement and surveillance. To fidelity understood as a strict discipline maintained to protect against variety of experience. To desire understood as inevitably dangerous and the certain pathway to transgression. All this without question so far from the way most of us—I include myself—now think and live as to seem at best ridiculous and, more than that, pernicious. For who among us can now believe that desire is a certain pathway to sin, or that we can be faithful only by shunning temptation? As with doubt, we now believe—most of us at any rate—that life presents innumerable openings to betrayal, and that to live as an adult in the world is to want not protection but the courage to see things as they are.

And yet I did find, when first I heard "sin" used in this peculiar, unpromising way, some reason to ask whether even someone like myself might find a way to make it fruitful. Some way to think sin and the occasion of sin without simply laughing it away. So that I turned, at once, as if it were the most natural thing in the world, to the simple fact that certain things disgust me, incite in me a powerful revulsion, and that this capacity for revulsion goes back to something deep in me, deeper than my own enlightened commitment to openness and toleration. When I say that something disgusts me, I am drawing on a response that must have originated in taboos and prohibitions underwritten by orthodoxies no longer alive for me. And yet the disgust is real. It is occasioned by a sense—my sense—that certain things are foul or indecent. If we recoil— I recoil—from the use of the word "sin" even for things that occasion disgust, I cannot deny that, at another time, in another place, "sin" would surely have seemed to me an appropriate term for certain deeds that now move me to revulsion.

Just so, though the strict prohibition against putting oneself in the occasion of sin must now seem, to people like myself, quaint or misguided, I can also concede that it does potentially point to something I would do well to consider. Set aside, just for a moment, the idea of a formal prohibition or an enforced exclusion from ordinary interaction. Set aside, if only provisionally, the objection that the occasions and prohibitions envisioned by Puritans and church fathers in the past were directed chiefly at women, who were presumed to be especially vulnerable and defenseless. The fate, or history, of ideas, as John Gray reminds us, "obeys a law of irony." Ideas rarely have the consequences "their authors expect . . . and never only those." The injunction not to put oneself in the occasion of sin may even now point us in a promising direction, if only we allow ourselves to think it.

For what may now be suggested by this injunction—so I conclude—is simply my willingness to live my life as if there were some things I am obliged to take seriously and some things I should want not to do. Again fidelity, in this sense, less a code of conduct than a disposition, less a rigid discipline than a habit of being. Not to put myself in the occasion of sin is to proceed with some sense that I am not, or not exclusively, a sovereign self. Though I have a hard time speaking of the sacred and cannot really worry about what will become of my immortal soul, I do hope to live as if some things were indisputably important, as if there were dangers to which I am, like the rest of us, susceptible, dangers to which I ought not too blithely or thoughtlessly to succumb.

One of those dangers is that I will become, through carelessness or indifference, the kind of person who will not think there is anything terrible enough to keep him awake at night. No sense, in acknowledging such a danger, of an unduly exalted order of obligation or of "powers" insisting or demanding or accusing. Simply a sense that an untroubled lightness of being is not—not for me at least—an attractive option. A form of knowledge and of power, to be sure, the power that will allow someone to say—one of many such things that Adam Phillips can bring himself to say—that "most infidelities aren't ugly. They just look as though they were." A view of things from afar, from on high, enviable in its way, compatible with the hopeful perspective of Italo Svevo's Zeno, who is tempted to feel that the thing "which leaves no trace does not exist," and that his own modest transgressions must then be as light and fleeting as air.

But then the charming and brilliant words of my friend Phillips, and of Zeno, do not here answer to the reality of the life I live. Choose to live. For they do not sufficiently concede that injuries, betrayals, and disappointments do not always vanish without a trace. Yes, the "reckless" and "impulsive" and "incontinent" may sometimes be "the heroes and heroines of our imaginations," as Phillips says. But then often they are not at all heroic, and their actions may seem to us shabby, or cruel, and when we think about what we want for ourselves and for those we love, we may well turn to other models. Is it true that our culture—what used to be referred to as our "high culture"—is largely committed to what John Gray calls the "dogma" of "inordinacy"? If so, it is not quite so certain that most of us are prepared to accept the consequences attendant upon the playing out of that dogma.

Richard Rorty once said that "the only way to figure out whether what you have been told is true is to see whether it gets you the sort of life you want." In support of this, Rorty also cited Lionel Trilling, who suggested that "the modern way of judgment" turns inevitably on "what sort of person one wants to become." Of course we don't all want the same sort of life, and we are sure also to differ—even with our closest friends—on what sort of person we would most like to become. And yet I must suppose that, where "fidelity" is concerned, even the most "modern" way of judgment can point—with very rare exception—only in one direction. Can I want to become the sort of person who fails to keep his promises or to regard any of his promises as important? Would anyone recommend to a son or daughter that they model themselves on—or attach themselves to—such a person? Even to try to resist the judgment entailed in these questions would require a perverse refusal to think seriously about them. Like it or not, the sort of life any of us will conceivably want will require that we acknowledge the crucial difference between faithfulness and indifference.

To be sure, fidelity remains an idea that carries with it a freight of unwelcome or unpromising associations. Often it has been used as a weapon to indict the character of persons who are unconventional. In itself, as we have indicated, fidelity too often seems the recourse of those who are weak, or timid, or puritanical. And yet, for all of its unfortunate—and sometimes deserved—associations, fidelity persists, as an idea, a goal, an ideal, a provocation. It is, in its way, an indispensable cultural marker. It signifies that our liberty does not require the elimination of our common wish to differentiate and to prefer one sort of thing to another. To say, with some confidence, that this is good while that is not, or at least not good enough. And it signifies, more particularly, that a culture is most healthy, and most open, when fidelity is not most of the time regarded as a bar to experience or a dismissible anachronism.

[5]

SAVING BEAUTY

PART ONE: A BEAUTY

And yet I cannot think of anything to say about it except that
it is wonderful. . . . You can merely say over and over that it is
very good, very beautiful.

—ELIZABETH HARDWICK

The most beautiful man I ever knew was Charles Newman,
once the editor of the quarterly journal *Tri-Quarterly*, a gifted
novelist and man of letters. When I met him he was almost forty,
the possessor of a large, intelligent, perfectly ordered face in
which there was no discernible trace of turbulent emotion. His
hair lifted softly above an unruffled forehead, and though, as I
later learned, he had recently been through a period of stress
and agitation, his eyes were radiant with confidence, unencum-
bered. What might have been taken for indifference in another
countenance in his was clearly the conviction of a sumptuous
sufficiency. The beauty was carried lightly, as if its possessor had
never known the need to tend or promote it. To win or shine
was not his ambition. Somewhere, some time, you felt, he had
promised not to be vain. In his own beauty he had discovered
an endowment not to be overvalued or abused. What came to
him as a result of his beauty would be accepted gratefully but
without any accompanying sense that he had done anything to
deserve it.

I had known other men who seemed to me too beautiful, men whose beauty overshadowed every other feature—of character or wit or intelligence. Charlie's beauty did seem that way to some of our friends, and I'll not forget the words of a colleague who said, not a minute after she had set eyes on him for the first time, that no man had a right to look that good. Who does he think he is? she asked. Others, by far more numerous, were impressed, struck dumb, or amused. Our friend Richard Howard declared him impeccable. He looks, Richard said, the way a man ought to look. Of course Charlie was not for him. Charlie was for women. At the Chinese restaurant on 58th Street before a dance performance at Lincoln Center, the striking twenty-something who showed us to our table carefully brushed his wrist when she handed around the menus. She likes you, I said, when she had moved a few steps away, but Charlie didn't answer. He took out his pipe and began to clean the bowl as if he hadn't really noticed the young woman at all.

He was between marriages then, and his new girlfriend was away at a business conference in San Francisco. Renata was her name, and Charlie had brought her to us for a "quick impression" only a week or so after they had met. She was a good deal younger than he was, late twenties, but you could see that there were some miles on her, and though she said that she'd never been married, or, for that matter, in love, I guessed that she wasn't in the market for anything permanent. Charlie was for her a trophy guy. With her long, bright red fingernails and her thick, reddish brown hair tied back in an unfashionable ponytail, she laughed a lot and batted her flirtatious eyelashes at her benevolent, blue-eyed stallion.

I figured right away that the girl in the Chinese restaurant would know perfectly what to do with Charlie, whose beauty was a match for hers, and sure enough, she struck up a conversation with him about the duck she'd sliced before his quietly admiring eyes and asked whether the martini wasn't too dry. By the time we left the place an hour later, Charlie had jotted his unlisted phone number on the back of our bill and dropped it meaningfully in front of her. I'm not in the book, he said to her, but you can leave me a message any time.

This was a scenario to which we'd grown accustomed. Charlie's beauty inspired intensities of admiration and interest. Though it might occasionally seem almost too good to be true, it was not intimidating. If his was an ideal beauty, a composite endowment of physical attributes that expressed poise, well-being, and lucidity, the beauty was at the same time, surely for most observers, entirely human, approachable. It conveyed little evidence, one way or another, of inveterate kindness or sensitivity, but it bespoke a measure of alertness and vulnerability that might in the long term prove an indispensable aspect of its charm. Women especially were drawn to this beauty as to a quality inordinately precious, as if the prospect of becoming its possessor might miraculously confer upon them a sense of comparable endowment, not otherwise available to them, in spite of their own substantial attributes. In the great violet eyes of the Chinese beauty brooding gamely at our restaurant table, we could see an avidity almost breathtaking in its hopefulness and candor.

Of course there are those for whom beauty is conventionally said to reside only in the eye of the beholder. On this estimation, my friend was creditably beautiful only because he clearly moved others to declare him so and to cite as evidence their own sensations of pleasure and longing. I don't know how to contend against this view of beauty, which is in its way as unanswerable as the alternate view, which insists that beauty exists as an objective fact irrespective of any particular impressions or sensations it inspires. It is tempting to cite as authority on this matter Oscar Wilde, who famously quipped that "It is only shallow people who do not judge by appearance." But appearance is not quite as self-evident a quality as Wilde supposed. In his indispensable book on beauty, *Only a Promise of Happiness*, Alexander Nehamas notes that "what counts as appearance doesn't remain constant" and proposes that appearance can be reliable as a gauge only when accredited by "the members of a particular group with similar background" who will agree "immediately when presented with the same phenomenon." This was, in my experience, the case with my friend Charlie, whose appearance was reliably compelling to all our friends who knew him. It was with him as Arthur Danto observed, when he wrote that beauty is "really as obvious as blue: one does not have to work at seeing it when it is there."

I knew Charles Newman for almost thirty years, and until he grew ill in his early sixties, I met no one who did not think him beautiful. Nothing remotely theoretical or problematic about it. In this sphere, the case for the more or less self-evident has long seemed compelling, if by no means flawless. Consider, as but one famous example, a passage from the *Pha-edrus*, in which Plato describes the response of a man to a beautiful boy as follows: the man, he writes, "shudders in cold fear. . . . But gradually his trembling gives way to a strange, feverish sweat, stoked by the stream of beauty pouring into him through his eyes and feeding the growth of his soul's wings. . . . He cares for nothing else. . . . He gladly neglects everything else that concerns him." The inflamed language will no doubt seem to many of us excessive, perhaps even embarrassing, and the superstructure Plato erects to exalt, or justify, the susceptibility to beauty—here reflected in the allusion to "his soul's wings"—may well seem irrelevant or spurious. But we ought not too readily to disdain the impression of a "stream of beauty pouring into him through his eyes." For Plato invites us to believe that there is in fact such a thing as beauty and that we know beauty exists even where the theory to which we subscribe may tempt us to doubt it. Sophisticated people who pay little attention to beauty as an issue do none-theless casually refer to the beauty of a familiar musical work—say, the adagio movement of Dvorak's "American" quartet or the *Primavera* of Bot-ticelli, or the clean lines of a Marcel Breuer chair in a Bauhaus exhibition. When they do so, they do not think of the beauty to which they refer as in any way disputable. They believe in that which pours into them through their eyes or ears. Their ardor is real to them, and they know it to have been occasioned by something real out there for which they are grateful.

To be sure, there will always be persons who are indifferent to beauty, who regard it as superficial or refuse ever to be taken in by it. In an essay on Elias Canetti, Susan Sontag noted that "the great limit of Canetti's sensibility is the absence of the slightest trace of the aesthete. Canetti shows no love of art as such," she goes on, and "he does not love any-thing the mind fabricates for its own sake." Though he was an "unre-generate . . . materialist," the merely material, fleshly beauty of Charles Newman would not have seemed to him at all irresistible. Would he have agreed, in the name of a hypothetically disinterested assessment, that my friend was endowed with the attributes conventionally associated with beauty? No doubt the very idea of such an assessment, mobilized simply to arrive at an empty verdict, would have seemed to Canetti irrelevant, adolescent. By contrast, Sontag herself was an insatiable beauty lover, and often she allowed herself to swoon playfully, openly, generously, girlishly at the mere sight of Charles Newman as he entered an auditorium or took a chair at the dining table in my own Saratoga Springs home. A 2002 email letter from Sontag, responding to something I'd written her about Charlie's novel-in-progress, asks if he's "still beautiful."

Though I often disapproved of my friend, his beauty never seemed to me diminished by anything he said or did. Perhaps that marks a limitation in my own equipment, a flaw, or worse, in my own moral sensibility. The thing I liked least about Charlie was his way of carrying on with several women at a time and letting me in on what he was up to. At a time when he was married to an obviously doting and substantial woman named Edith, he was going around with a very attractive younger woman in St. Louis, where my wife and I often visited one of our children and his growing family. Though in New York Charlie lived with the wife—his fourth—in a high-rise near Lincoln Center, he spent the spring semester each year away from her and had made the St. Louis companion something of a significant other there. The wife clearly had no idea what Charlie was up to, and though you might say that anyone married to Charlie who remained clueless about his predilections deserved whatever he handed out, it was hard for us to be cavalier about Charlie's cheating ways. We knew and liked Charlie's wife. We spent time with her and were pleased that she regarded us as friends to whom she could occasionally appeal for help or advice. She was an open and sometimes ebullient woman who might well, at the start of an intimate dinner party at their apartment, entertain her guests with fifteen or twenty minutes of a piano piece she had recently mastered. She obviously liked her husband and forgave him for what she took to be merely an inveterate habit of flirtation toward available women. Why shouldn't he flirt, she once asked us. He likes it, and the women all seem to like it too. She knew herself to be both doting and beautiful, and Charlie had given her no reason, she felt, to be insecure about their future together. He drank too much, but that had little to do with his feelings toward her or their marriage.

In truth, my wife and I often felt uncertain about what to do where Charlie and Edith were concerned. In spite of everything, Charlie continued to treat his wife with courtesy and affection. Often he spoke of her professional exploits at an architectural firm with unconcealed admiration. In their company it was remarkably easy to forget, at least for a while, that Charlie was involved with another woman in St. Louis and likely had other women he saw from time to time in New York as well. Even in decline, Charlie dressed elegantly and seemed in every way a refined, beautifully educated specimen, in bearing impeccably upright, correct, a pure example of the *danseur-noble* type we would admire together at performances of the New York City Ballet.

But Charlie's beauty did not help us much when we were forced to confront his tall, willowy companion in St. Louis. He brought her to our son's house for brunch one Sunday morning and was courtly and solicitous around the compact wooden table crowded with fruits and bagels and platters of fish and cheese. That evening, on the phone, I told Charlie that none of this seemed to me a good idea, not where we were concerned. After all, we'd soon be seeing him with Edith in New York, or at our place in Saratoga Springs, and we'd have to pretend to her that we knew nothing about the other woman.

You don't have to pretend anything, Charlie shot back, as he did again and again when we walked around in Central Park together later that spring. It's not as if Edith is going to ask you about my girlfriend and you'll be forced to lie. Jesus, he went on, you don't go around blurting everything to everyone you meet.

Bad faith, I said, reaching for a platinum-plated idea that Charlie and I had debated maybe twenty years earlier when people still talked earnestly about such notions.

Bad faith my ass, Charlie said. Tell her anything you want. If you think Edith needs to hear from you about my love life, by all means, let her have it. It's not as if she hasn't harbored a suspicion or two. Might be good for her to think my best friends are looking out for her.

Sometimes with Charlie you forgot that he was one of the smartest guys you knew. Or you forgot that he was in many ways a gentle soul. But then you looked into those steady, steadying eyes of his and found something reassuring. Didn't know quite what to call it, but it did, you felt, have much to do with whatever in him continued to seem ineffably beautiful. He was not, to be sure, what typically passes for a beautiful character, not if that epithet is intended to identify an exalted moral stature. At times I felt that Charlie's beauty got in the way of any reasonable estimation I might make of him as a person, and I wondered—only a little—at my own ability to be moved, consoled, by a beauty that could seem, at such moments, mainly skin-deep, as others would have it.

It's not so easy to abandon the idea that beauty can never really be skin-deep, that genuine beauty is not only unproblematic but also somehow a sign of an essential goodness. "If the goodness of your heart was visible," Jenny Diski writes, "it would surely look like Audrey Hepburn or Johnny Depp." There was, I felt, in my friend, some indiscernible correspondence between his looks, his demeanor, and his true self, which had to be "good" in a way not always apparent even to those of us who loved him. I would not have known how to defend this impression had I been forced to do so, and it seemed to me the sort of lazy notion I typically despised.

Useful, perhaps, to recall at this point something from Doris Lessing that may have some bearing on the question of beauty. Lessing noted what she called "a basic female ruthlessness in herself" and went on to disdain the notion that gender is, in its essence, "socially constructed." How, she asks, did she acquire her husband? She stole him from another woman. And how did she feel about that? She felt, she said, that it was "my right": "When I've seen this creature emerge in my self, or in other women, I have felt awe." No need, at this point, to pursue the question of what was, or was not, a "basic female ruthlessness" in Lessing. No need, in fact, to ask whether anything in Lessing's description has more to do with women than with men. Critical, however, to consider that the awe Lessing cites—a quality others might describe as pride, pride in being what one is—may well have much to do with the experience of oneself as a being sufficient, whole, indisputable, and yes, beautiful in one's felt disdain for standards not of one's own choosing, as for example moral standards that have something to say about a woman's setting out to steal another woman's husband. Lessing's awe rests upon a felt indifference to ways of feeling and judging that would interfere with pure enjoyment or with the appreciation of a beautiful sufficiency aloof from the trivial misgivings of assorted scolds and moralists.

My friend Charlie was not—not in any way I could get terribly worked up about—a bad man. He took no special pleasure in causing pain. But betrayal was not for him—certainly in the domain of ordinary relations between men and women—an operant concept or lurking sentiment. Though he would not describe his own somewhat predatory attitude toward women as ruthless, he moved with the certain sense that he was somehow bound to behave as he did. I never heard him speak of the awe he felt at the display of his own seductive gifts, but he had about him an enviable freedom from the misgivings and reluctances that often inhibit the projects of less headstrong and confident lovers. If our sense of what is beautiful, truly beautiful, always derives from some idea or impression of what is natural, fully consistent with its own intrinsic laws, then it was legitimate for me to think of my friend as beautiful, even where his behavior seemed to me reprehensible.

Would I have continued to think him beautiful had he been openly or slyly flirtatious with my own very beautiful wife? No doubt my estimation of Charlie's beauty would then have been fatally compromised, for it would surely have seemed to me unnatural for this intimate friend of ours to ignore the obvious distress to which he would then have blithely subjected both of us. The attentions in that case, had Charlie paid court to my wife, would then have seemed to me not an expression of supreme self-confidence but of a desire to wound, and it would have seemed to my wife not merely a testament to her own attractiveness but a symptom of Charlie's dark and complicated relation to me. The impression of our friend's beauty would then, I suppose, have given way to an impression of him as more than a little bit fucked up, driven and unpredictable and reckless, rather than healthy in the steady pursuit of his own pleasures.

Natalie Angier, among many other science writers, has studied the relation between health and the capacity to experience "unfettered joy." She notes that "sensations like optimism, curiosity, and rapture . . . not only make life worth living but also make life last longer." The surge of awe Lessing described in acknowledging her own right to proceed in accordance with her desires is, in this sense, rightly understood as entailing an optimism about her prospects. Lessing—so we may say—felt rapture at the absence of impediments associated with anxiety or reluctance. She seemed beautiful to herself in her healthy, uncomplicated understanding of strength and appetite. Angier would appear to ratify this sense of the case when she writes that "real joy, far from being merely a lack of stress, has its own decidedly active state of possession, the ripe and gorgeous feeling that we are among the blessed celebrants of life. It is a delicious, as opposed to a vicious, spiral of emotions." If there does seem something primitive about the state so described, health a condition in which a whole range of civilized sentiments (guilt, regret, pity) are simply not in play, it is a state that aptly embodies what we witness when we are in the presence of certain kinds of beauty.

Think, for a moment, of Stendhal's extraordinary Sanseverina in *The Charterhouse of Parma*, a figure who seems to us worldly, witty, robust, assertive, and desirable, in every way a magnificent woman, indisputably beautiful though also scheming, corrupt, and openly disdainful of the standard moral sentiments. Her physical beauty we accept on the basis of the passions and transports she inspires, though, as a woman past thirty, she takes herself to be already "old" and to have passed beyond the stage at which mere looks in a woman will suffice. Stendhal is clearly in love with her, however much he pretends, playfully, to be appalled at her stratagems and duplicities. She seems to him, we feel, an epitome, the incarnation of everything that would make a woman seem to us desirable and therefore indisputably beautiful. Though she can be, at times, genuinely compassionate, she is by no means routinely so, and no one alert to the full range of her thoughts and propensities would think her conventionally nice or sweet. She is clever, to be sure, though Stendhal does not, clearly, regard her as an embodiment of spiritual beauty. Her attractiveness, all apart from the physical attributes duly noted by men and women of her acquaintance, has to do with her confident rejection of the fastidious conventions of feeling and manner associated with ordinary decent women. To be in her presence is to feel a certain uneasy gladness, where our senses are preternaturally alerted to a beauty not uplifting but troubling. Though Gertrude Stein once said that to call a work of art beautiful is to say, in effect, that it is dead, there is nothing remotely dead about the Sanseverina, who is not, of course, a work of art, but who is in her way a perfected emblem of a beauty that is bracing, not at all superficial or ephemeral.

My friend Charlie was, in his way, a much more elementary embodiment of the beautiful, his physical endowments consoling, obvious. Admirers did not need, certainly not at first, to overcome in themselves a reluctance to give themselves over to his beauty. I never felt that his beauty required of me an exercise of taste presumably lacking in others. The few friends with whom my wife and I discussed Charlie's inconstant ways thought his infidelities irrelevant to our common impression of his

beauty. Charlie's character simply did not play any part in our estimation, perhaps because in most respects he was likable, not at all given to
the plottings and subterfuges that so preoccupied Stendhal's Sanseverina.
Charlie's was a more moderate temperament. His confidence required
little in the way of testing or reinforcement. His health lay in the habitual
exercise of faculties he knew to be firmly in his possession and rightly his
to use as his instinct dictated. Though he was a learned and sophisticated
man and knew that among educated persons beauty itself had become an
unpopular and retrograde idea, he could allow himself to take pleasure
in beauty where he found it and did not regard simple ingratiation as
a despicable sentiment. Had he been asked, he would not have agreed
that the easy consolation derived by others from the contemplation of
his own good looks was an unworthy satisfaction. No more would he
have regarded the fact that judgments of beauty are often "subjective" as
a reason to doubt their authenticity.

Charlie was, in the true and somewhat old-fashioned sense of the term,
an art-lover. A brilliant fiction-writer and essayist, he worried over the
fate of the arts in a culture he had reason to mistrust and devoted a controversial book-length study to what he called "the Post-Modern Aura."
There he displayed his own fondness for the difficult and his suspicion of
the accessible pleasures afforded by straightforward realist fiction. He was
a man in search of more rarefied pleasures, and he appreciated that, in art
especially, persons like himself were more apt to regard as beautiful what
others might regard as unduly complex or self-conscious.

At the same time, he was unapologetic about his own appetite for
accredited masterpieces and insisted that the beautiful was obviously
preferable to the ugly. Though he understood perfectly that works once
thought to be awkward or ugly—from the poems of T. S. Eliot to the music
of Igor Stravinsky—could in time come to seem "beautiful" by virtue of
their familiarity or their status as revered modernist artifacts, he resisted
the view that taste was merely a matter of convention and that efforts to
differentiate between the beautiful and the ugly were hopelessly naive.
Though he was an adept of interpretation, he was also drawn to Susan Sontag's famously provocative assertion that it was "the revenge of the intellect
upon art," and he despised what she had designated the "overt contempt for
appearances" that often figured so prominently in fashionably "advanced"

readings of books and other artworks. In music he preferred the ravishing to the atonal and withholding, and he saw nothing limited or embarrassing in the canvases we examined together at an exhibition of Matisse's Moroccan paintings in New York. Theoretically he was inclined to agree with the critic Clement Greenberg that beauty, as commonly understood, is mostly irrelevant to the value of art. But he was, all the same, an inveterate beauty lover, and he was loath to accept that beauty has nothing at all do with the success of particular artworks. We were not at all surprised to learn, when Charlie died in March 2006, that he had left his money and possessions to the Chamber Music Society of Lincoln Center, whose programs he had enjoyed for many years. Did the beauty he found in the performances he attended of chamber works by Schubert, Haydn, Ravel, and others inspire him to feel beautiful beyond what he would otherwise have felt upon gazing at his own reflection in the mirror hung above his dressing table? I would imagine so. Though Elaine Scarry may well be right when she says "it does not appear to be the case that one who pursues beauty becomes beautiful," Charlie was always inclined to Plato's view in the *Symposium* where, as Alexander Nehamas reminds us, he explained that "life is worth living only in the contemplation of beauty."

PART TWO: THE ATTACK ON BEAUTY

> . . . things disposed to perfection.
>
> —MARK STRAND

The derogation of beauty is not a recent phenomenon. Puritans, old style and new, have long decried the attention paid to the gratification of the senses. Others have bristled at the very notion of taste as a cultivated faculty required of persons who hope to recognize genuine beauty and to resist the appeal of trivial embodiments—serene vistas, brilliant sunsets, purple prose. The futurist Marinetti in 1912 railed against "lulling harmonies" and "soothing cadences" as if beauty were by definition bland and elementary. Others—Virginia Woolf among them—have worried that an appetite for fine sentences and elegant metaphors might cause us to shut ourselves off to what Woolf called "the spasmodic, the obscure, the fragmentary, the failure." And yet Woolf herself was no enemy of beauty, and many of those who have warned us against surfeit and infatuation have been drawn in their art to ecstasies of language or pigment.

The most serious and sustained attack on beauty has taken shape within the domain of art. Modernist artists—though with notable exceptions— have dismissed all things relaxing, easy to take in and enjoy, and therefore inimical to the spirit of an art intended to be rigorous, difficult, unpopular. To be impressed by what passed for beauty was felt by many modernist writers and artists to be philistine. A respectable work might sport the look of beauty or finish so long as its primary intentions were subversive or obscure. Though beauty is unmistakably an aspect of high-modernist works by Woolf or Wallace Stevens, no one would suppose that their creators aimed simply to make things easy or enjoyable.

Earlier generations of artists had their own very different quarrels with beauty. Often, in fact, they made art whose beauty now seems to us indisputable, though it seemed anything but obvious to their contemporaries. Is beauty at issue in the paintings of Tintoretto? The massive canvases made for the Scuola San Rocco in Venice now seem plainly ravishing. What is vertiginous and eccentric in Tintoretto's handling of space presents no problem at all to a contemporary viewer. And yet, as E. H. Gombrich reminds us, Tintoretto's paintings are often distinguished by jarring or inharmonious "contrasts of light and shade, of closeness and distance." In sacrificing what Gombrich calls "that mellow beauty of color that had been the proudest achievement of Venetian painting," Tintoretto's work suggested to some of his contemporaries that beauty was henceforth to be regarded as irrelevant to the purposes of art. Gombrich writes that Tintoretto "had tired of the simple beauty in forms and colors which Titian had shown to the Venetians" and speculates that Tintoretto "seems to have felt that . . . [Titian's] pictures tended to be more pleasing than moving." Though he was by no means the first painter to operate from a conviction that to please could hardly be the sole or primary function of the artist, Tintoretto was one of the first painters to call into question the virtues of harmony, proportion, and mellow perfection of color. Gombrich notes that Tintoretto's contemporary, Giorgio Vasari, criticized him for his "careless execution and eccentric taste" and wondered at the lack of "finish" in paintings that could seem "crude" or indifferent.

No doubt it is impossible now to suppose that such a painter could have been casual or careless about anything in his own intricate compositions. But Vasari was not inclined to appreciate the tension so prominent in the works of an artist for whom beauty was an expression of instability, the virtuosity an effect of the painter's need to dramatize the body's capacity to extend and coil.

In the history of beauty we do not find that tension itself has invariably played a significant role. Even the modernists were by no means at one in the valuation they placed on it. To be sure, the rejection of a particular kind of art or of a particular artist is by no means what we usually have in mind when we speak of the attack on beauty. To see only crudity or exaggeration in Tintoretto is not to dismiss the possibility or validity of beauty everywhere. Quite the contrary. Those who have raised questions about the durability of beauty have often tried, in their several ways, to make a case for it as something real, a set of qualities inhering in many works of art in spite of the fact that ideas of beauty change. Even a thinker like Arthur Danto, who regarded beauty as an "optional" feature of artworks, attempted to locate the legitimate uses of beauty in underwriting the effectiveness of certain kinds of painting.

But there is a line of thinking that rejects entirely the idea that beauty can ever be other than a sensation in the eye of a beholder. From this perspective, the taste of a particular viewer—by definition neither good taste nor bad taste—would then wholly determine our "personal" assessments, which would therefore have no authority whatsoever. The "evidence" typically brought forth to support such a view includes the following:

- Works once thought to be ugly or disgusting often come in time to seem pleasing and beautiful.
- Beauty has been defined in so many different ways, even within the confines of a single period or culture, that it is hopeless to suppose it can be associated with any particular class of objects or features.
- Because we accept that beauty is not in itself an absolute requirement or criterion for works of art, judgments about what is or is not beautiful are obviously of little interest in the domain of aesthetics and are apt to be "personal" or "accidental" or "merely subjective" when invoked outside of that domain.

- The language employed to describe beauty is so obviously slippery and unreliable that it cannot possibly refer to objectively discernible qualities. What Yeats called "sweet sounds together" are to another auditor artificial and cloying; what the film critic Pauline Kael called "rapturous" in Visconti's *The Leopard* is to another viewer lugubrious and overheated.
- Because beauty has long been associated with qualities of refinement, finish, and perfection, it will always hinder our appreciation of other, more important qualities, such as audacity, spontaneity, vehemence, and what Clement Greenberg called a willingness to proceed "by way of errors of taste, false starts, and overrun objectives."

It is tempting to concede something to each of these arguments and then to go on as if none of them could possibly blunt our estimation of beauty or its claims to "objective" status. No doubt the word "beautiful" can mean nothing or everything. Even a work intended to provoke or offend—say, Duchamp's "urinal"—may rapidly come to seem familiar and even beautiful by virtue of its form or its smoothly gleaming surface. The face in a Soutine portrait, which can resemble a slab of raw or undigested meat, may signify "beauty" where vileness is felt to be cathartic and inversions of the sacred are thought to excite our appetite for the good. The case against beauty, for all its reasonableness, will never quite banish the visceral attraction to particular objects or experiences that inspire a pleasure distinct from mere interest or curiosity. Artists like Barnett Newman, who believed that the idea of beauty had been put successfully to route, nonetheless found themselves referring to qualities that might just as well have been marshaled under the heading of beauty: "the artist," said Newman, inevitably asks himself, again and again, "to what extent are you charmed by [the] inner life" of the work you are making—a concept to which he might well have referred by invoking the "spiritual" beauty of the work. Likewise the critic Robert Hughes, who rarely assessed works in terms of their beauty, nonetheless extolled the merits of paintings often unpromising, inchoate, humble, neither suave nor decorous, whose virtues seemed to him hard-won and therefore oddly ravishing. So that one imagines him very much at one with Frank Kermode's response to E. M. Forster's novel *A Passage to India*: that book, Kermode writes, "does not founder, is difficult in some of the ways India is difficult, and like India, can on occasion be menacingly foreign as well as strange and beautiful." Beauty, then, where the thought if not the fact of foundering is present, where difficulty is apparent in the unresolvable conflicts inherent in the work, and where that which emerges can seem strangely beautiful because it exists in tension with all that threatens to unsettle or dislodge it. Beauty, perhaps, as tendency rather than as system, as reluctance more than complete gratification of the senses.

And thus we may say that the attack on beauty belongs to a long history of mistrust and misgiving and has inevitably generated a wide range of compensatory strategies and embodiments. If we cannot find it in ourselves to receive beauty as a gift, pure and simple, then beauty, we insist, must be apprehended in some other way. When Duchamp complained that "too great an importance [was given] to the retinal," he meant that art itself was too beholden to ideals of beauty and too committed to giving simple pleasure. Though Duchamp was fundamentally mistaken in his assessment and did not imagine how successful his attack on beauty— on art itself—would be, he also could not imagine how inventive artists would be in clinging to improbable versions of the beautiful. "To make beauty in some sense imperishable required a lot of conceptual tinkering," Susan Sontag once wrote. "The aim was to multiply the notion, to allow for kinds of beauty" that might well bypass "what ordinary language extols as beautiful—a gladness to the senses." If, as Sontag concedes, "beautiful has come to mean 'merely' beautiful," at least among those in the arts dedicated "to drastic projects of innovation," the innovators have much of the time aimed to discover possibilities of beauty where none were assumed.

To be sure, beauty lovers over the past century have often found themselves on the defensive. Accused of favoring the obvious, the pretty, and the pretentious, they have often found it useful to deny or to disguise their predilection for the beautiful. Did Kandinsky concern himself with beauty? Describing his own beginnings, he sounds like a sophomoric infatuate drunk on the beauty of a Moscow sunset, drinking in "the deeper tremolo of the trees, the singing snow with its thousand voices on the allegretto of the bare branches." But Kandinsky's progress is typically discussed in terms of his lofty ambition—signaled in the language of the quoted passage—to "apply the methods of music to his own art" and to capture "the spiritual in art." The naive ambition to paint, and thereby experience "the most impossible, the greatest joy," a joy expressive of his own rapturous discovery of unmediated beauty, is translated into more acceptably sophisticated terms. The movement in his work from recognizable forms and images to abstraction is thus accorded the respect reserved in the modernist era only for those who were determined to take risks and to break with conventional ideas of representation and beauty. Though Kandinsky himself feared that abstraction might in time decline to a merely decorative or trivial routine, he defended his own procedures while avoiding any reference to the sumptuousness of his texture or coloration. The vocabulary of appreciation lavished on Kandinsky's mature work follows the painter in emphasizing its commitment to the kaleidoscopic and bottomless, to sensations and the spiritual. Beauty, which is unmistakable in Kandinsky's best work, is simply not on the table.

Sontag notes that beauty necessarily applies "to some things and not to others." It belongs, she argues, to a category of ideas dependent on "discrimination." Those who are comfortable making judgments about beauty are "unapologetic" about their willingness to rank and exclude. The attack on beauty, she contends, is an aspect of a larger attack on discrimination itself, which is felt to be "elitist" and to entail "prejudice." Our "appreciations," she says, or so "it was felt, could be so much more inclusive if we said that something, instead of being beautiful, was 'interesting.' . . . To name something as interesting implies challenging old orders of praise." Beauty, which is central to those "old orders," would then seem, at the least, not only "elitist" but not so very interesting. Though it is true, as Sontag contends, that "long use of 'the interesting' as a criterion of value has, inevitably, weakened its transgressive bite," the category has remained viable, central as it is to "the promiscuous, empty affirmations" that now stand in for what were once judgments based on shared convictions about the difference between good art and bad, the beautiful and the ugly.

Though most of us routinely make such judgments in our daily lives, preferring this to that, recommending a good film and dismissing a bad one, we have learned to be uncomfortable with judgments based on clearly articulated standards. We mistrust standards, know them to be anything but fully defensible. Understanding that ideas of beauty change and that works once thought ugly or poorly executed can come to seem attractive by virtue of their originality or complexity, we are loath to commit even to deeply felt impressions. The interesting seems to us more reliable if only because it entails a verdict that regards issues of value as naive or spurious. We may incline, like Jenny Diski, to believe that though "beauty's shape shifts. . . . it is always in some ways recognizable to later viewers" within a culture. But we are reluctant to sign on "officially" to such a view, in part because we have lately been taught to sneer at "universal" values and to mistrust the authenticity of impressions that are "culturally conditioned." If beauty really is, or seems to be, "in some way recognizable," that is no reason to believe that it exists as an objectively credible attribute. So the culture of modernity would seem in a thousand ways to insist.

The critic Wendy Steiner puts it this way: "For a start," she proposes, "we must stop treating beauty as a thing or quality," accepting shifts and differences in valuation as "meaningful and valid, and not 'fallings away' from some 'truth' or 'higher taste.' Beauty is an unstable property because it is not a property at all. It is the name of a particular interaction between two beings." Steiner's view of the matter is a good deal more complex than the passage may suggest, but it does sharply affirm the current, enlightened tendency to mistrust discrimination where the term entails an effort to differentiate between good and bad, more or less beautiful, taste and the absence of taste. The idea of beauty as nothing more than "the name of a particular interaction" is a nice evasion of the question and leaves us wondering why artists remain committed to discrimination, however they feel about issues of "higher" and "lower" taste.

Consider, in this regard, Gerhard Richter's notes on a 1985 Anselm Kiefer exhibition of "so-called paintings." "Of course," Richter writes, "this is not painting at all." Why not? Plainly, because "they lack this essential quality." What quality? The one essential to painting when it deserves to be treated as such. How do you know that Kiefer lacks the essential? You have only to look at his work and see that it features "formless, amorphous dirt as a frozen, mushy crust, nauseating filth, illusionistically creating a naturalism which—while graphically effective—has, at best, the quality of a striking stage set. The whole thing," Richter concedes, "is delivered with panache and undoubted self-assurance—as well it may be, because its motivation is literary: it's all in the content. Every lump of filth stands for one scrap or another, snatched from the bran chest of history."

Richter's notes on Kiefer are saturated with the language of disgust, a sentiment not at all diminished by the felt effectiveness and panache of Kiefer's work. Are "dirt" and "filth" and "crust" the source of Richter's disgust? Or is the source identified in words like "formless," "amorphous," and "literary"? The final sentence in Richter's "Notes" to the Kiefer exhibition is definitive: "The one thing that frightens me," Richter writes, "is that I might paint just as badly." Though he is himself an artist who knows not what his own works are to look like, nor even what he "aims at," proceeding like a "blind" and "desperate" man, for whom it is possible that "anything goes" and nothing can be, strictly speaking, "wrong," he is sure that Kiefer's works ought not to be called paintings and that to paint like Kiefer is to paint "badly."

I do not at all share Richter's view of Kiefer, whose best work seems to me neither formless, nor amorphous, nor nauseating, nor unduly literary. But Richter's critique is important because it is informed by a sense that genuine painting does betray certain qualities, though it may take shape under the hand of an artist who has no aim, who proceeds blindly, and whose work will remain largely "incomprehensible." Impossible to say in advance what any given painting will look like, though, Richter insists, it is possible to say that the work we admire—if we are to admire it—will be "just as right, logical, perfect" as a work by "Mozart, Schoenberg, Velazquez, Bach [and] Raphael." Right and perfect, then, as a work by Kiefer clearly is not.

No doubt it is too much to suggest that the quality chiefly lacking in Kiefer, so far as Richter is concerned, is beauty, though the word "perfect" at least has often been invoked to signify the harmonious completeness and balance of a work made to generally accredited standards of beauty. What Richter misses in Kiefer's work is some sense that it has sought, however blindly, the perfection consistent with its own nature. He misses not a particular kind of beauty, not a conventionally serene or polished surface, but the signs of struggle that bespeak some sense that there is a difference between getting something right and not getting it right. Richter's disgust would seem to have been inspired by his impression that at some level Kiefer was indifferent to the intrinsic logic of his own work, indifferent to the prospect of beauty as a quality we love and admire in a work that is, in every particular, true to its own intention. Though we can never say with confidence—not in so many words—what any work intends, we feel, now and then, that we may know what a given work is supposed to be because there is nothing in it that seems to us lax or ostentatious or superfluous or trivial. Only in that sense, perhaps, may we say that Kiefer's work inspires in Richter a disgust that has principally to do with Kiefer's presumed indifference to the prospect of beauty.

Of course there is danger in presuming to speak of beauty, which requires that we trust our own instincts more than we have any right or reason to. Often, as we know, we ourselves will change our minds about a thing whose beauty or logic had seemed clear to us only a month or a day earlier. A new piece of information, an idea will come suddenly to bear upon a long-held impression in a way that will loosen its hold on us and force us to revise what had been an all-but-certain attachment. Someone, a philosopher it may be, will explain how stacks of Brillo boxes, turned out by someone named Andy Warhol in 1964, at once acquired the power to call into question everything we thought we knew about art and thereby raised questions about quality and intention and technique so that nothing—so many of us now believe—can ever again be what we thought it was. Beauty, regarded as one of those perennial "questions" now forever altered, has thus come to seem to many of our contemporaries at once irrelevant and out of bounds. To insist that we cannot and must not ignore it is to fly in the face of ample evidence to the contrary.

But there is another sort of danger in these precincts. Call it the danger of insisting on the value and meaning of something you don't quite believe in yourself, the danger of lying. You say, to yourself at least, that beauty is real and point to this or that indisputable instance. You identify, as scrupulously as you can, those instances in which the beauty is essential to the effect of a work and those in which it is incidental or spurious or misleading. You flatter yourself on your ability to make such discriminations and suppose that such an activity is one of those necessary and valuable things we do within an ostensibly advanced civilization. Some of us may go so far, perhaps, as to talk, or to think to ourselves, about taste, and to deplore the absence of that faculty in the life of our society. We note that most of what gives pleasure to our contemporaries is contemptible and feel somewhat embarrassed to have entertained such thoughts, wondering about the source of such disdain, and think ourselves more than a bit ridiculous to feel, in this way, superior. The insistence on the validity of beauty is but one of a range of activities that may be fatally tainted by the suspicion of a most unbecoming self-regard. And that very suspicion may well point the way to the suspicion that there is something false in our insistence on beauty.

T. S. Eliot wrote, many years ago, of those who strive, as he himself had often done, to arrive at "the objective order of merit" of works of art and to preserve and cultivate the "taste" required to appreciate beauty. Is not this striving "to pursue a phantom," he asked, "the chase which should be left to those whose ambition it is to be 'cultivated' or 'cultured,' for whom art is a luxury article and its appreciation an accomplishment"? Is there not, in the pursuit of such a "phantom," Eliot wondered, the danger that we will forget that we are, all of us, "imperfect" people with "imperfect taste" whose sense of the value of things must necessarily be founded on "the development of [our own peculiar] personality and character"? To pursue the phantom of beauty may well be, as I follow out the arc of Eliot's logic, to presume "to have better 'taste' in poetry [or in art more generally] than belongs to one's state of development" and thus—here is the real danger—"not to 'taste' anything at all."

And yet we may also remind ourselves, by way of encouragement and consolation, that "beauty is part of the history of idealizing." Susan Sontag's formulation has the virtue of confirming what in general beauty-lovers must believe: that their infatuation with beauty has a long and noble pedigree. To idealize is to attempt at least to be in touch with an idea of perfection, to suppose that *what might be* is more than what is, that the fact of the ordinary is no final bar to a conception of the extraordinary. Idealization proposes that there may be in this world something to which we may feel drawn to offer our admiration or allegiance because it is apart from us, better than we are, more wholly what it is and needs to be, something we cannot suppose can be better than it is. Our own sense of smallness, limitation, imperfection, vanity—call the defects what we will—cannot banish our instinct to imagine something not fatally flawed as we are. In idealizing, we do not suppose that perfection is easily come by. It may appear to us in the guise of an enviable self-assurance, an air of sufficiency, but we admire it in proportion to our sense of how fully it has been tested, how far it has had to contend with what is ordinary or ugly. We admire beauty, in works of art especially, because they embody a successful mastery of everything that says *no* or *impossible* to every effort at an ideal, unimpeachable sufficiency.

What we have learned, however, is that idealization cannot pursue its chosen phantoms where the thought of taste is allowed to intervene. Taste levels preference to the status of the merely individual and accidental. It eats the heart out of idealization by instructing us to feel that our dreams are tainted by their origin in accidents of habit or fortune or psychology. To believe, with whatever misgivings, in the actual existence of beauty is to believe that taste does not alone account for what seems to us authentically beautiful. Further to believe, with Gerhard Richter, that there are actual qualities without which a work by even so original an artist as Anselm Kiefer cannot be called "a painting" is to operate from the basis of an idealization that is felt to be legitimate and, in ways that must remain mysterious, binding.

We acknowledge, all the same, the limits of our ability to identify exactly what we mean by beauty. We accept that the introduction of the matter of *taste* in these precincts fatally challenges our conviction that beauty is more than "a particular interaction." And yet we are tempted to reach a kind of "proof" that will settle a matter that cannot be settled. We know—how not to know?—that *for example* is not proof. And yet there is—absent abstraction and self-canceling argument—nowhere else to go but to particular examples. Hard not to point and refer, to insist, with Sontag and other beauty-lovers, that "the capacity to be overwhelmed by the beautiful is astonishingly sturdy." Hard not to agree with her that in the end, with all the arguments tallied up, "beauty regains its solidity, its inevitability, as a judgment needed to make sense of a large portion of one's energies, affinities, and admirations."

Too much, maybe, to stake a claim to "proof" on the basis of "masterpieces," which belong to a category itself much disputed, however foolishly, in the course of at least two or three generations. Better to look, briefly, at a beauty more modest in scale and ambition. A beauty made and yet revealed to us as if it were a brief miracle, decisive and unaccountable. And so why not, then, the beauty of aphorism, which must move on the brink of inconsequence and yet seem necessary, which, at its best, will state or suggest a meaning, may even reveal a "truth," while seeming to

exist principally for its *way* of saying what it says. To happen on a striking aphorism is to experience an improbable thrill, so audacious is the
formulation in its impossible brevity. The critic Kenneth Burke wrote that
"eloquence is simply the end of art, and is thus its essence," which may or
may not be true but does point to a quality indispensable to aphorism,
which is eloquence. And what is eloquence? It is what Nietzsche called
"a beautiful folly," what Denis Donoghue calls "the dancing of speech,"
where "the aim of [the] dance is not to get from one part of the village
green or the stage to another." Eloquence, Donoghue says, "is a play of
words or other expressive means . . . , a gift to be enjoyed in appreciation
and practice." Its main attribute is said to be "gratuitousness," and "its
mode is to be intrinsic. Like beauty," Donoghue goes on, "it claims only
the privilege of being a grace note in the culture that permits it."

More to be said, of course, though not here, about varieties of eloquence and about the relation between context and apparently autonomous self-pleasuring expression. But the proof I am after is discernible,
I believe, in aphorism considered apart from context. An aphorism may
have a part to play in an essay composed to develop an idea or argue a
proposition. A line or a passage in a poem may have the force, the shape,
the wit, the concision of aphorism and participate in the larger rhetorical
design of the poem. And yet the brilliant, commanding aphorism will
seem to us somehow also to stand free of its context and to delight in its
own autonomous perfection. The aphorism will thus draw our attention
to its own concise formal comportment. It will, as Alexander Nehamas
says of the beautiful generally, "stand out against its background," and it
will press us to ask "how it differs from other things." This will have little
or nothing to do with a critic's passing of verdicts or the impulse to rank.
It will also bypass the issue of whether or not the thing before us is a
work of art. The aphorism, considered, received, as a thing of beauty, will
require simply that, in noting that it differs from other things, we do our
best to understand why it is beautiful.

Consider, to begin, a sentence from Emerson that may, alas, reflect
somewhat on our own little exercise: "If you go expressly to look at the
moon, it becomes tinsel." Nothing especially remarkable there in the way
of metaphor. No special marks of eloquence or formal originality. The sentence has going for it merely conviction and brevity. Is it at all beautiful?

It has the decisiveness and clarity of a good aphorism, but it lacks the dash, the brio, the sting of a really first-rate aphorism. In their foreword to *The Viking Book of Aphorisms*, W. H. Auden and Louis Kronenberger attest that a good aphorism must be "valid," must "convince every reader that it is universally true," and I suppose that Emerson's aphorism succeeds, more or less, on that score. But it is, if not tedious exactly, or obvious, at least near enough to tedious and obvious as to inspire no sensation whatever of beauty. The best I can say of it is that it makes me uneasy about my own search for the beautiful in aphorisms, which may, as a result of my earnest pursuit, come to seem tawdry, shopworn, obvious, no matter their potential capacity to astonish if happened on in some other way.

There are aphorisms that, on first blush, seem surprising, and thus promising, and yet turn out to be easy, mechanical. Here is George Santayana: "Music is essentially useless, as life is." The turn, from music to "life," is promising, in the sense that we had not thought before to compare music to life and surely had not been tempted to anything so sweeping as the assertion that life is useless. But the promise disappears when we remember that "music is essentially useless" is itself an uninspired commonplace and reflect that life is not for most of us useless, and that the more we think about it, the emptier the assertion must seem. Maybe a good aphorism need not be "universally true," but it cannot be good if it is merely the expression of an author's desire to say something more, or other, than we usually say.

In fact, a beautiful aphorism, as I have suggested, will necessarily demonstrate the quality of eloquence, will embody "the dancing of speech," will deliver an "improbable thrill," and will seem to exist "principally for its *way* of saying." Would this be the case with Nietzsche's declaration that "convictions are more dangerous foes of truth than lies"? The statement has the virtue of calling into question the very thing—convictions—that ostensibly decent people are accustomed to claiming for themselves. It has the further virtue of declaring an inevitable opposition between "truth" and convictions and thus emptying convictions of any validity we might impute to them. The statement is thus subversive and, in its way, stirring. Auden and Kronenberger say that "aphorisms are essentially an aristocratic genre of writing" in the sense that the "aphorist doesn't argue or explain" but simply "asserts," implicitly operating on the assumption "that he is wiser or more intelligent than his readers." No doubt Nietzsche fits this profile, and no doubt the force of aphorism has always to do with a refusal to argue or explain. The successful aphorism must seem peremptory, definite, unapologetic, a law unto itself. And by that standard, Nietzsche's assertion would seem, at the least, adequate.

But is it beautiful? Is it eloquent? Surely its language is by no means distinguished. It does not seem to take pleasure in its own expression, clearly does not exist for the sake of its own expressive vitality. Its essential aim would seem to have more to do with correcting an idea than with bringing forth a statement that, in some indisputable way, will be its own delicious reason for being. It doesn't create what Donoghue calls "an eternal present moment," the moment when the sheer unanswerable beauty of a thing stands forth and seems, miraculously perhaps, more important than anything else. The fact that the impression of "an eternal present moment" is impossible to certify with perfect authority doesn't make the impression any the less real for those who experience it. Not, of course, possible to suppose that any free-standing aphorism will have the indisputable incantatory beauty "exempt from duty or obligation," as Donoghue says of perfect eloquence, of the stanzas in Wallace Stevens's "Sunday Morning" or Auden's "In Memory of W. B. Yeats," which remind us that "poetry makes nothing happen: it survives / In the valley of its saying where executives / Would never want to tamper. . . . it survives, / A way of happening, a mouth." To which we can only say, yes, precisely, and know that thereby we have pointed at least in the direction of the beauty we wish to acknowledge.

Is there beauty in the following aphorism of Karl Kraus? "My language is the universal whore whom I have to make into a virgin." We note at once—should note—that the sentence is a striking, memorably compact expression of an idea, a thought complex, that might have been developed, played out, over many sentences. It is the expression, moreover, of a ferocious intelligence that has found a way to embody its thought in an improbable yet utterly compelling metaphor, in terms of which a "universal whore" can be made "virgin." The force contained in each of the primary terms is palpable and is the result of their being used in this improbable way. We may well subscribe to the idea that possessed Karl Kraus throughout his lifetime, the idea that reality itself is cheapened, made unreal, by the language of newspapers and commerce, that every thought we have is a lie because it is the creation of the information industry. But what seizes us, as readers of the aphorism cited here, is the rigor of the formulation, the way the language obviously delights in its own subversive rightness while containing, controlling, an unmistakable rage. The exaggeration intrinsic to Kraus's statement is here invulnerable to criticism because it is so obviously the servant of the impulse to astonish and delight and affront. Kraus's aphorism is of course "conceptual," but it has none of the aversion (or indifference) to pleasure and sensation that made so-called conceptualist art a bore and a dead end. Though influential thinkers like Ludwig Wittgenstein drove many artists to believe that "beautiful" is a meaningless term and that the words we intend are "right" and "correct," we see in Kraus's aphorism that "beauty" does in fact get at something we want. The alternative terms, "right" and "correct," say merely that Kraus found a way to say precisely what he meant to convey. The emphasis there is on the content of the aphorism. But we admire Kraus's aphorism chiefly for its invention, its compact intensity and suggestiveness, its ability to hold and express a great deal in a single reflex. I don't care in the least what Kraus himself might have said about the relevance of "beauty" to his writing, which is never beautiful in the sense of *lovely* or *mellifluous* or *delicate*. But I like to think he'd have been moved, as I have been, by a brief exchange between two exceptionally smart and gifted painters by the name of Larry Rivers and David Hockney.

LR: Now let me ask a serious-type question: Would you prefer your work to be thought beautiful or interesting?

DH: Putting it like that I think I'd rather have it thought beautiful. It sounds more final, it sounds as if it did something. Interesting sounds on its way there, whereas beautiful can knock you out.

Is that it, I ask myself? Is it that "beautiful can knock you out" as nothing merely correct or interesting or right-minded can do? No one will doubt that a piece of crap intended to shock may also have, at least briefly, the ability to knock you out. Duchamp and his legions found ways to knock out their audiences without committing deeds remotely related to beauty. In the end the critical difference may lie in our sense that a work merely interesting knows all too well what it wants to accomplish, while something beautiful is informed by a desire to express something as if expression itself were of paramount importance. Duchamp's works are essentially polemical, persuasive. They press us to draw conclusions they are contrived to enforce. By contrast, Kraus's aphorism, which looks like it shares that polemical intention, is yet, in another way entirely, its own reason for being. Duchamp's urinal or bicycle wheel, like Warhol's Brillo boxes, can have no reason for being other than the points they aim to make, and whatever features they may happen to share with genuinely beautiful objects, those features are entirely incidental to the effects they aim to produce. If they knock us out, that is because the idea they express seems to us shocking or unfamiliar or clever. Kraus's aphorism is an instance of the beautiful because it is not reducible to its "idea" or "concept" or "argument" and because it seems to us perfect in its freshness, its willingness to take delight in being what it is. Though the aphorism seems purposeful, it participates in what Denis Donoghue calls "the gratuitous authority of freedom, play, and pleasure" and is content to exist within its own perfectly constructed precinct. It seems to us, in this way, beautifully self-sufficient. It wants for nothing, and it inspires in us nothing more than the desire for further instances of beauty, for the satisfaction we feel in the presence of objects or expressions that are completely themselves.

[6]

MY "OTHERS"

Be that as it may, I cannot pretend to be what I am not.
—PRIMO LEVI

Never for him the tyranny of the we that is dying to suck you
in, the coercive, inclusive, historical, inescapable moral *we*
with its insidious *E pluribus unum.*
—PHILIP ROTH

But in my account, love—that is, caring—is a thick relation
that can be directed to others only insofar as they are worthy
of our love.
—AVISHAI MARGALIT

In 1954 I met "The Other." Like me, he was then twelve years old, a student at John Marshall Junior High School in the Bedford-Stuyvesant neighborhood of Brooklyn. Like me—this I learned some months after our initial encounter—he was exceptionally good at hitting and fielding baseballs. The first time he approached me he announced his name and commanded me to take off my shoes. When I hesitated and backed a few steps away he rushed forward and smacked me hard on the cheek, then smacked me again when I tried to get up off the playground asphalt. Though I was stunned, it occurred to me to be grateful that this black boy had hit me with an open hand, had not used a fist or a weapon. It also occurred to me that the expression on his face did not betray anger. If I was not mistaken, he was but barely suppressing a smile, and I imagined that he would like nothing better than for me to get up, so that he might smack me again. Would he be satisfied with the money my mother had deposited in my right shoe so that no bully would take it from me? I resolved, with not a little fear and misgiving, to test him and reached, without saying a word, to pull off my shoe. Punk, was what he said. You're a punk. And with that he himself stepped back and ordered me to stand up. Now run to your mother, punk, he further commanded, and get the fuck out of my sight.

I didn't know what to make of this boy, no bigger than I was, but I thought him no doubt finished with me. When I pictured him, as I did often in that year, I tried to reconcile that incipient smile with the sense of something implacable in his demeanor. Might I have found words to please him? I didn't think so. He was as little interested in my thirty-five cents as in the leather baseball glove strapped to my book bag. He was interested in me, a well-behaved white boy enrolled in a ghetto school, segregated in a "special" class of students doing three junior high school years in two. Smug, he would have thought me. Intolerably secure in my whiteness, my thin long nostrils, and my elite academic status. Interested in me the way you might be interested in someone you know to be irrevocably alien to what you are and hope to become. Wanting only to confirm, so that neither of us might have any doubt on this score at least, that nothing could conceivably be done to close the gap between us.

I suppose I have always felt that we live, all of us, among others who do not wish to join hands and dance with us in a circle, who have no desire to make nice. Often we are told to mistrust the evidence of our senses and to think more optimistically, even about those who clearly have no use for us. But I have found infinitely more compelling the testimony of those who see little reason for a comprehensive optimism, who can accept that often the other is, in every important respect, beyond us. Consider, as but one brief example, this passage from Ryzsard Kapuscinski's *Travels with Herodotus:* "I am witness in Tehran," Kapuscinski begins,

> to the last weeks of the Shah's regime . . . traffic is paralyzed by endless daily demonstrations . . . every now and then armored trucks dive into the streets and squares and fire at the demonstrators . . . sometimes,

white clad girls and boys march at the front of the columns, their foreheads encircled by white headbands. They are martyrs—ready to meet their deaths. It is so written on their headbands. On occasion, before the procession starts to move, I walk up to them, trying to understand what their faces express. Nothing—in any event, nothing that I would know how to describe, for which I could find the appropriate words.

Of course Kapuscinski is not alone in discovering that often the other is indecipherable, out of reach. Even when we have the courage to "walk up" to the other, we are struck—more often than not—by how little we have to say to him that he would be willing to hear. By now, sixty years after my unsatisfactory encounter with the boy who told me to take off my shoes and then bluntly, with almost aristocratic condescension, dismissed me, I have an arsenal of terms and concepts that might well account for his enmity. And yet, try as I may, that disdainful countenance, that quality of contempt, will forever seem to me alien, the expression of a fixed determination, a coolly intolerant dignity beyond anything I have ever been able to summon or adequately decipher.

Just so, the martyrs, "ready to meet their deaths" in Kapuscinski's Iran, are at once susceptible to analysis and yet irrevocably beyond me, almost as if as they belonged to another species. I am aware that, like the rest of us, martyrs too may have a change of heart, that even the strangest of the strange may come to seem less strange to us when we make some effort to see the world—to see ourselves—as the other does. But these are platitudes, and they are nowadays routinely promoted by a cadre of thinkers—wishful thinkers—who want, like Kapuscinski in his last book, *The Other*, "to free us from the restraints of selfishness, from indifference, [to] keep us from the temptation to be separate."

And yet indifference is by no means an inevitable concomitant of separateness, and selfishness may have nothing whatever to do with the impression that meaningful dialogue or interaction with the other is often difficult, and in some cases impossible. I am not indifferent to the Islamic martyrs who assemble in the streets of Jakarta or Kabul, or to the Israeli fanatics who blithely promote "population transfer" for Arab citizens long resident in the state of Israel. I wonder at their fanaticism, and now and then I actively fear them. Wanting to find them comic or pathetic or inconsequential, I find them instead vicious and perplexing. When I wait for an elevator in a Boston high-rise and see myself standing next to a hijab-covered woman with a lock clamped firmly over her mouth, I am astonished and appalled and wish that I might summon the words to tell her that she has made of herself something monstrous. Kapuscinski quotes with approval those who believe that "there are no superior or inferior cultures— . . . just different cultures, which satisfy the needs and expectations of their members in different ways," so that the other is simply "an individual whose behavior, just like that of every one of us, is typified by dignity, respect for recognized values, and esteem for traditions and customs." But the dignity of the woman with the lock on her mouth is something so far inferior to the dignity of women who are free to speak as they wish as to deserve to be called something other than dignity. I am admonished by legions of right-thinking men and women to "esteem" traditions and customs unlike my own, and yet I find no reason—apart from the wish to pass muster with such persons—to esteem what often seems to me grotesque.

And yet there is, unmistakably, another way to think about such matters. The injunction to think well of the other, however inscrutable or forbidding he may seem, is not merely a reflex of misguided generosity. Kapuscinski recommends, as a way of understanding this requirement, that we look to the works of the influential French philosopher Emmanuel Lévinas. Lévinas responded to the "atrophy of interpersonal relations between the self and the Other" by proposing that each of us slow down, "look at the other's face," and learn to see in it one's own. Ignore the other and we cannot know who we are. Take responsibility for the other, accept that the other can be "rich and valuable," a "sacred book in which good is recorded," and we will avoid the fate of those who fear to see themselves mirrored in "the culture of others" and thus obstinately shut themselves away from any prospect of contamination.

We have, all of us, encountered versions of this outlook, in a thousand different places. Did Flaubert not suggest some such thing when he famously declared, "Madame Bovary, c'est moi"? Was he not moved, in spite of his savage disdain for her and her kind, to see in her something like an uncommon fate, the impulse to surmount what seems insurmountable, to say no to the boring, safe, settled life to which ordinary persons are usually consigned? Emma Bovary was, in the eyes of her creator, an other: delusional, unprincipled, grasping, easily duped. But he did not allow himself to resist her, looked into her face and saw in it something he recognized and feared and detested and could almost—almost—bring himself to love. Would Lévinas have been content with Flaubert's exertions along these lines? Perhaps he would have thought them—did in fact think them—insufficient, the impulse to judge and condemn and hold himself apart from his struggling creature more prominent in Flaubert than was healthy or essential.

In Robert Musil's novel *The Man Without Qualities*, a criminal named Moosbrugger, a central figure in the work, is allowed to haunt the dreams of his contemporaries. One character named Ulrich regards Moosbrugger as "a closer concern of his than the leading of his own life," one who "held him spellbound like an obscure and somber poem in which everything was faintly distorted and displaced." Ulrich's wife hopes that he will liberate something in her which she knows not how to release, and supposes that, to accomplish that liberation, she may need "to be destroyed by him, [that is] by the Moosbrugger in him." There is, to be sure, something unsavory in this sort of advanced reflection, the tendency to be impressed by a destructive force whose actual violence and ferocity one has never actually felt. The imagination of disaster, of criminal defiance, is a paltry thing when it remains merely theoretical, fashionably "advanced" but unserious, and Musil was alert to the danger of mere ideas when they were permitted to circulate more or less undangerously among otherwise reflective persons. All the same, he entertained, as insistently as he could, the idea of difference, and he was drawn, inexorably, to the collision of values and perspectives, to what he called the "one great rhythmic throb . . . of all opposing rhythms." He believed, as he often wrote, that "man's most deeply felt association with his fellow men consists in disassociation from them," and yet he studied, again and again, the transition, conscious or unconscious, from a stable sense of self toward the sensation that one is inhabited by alternative selves, all of us therefore participants in what another writer once called "a great carnival of transit."

This sense of one's relation to the other recalls the familiar notion that each of us contains multitudes. In Musil it is associated with "the capacity to think how everything could 'just as easily' be, and [thus] to attach no more importance to what is than to what is not." Thus the other will wear the face I might "just as easily" wear had I been born in different circumstances and endowed with a nature closer to his than to mine. If I were not, for whatever complex of reasons, inclined to be passive, or tolerant, or forgiving, I might—like the other I condemn—respond with rage to each provocation I receive and perhaps then display the kind of violence I deplore in predators or criminals.

To contain multitudes thus may unfortunately suggest that no one is really, truth be known, one thing rather than another. All of us would then be merely human, all too human, differences merely apparent and trivial. The criminal Moosbrugger in Musil's novel would be understood as the incarnation of a possibility that belongs to me about as much as to him. In important respects—so this line of thinking has it—he is to be acknowledged as superior to, more admirable than those who lead respectable lives. Why? Because there is in him less of the spirit of accommodation that marks well-behaved, law-abiding persons. The Moosbrugger in us is less deferential than we are to assigned or prescribed limits. He may well have a sharper awareness than we have of his true wishes and the dynamic thrust of his own personality. Musil's Moosbrugger believes that his actions reflect a "grand attitude to life," and he can say of himself what many of us, apparently, cannot, that he has a worthy story to tell, and more, that the story of his life is in fact told, and told, and holds others "spellbound."

The other as criminal, or underground man, or repressed self—the self who, whatever its flaws, is felt to have more life in it than the conventionally well-adjusted can claim—is by now a standard figure in our culture. Orwell, many years ago, writing of Graham Greene, noted that he "appears to share the idea, which has been floating around ever since Baudelaire, that there is something rather *distingué* in being damned." Think, if it occurs to you to take this seriously, of all the well-brought-up late adolescents and graduate-school students of your acquaintance who routinely invoke the names of Georges Bataille and the Marquis de Sade while gingerly toeing every politically correct line set down by the commissars of correctness in the academy. *Epatisme* and defiance continue to be growth industries in the rock universe and in the several domains belonging to popular culture, while the other, as sexual inebriate or desperado, remains a thrilling figure embodying the prospect of pleasures or cruelties or devastations rarely tasted by persons condemned to be moderate. The other, conceived in this way, consists principally as an incitement to tourists of the abyss who hope to liberate in themselves a fantasy of derangement or transgressiveness without actually risking anything beyond a mild hangover.

If it has, for quite some time, seemed attractive to play at "being damned" or at least to dabble in pretentiously *outré* ideas about the other as outsider and as secret self, the "other" has also served our purposes in dramatically different ways. As a boy growing up in a mainly black neighborhood in Brooklyn in the 1940s and '50s, I was witness to the usual contradictory signals and impressions. The son of liberal working-class Jews, I had every reason to think of the black people I met every day—of course they called themselves negroes, or colored people, not black people, or African Americans—as persons even less advantaged than the members of my own family, who worked long hours six days a week in a small store selling dry goods mainly to black customers, many of whom came on Saturdays to pay down their charge accounts with nickels and dimes. On Saturdays and in holiday season after-school hours, from the age of eight until I reached twenty-two, I waited on customers, knew many of them by name, and thought of them pretty much the way I thought of everyone else. Some were friendly, some were not. Some asked about my grandfather's health problems, others were surly or drunk. Though we had our share of holdups and petty thefts, most of our customers were as outraged about crime in the neighborhood as we were. When at closing time I stood outside the store and helped my father or my uncle to roll down the steel gates that protected our display windows out front, we were often joined by customers who companionably recalled that not many years earlier my grandfather had not needed to roll down those heavy gates and that the Safeway supermarket across the street hadn't needed armed guards to patrol the aisles.

Little sense in any of this of the black person as an other. I was aware that the black kids in my school, with whom I played on schoolyard stickball or punchball teams, did not think themselves college-bound. The black friends I made on school softball and basketball teams usually cared little about their studies and seemed—so far as I could tell—indifferent to the books we were assigned. When I noted this to my own parents, who never read books or magazines, they explained that Jews wanted their kids to have lives better than the lives of their parents, but that other people—"poor working people like us, but not Jewish"—didn't think it realistic to hope so much for their children. In this view the black kids were much like the children of the Irish and Italians who, in dwindling numbers, also lived in our neighborhood.

In fact, the black, man or woman, became for me an other not in the course of long hours working in the store or in a schoolyard but in my junior high school classroom. There, on my first day, at the age of twelve, I met my homeroom teacher, a fiftyish, bosomy, impeccably well-dressed black woman named Mrs. Ethlyn Rutledge, who also happened to be my English, history, and mathematics teacher. I had never met anyone like her and knew at once—within a week—that I wanted to be worthy of her, only her, and that she alone would understand either that I was worthy or not. She was the other as I could only have dreamed her up: erect, eloquent, alert, beautifully coiffed, clothed in floor-length clinging dresses with almost-plunging necklines. Between her breasts she held a colorful handkerchief which, very occasionally, she lifted from its nest and used to dab her perfect nose or mouth. Where the lively women in my own family were good at generating great flashes of feeling which usually felt menacing and excessive, Mrs. Rutledge displayed what I can now only think of as an Anglo-Saxon restraint. When, very rarely, she was moved by something I or another devout student had done, she would discreetly grapple us to her and permit us to nestle in the vicinity of her great operatic breasts, but even these clinchings never seemed anything but dignified. At such moments, though I was not unhappy to belong to my own tumultuous, often unlovely family, I sensed that I might in fact be destined for something better, and I marveled at the fact that the source of these intimations should be a woman whose people were routinely said, by my own right-thinking parents and grandparents, to be downtrodden and very much to be pitied. When I looked up at Mrs. Rutledge, poised with an open book in hand at the front of her classroom, I wondered at the fineness of her profile, the delicacy of her nostrils, and when she passed nearer to us, up and down the long aisles flanked by rows of seats, I swooned at the fragrance of the perfume she wore, which seemed to me to bespeak a worldliness and sophistication I obscurely admired. Her body, near and far, gave off what seemed to me a steady, always pleasant heat, and when she spoke in what seemed to me sentences longer and more complex and perfectly formed than any I had ever heard or read, I thought that this must have been the speech of the blessed, the elect.

In the two years I studied with Mrs. Rutledge, I encountered nothing to alter my view of her. I remained an infatuate, though I do not think I did anything to betray how entirely she held me under her spell. I compared her, again and again, to others I knew, and I found, of course, that no one could hold a candle to her. When my parents went to meet her at open school night, they came home to declare her "a beautiful woman" and "a credit to the teaching profession." Of course they could not envy someone whose endowments, in their view, were so far beyond their own and who must have enjoyed "advantages" unavailable to them. Nor could my parents want to undertake anything that Mrs. Rutledge might have recommended or inspired. She was, certainly as my father understood it, out of their league, and though my mother entertained certain unspoken "suspicions" about so "high class" a schoolteacher, my father was always pleased that I should have found myself assigned to her classroom, where she might work her magic on me and lift me above the life they led.

To speak of Mrs. Rutledge as the other is to engage with this idea in ways that are obviously promising, though also elusive, even dangerous. It is by now customary to think of the other as a provocation, as a menace, a challenge to one's stable sense of self. It is also customary to think of the other not merely as a challenge or affront but, most frequently, as an unfortunate, a victim whose misery we find fascinating. Almost routine by now, when the subject of the other is on the table, are citations from Lucretius ("Tis sweet, when the sea is high and winds are driving / To watch from shore another's anguished striving") or Montaigne ("In the midst of compassion we feel within us I know not what bittersweet pricking of malicious pleasure in seeing others suffer") or La Rochefoucauld ("We all have strength enough to endure the troubles of others"). Tzvetan Todorov reminds us that Georges Bataille "admitted that he gazed at least once a day at an especially atrocious photograph from China in which one sees a man skinned alive." The other as absolute victim, the one whose misery pleases us, presumably in the degree that we can think ourselves exempt from any comparable intensity of distress. Though of course there is the very different kind of pleasure when the images of suffering or victimization, placed within a sufficient explanatory context, "remind us," as Todorov writes, "of the evil of which one and those like us are capable" and thereby "shake us out of our complacence about ourselves."

Mrs. Rutledge, as my own peculiar, emblematic other, likewise served to shake me out of my own early adolescent complacence. Is not the view of black people—even in their most attractive and fortunate incarnations—as essentially victims a deeply complacent and degrading view? This was the enlightened view of black people served up to Americans of my generation. But then it was not possible to think of Mrs. Rutledge as any sort of victim. No more was it possible to think of her as my familiar, one who might readily fit in at a Boyers family gathering on a Sunday afternoon. Oh, she would have known how to put my family members at their ease, quite as she knew how to press and test and provoke the children she taught without any trace of condescension. In the class notebook I have kept for sixty years, I see—the key words are circled—that Mrs. Rutledge actually uttered the words "and there the muse must draw her veil," thereby admonishing us not to go too far in making explicit what, even in a junior high school personal essay, should be no more than suggested. Elsewhere, I note, she advised us to regard the short essay a student in the class had been asked to copy out on the blackboard for our collective edification as "intelligently unambitious," thereby introducing a concept I could not have encountered before and, in effect, shaping forever my sense of the difference between merely acceptable and distinguished work. But never, as I recall, did Mrs. Rutledge offer an insight or an admonition with the effect of having hardened the line between herself and others. The act of judgment was—so she made it seem—an act that needed to become as natural as the act of breathing, but it was not intended to confirm the status of an elite minority. What made her seem to me an other was her relentless attentiveness to implication and intention, her quiet insistence that everything mattered. If she feared that children of twelve or thirteen would be indisposed to follow her lead, she never let on. Was it reasonable to suppose that a kid like myself, raised in a household almost entirely without books or magazines, would be able to grasp a distinction—Mrs. Rutledge made it—between "mere banal liking" and "real appreciation"? Surely the distinction must have seemed to me difficult. Very likely I would not have known, at the time, how to use it to think about my own aversions and enthusiasms. But it would have served as a reminder of something high and out of reach to which it was worth aspiring, and I knew, at some level at least, that I was honor-bound to aspire to the high and distinguished company of the black woman whose confident, unhurried arpeggios of sentences emerged unfailingly from her lips.

Was it important, in my sense of Mrs. Rutledge as the other who defined for me my own limitations and, in consequence, the largeness of my inchoate ambitions, that she be a person of color? Hard to know with certainty about that. If color represents, in the most crude and obvious of ways, a mark of difference, it must also carry with it some aspect of enigma. The other, if she is to be regarded as such, must embody mystery. As a black woman who had miraculously managed not to bear any discernible mark of weakness or victimization, Mrs. Rutledge surely seemed to me, on that score alone, remarkable. Her beautifully teased jet-black hair was, to me, a notable signature, as notable, certainly, as her long, meticulously painted fingernails, which rightly belonged to the woman who each day after school slid behind the wheel of the long, black, distinguished Packard automobile parked up the street from the front doors of John Marshall Junior High. What was the name of the mystery that was my Mrs. Rutledge? Say that I had no way of accounting for her, that though she was a negro and belonged to an identifiable group with a presumed collective identity, she was, unmistakably, always an individual who could never have represented her group or any other group. She was, in addition, an other in the face of whom it was not possible to feel indifferent. She was a standing affront to everything ordinary and mean I had ever learned to accept as real. After some months in her classroom, rising as best I could to the challenges she set before me, I could no more have regarded the quotidian experience I had known as the measure of all things than I could ever again think of black people as being defined absolutely by the conditions in which they were constrained to live.

To be sure, one's sense of these matters never quite remains exactly what one thought, perhaps, would never alter. Our lives are marked by encounters with a multitude of others. Though professional travelers like Kapuscinski often write of persons determined not to risk encounters, the world is such that it is increasingly difficult to avoid the other and to think, however reluctantly, about difference. Some contend that transient, peripheral contacts with unfamiliar persons have nothing to do with a genuine experience of the other, and that seems more or less persuasive to me. It is, in the words of another Polish thinker, named Tischner, "only in dialogue, in argument, in opposition, and also in aspiring" that there can be genuine encounter with the other. Had I not been forced to take seriously my own brief but violent encounter with the student who many years ago slapped and insulted me, had I not felt the need to measure my own sense of possibility against his, he would not have existed for me as an other in the sense that seems relevant here.

My sense of the black person, and of the possibilities associated with blacks as very significant others, altered with the appearance in my life of other kinds of black people. The angry, eloquent, fire-breathing 1960s black activists I encountered could not readily be conflated with a black person like Mrs. Rutledge, who would have thought it—did think it—more than a little theatrical and pretentious for a writer like James Baldwin to come on all prophetic and fist-shaking about *The Fire Next Time*. When, as a graduate student at NYU in the '60s, I asked Mrs. Rutledge to join a group of us at a "Welcome Home James Baldwin" evening at the Village Gate nightclub, she smiled and said, "You go and tell me all about it." Nor would I have thought to invite her to join me at a public event featuring less gifted but decidedly angrier speakers like Eldridge Cleaver or Leroi Jones, though for a while she toyed with the idea of teaching Jones's plays in her classes.

One of the angriest books I have ever read—Salmon Rushdie describes it as "a jeremiad of great clarity and force that one might have called torrential were the language not so finely controlled"—is Jamaica Kincaid's *A Small Place*. Published originally in 1988, it burns still with a kind of cleansing outrage directed at the crimes perpetrated by colonialists and tourists upon the population of Antigua, a small island in the British West Indies where Kincaid herself grew up. Often the very thrust and slash of Kincaid's language feels heady, like revenge. It is deliberate, considered, judiciously mean-spirited, and it makes no allowance for innocence or stupidity or even good intentions. It spares no one, apologizes for nothing, and seems, in its odd, elegant, punishing way, to eschew any prospect of generosity. It throbs with its own mellifluous harshness and inspires in its reader the thought that the author of such a book must herself be hard and unforgiving, not malicious exactly, though possibly that as well. To submit to the spell cast by such a person, one thinks, would be to let oneself in for a protracted bout of self-loathing—not the same thing as humility—and I can only smile at the mostly bland words of approval cast at Kincaid's feet by the conventional reviewers of her little book, a book adeptly tuned to the pitch of venom, hurling its well-aimed anathemas at perpetrators and hapless victims alike.

An other, then, this author, "bitter" and "dyspeptic," as she calls herself, determined to be, for many of the comfortable, politically moderate readers who knew her in the pages of the *New Yorker*'s "Talk of the Town" years earlier, a decidedly less than accommodating presence. And what to make then, of this other, who had so fashioned herself in a book obviously designed to alienate and affright? We are not, after all, dealing here with a spokesperson for an unfamiliar culture whose essential difference her work encapsulates. Neither is hers the voice of an exotic whose accent can seem quaint or charming. Kincaid writes in a voice that is hers alone, and the scorn inscribed in her most characteristic utterances seems an expression of her own peculiar bilious disposition. If she is, for the reader she imagined here, an other, it is the other who, as Neil Ascherson once wrote, "is external to oneself and yet a reflection of oneself." An other, therefore, whose very unfamiliarity moves us to want to turn away from it as from something unpleasant or offensive but who, at the same time, holds us. Holds us how? With the communicated sense that, if we resist the desire to turn away, to flee, we may well see our own face.

But let us have a look at a few, a half-dozen, selected passages taken from *A Little Place*:

> Since you are a tourist, the thought of what it might be like for someone who had to live day in, day out, in a place that suffers constantly from drought . . . (while at the same time surrounded by a sea and an ocean) . . . must never cross your mind.

Will you be comforted to know that the hospital is staffed with doctors that no actual Antiguan trusts . . . that when the Minister of Health himself doesn't feel well he takes the first plane to New York to see a real doctor.

You must not wonder what exactly happened to the contents of your lavatory when you flushed it . . . the contents of your lavatory might, just might, graze gently against your ankle as you wade carefree in the water, for you see, in Antigua, there is no proper sewage-disposal system.

The thing you have always suspected about yourself the minute you become a tourist is true: a tourist is an ugly human being.

You make a leap from being that nice blob just sitting like a boob in your amniotic sac of the modern experience to being a person visiting heaps of death and ruin and feeling alive and inspired at the sight of it; to being a person lying in some far away beach, your stilled body stinking and glistening in the sand.

And since you are being an ugly person this ugly but joyful thought will swell inside you: their ancestors were not clever in the way yours were and not ruthless in the way yours were. . . . An ugly thing . . . an ugly, empty thing, a stupid thing, a piece of rubbish pausing here and there to gaze at this and taste that, and it will never occur to you that the people who inhabit the place in which you have just paused cannot stand you, that behind their closed doors they laugh at your strangeness.

And what of the people who inhabit the "small place"? How do they fare by comparison with Kincaid's tourists? Will they, properly considered, permit us to see our own face, the face we shudder to associate with the caricature of the tourist Kincaid assiduously assembles? In fact, Kincaid would appear in this work to loathe ordinary Antiguans about as much as those ugly tourists. Her Antiguans, after all, have no gift—none whatsoever—for a "careful weighing, careful consideration, careful judging, careful questioning." For them, "The division of Time into the Past, the Present, and the Future does not exist." They are, moreover, proud of their Hotel Training School, "a school that teaches Antiguans how to be good servants, how to be a good nobody, which is what a servant is." Clearly there is nothing to approve of in these small people. Decidedly, the Antiguans anatomized in Kincaid's book are not a promising mirror in which an earnest liberal like me might hope to see, with whatever allowance made for difference, his own reflection.

So that the promising other in this case—if there is to be one—must be, can only be, the author herself. One determined here not to speak as a nice person, not to give comfort nor to avoid seeming to speak out of a rage and bitterness that are, in every way, personal. Does this Jamaica Kincaid seem so much an other to me because so entirely antithetical to my own Mrs. Rutledge and the decorums entailed in her presentation of self? It is a question I cannot dismiss. And would Jamaica Kincaid have thought my old beloved teacher a female Uncle Tom, the other as comforter, not far enough removed from the status of exalted but reliable family retainer, bound to be there when needed but discreet enough to stay out of sight when not wanted? The very thought of Mrs. Rutledge as a veritable Uncle Tom fills me, even now, with unaccountable distress, so absolutely unfair does it seem, and yet just plausible enough to appeal to a certain sort of mind. By no means—of this I am certain—tempting to the mind of Ms. Jamaica Kincaid, the person who has written not alone *A Small Place* but works as chastening as *Mr. Potter* and *Autobiography of My Mother*, works that explore the far reaches of what it is to be human.

But then the mind on offer in *A Small Place* is not concerned with the far reaches of our humanity. It is not tuned to the key of moderation or forbearance, not teacherly in its instincts but obsessive, confrontational, operating from a reservoir of unmastered emotion. The other as the hand at your throat, not quite murderous but inimical. It does not propose that we calm down and stare soulfully into one another's eyes. Here there is no promise of sisterly or brotherly love. The other inscribed in the pages of *A Small Place* accords no dignity to tourists and has no respect for the so-called values of native Antiguans.

So that we can only ask what we are to do with this other, this palpable, fire-breathing Jamaica Kincaid. A writer friend, familiar with her books, says to think of her simply as a writer, in which case there is no need to take seriously what she says, only to commend the music of her sentences and the "integrity" with which she sticks to her guns. But this, I have responded, is to turn the writer into an exotic bird, an other exempt from adult criticism or censure. Better to begin by thinking of this other as a writer determined not to furnish a standard "sensitive" account of a charged subject and determined, therefore, to provoke. This is a writer, after all, who refuses to be an instance of anything in general. Who confronts us not with the actual prospect of correcting an injustice or altering an idea but with the spectacle of the author herself as unapologetically unjust, excessive, at least half in love with her own vituperation. The other, then, as unreasonable, out of reach of argument, not at all interested in the give-and-take of rational conversation. Not wanting to hear your objections and exceptions, not interested in the predictable drivel about tourists who may not be quite so "ugly" as the usual breed, or natives of small places who might actually think complicated thoughts, exemplary, out-of-the-ordinary tourists and exceptional native Antiguans. Old and familiar, those sorts of objections. So this other would regard them. This other decidedly not wishing to curry favor with the likes of her own compulsively fair-minded Western readers. An other, then, willfully, deliriously insensible to the peculiar moral authority often accorded to artists and writers speaking on behalf of the wretched of the earth—accorded to them, of course, only on condition that such writers appear at least to speak with compassion rather than with the eviscerating fervor of our Ms. Kincaid.

And is there anything at all to be learned or gained from the interaction with such an other? Perhaps it is useful to be reminded, forcefully, that there exists in the world an other at least as clever as you are, who is not well disposed to you and your customary fine discriminations. An other who believes that things are considerably simpler than you believe them, or at least that the essential truth of things is not to be softened or explained away. You will say that each of us is an individual whose habits of thought and feeling cannot be established by citing the group or class to which we belong. The other here declares that whether or not you share the particular predilections of "tourists" or "natives," you are guilty by association and by disposition. You say, perhaps, that you were never a tourist in a country like Antigua and thus cannot be "ugly" in the ways of such a tourist? Say, rather, that you might well have been, had you chosen to visit a little place, and had you gone, would have felt rising in you the unearned sense of superiority to persons small enough to have been born in such a place. That is what the other here would have you feel. Ashamed, then? If not ashamed then incapable of acknowledging what ought to be obvious even to you. The shame you ought to bear lies on you like a curse and cannot be argued away. That is what this other would have you understand. As also the fact that it is especially difficult to reclaim your honor, your pride of self, when you have been accused of participating in a historical crime you yourself did not commit. In this case the crime of having felt superior, or fortunate, or of having, willingly or not, supported, in your very manner of existence, the way of life denied to other human beings whose horizons are defined by servitude.

Does our other here in fact believe what she writes?

Perhaps it is helpful to speak of *A Little Place* as a work in which Ms. Jamaica Kincaid impersonates an other, that is, someone fundamentally unwilling to see things in what we regard as a reasonable and forgiving manner. The other, after all, as we have come to think of him, is often inimical because so inured to oversimplifying. Jamaica Kincaid's tourists and natives are, in this sense, deliberately, grossly oversimplified, so that we might know as we read what it is like to feel that there is no appeal we can make to this author, this resolutely out-of-reach other. The writer is here so adept at impersonating—or embodying with all her heart—the out-of-reach, unforgiving other that we may be forgiven for associating her, just for a moment, with the sort of fundamentalist for whom it does not matter whether any particular other person is well-intentioned, for whom with me or against me is the only consideration that can matter, and nothing you can say by way of complication or counterindication will be countenanced.

In this sense my experience of the Kincaid book is such that it hardly matters to me—as a reader—whether it is or is not a deliberate imper-sonation or an assault pure and simple. It puts me in mind of the other as what Kapuscinski calls "a very emotional person" who moves on the edge of hatred—cool or hot—for whatever is identified as its other. If I say—I say it here—that Ms. Jamaica Kincaid is well-known to me as a dear and generous person who in recent years has often dined at my table, that does not alter my relation to the persona devised to strike fear into the hearts of her readers. That persona, however writerly and seductive the sentences that bring her into our company, is a sinister presence, and it is entirely reasonable to associate her intransigence with the unyielding demeanor of the very distant, utterly different other whose singularity of purpose we can only wonder at.

Think, if only for a moment, of the female suicide bomber profiled a few years back on page one of the *New York Times*, one of many captured by the Iraqi police forces in that period. "Each woman's story is unique," we are told, "but their journeys to jihad do have commonalities." What stands out in the profile, however, is one simple quality perfectly articulated by the attractive, rather likable young woman named Baida, who frankly admits that her deeds are motivated by hatred and revenge and refuses to accept that there can be a difference between, say, "killing American soldiers and killing American civilians," or that there is a difference between "invaders and blasphemers" and Jews, or between her responsibility for her own two children and her "larger" responsibility to blow herself up. And what is the one utterly indispensable, simple quality that so stands out in the profile? Call it a sublimely impersonal quality of implacable enmity, such that Baida can direct at the interviewer, who has spent many kindly, inquisitive hours with her, a quietly murderous intensity. "As a foreigner," after all, "it is halal to kill you," she tells her earnest companion, and so she has been in touch with "friends" who will perhaps manage to grab her and then at least "to torture you and make lunch of your flesh." At this the interviewer adjusts her own veil and thanks Baida "for teaching me about Jihad and for making me understand how dangerous her world was." A courteous, apparently genuine sort of leave-taking, one would think. But "Baida was smiling again," we read: "If I had not seen you before and talked to you, I would kill you with my own hands," she says pleasantly. "Do not be deceived by my peaceful face. I have a heart of stone."

And that, we may well suppose, is what often, though not invariably, will distinguish the other. A heart of stone, or an unwavering commitment to something we cannot share, an enmity that cannot be fixed or cured by anything we can invent. Though there is, of course, the other as embodied in my own Mrs. Rutledge, whose otherness for

me—in my young eyes—was a quality of almost inconceivable refinement. No resemblance there to the heart of stone, but in its way a heart
ever so slightly remote. Generosity as a discipline, fellow feeling carefully rationed, intelligence poised to select and recoil, never too easy
with praise or agreement. The "other" years before the worldwide crisis
of identity and the rise of multiculturalism, allergic, in her bones, to
the demands that everyone be stroked and respected for what they are,
whatever they are. Mrs. Rutledge as certain to be amused and astonished
as young Baida by the idea that anything is owed as a matter of course
to views or persons of which she disapproves. By the demand that we
forget our differences and learn just to get along, as if getting along were
the most we might expect of one another.

Of course it is consoling to feel that the other is inevitably remote
from us and yet not so far that we cannot hope to close the gap between
us. We must hope—so we are admonished—that the other will reveal
his true face to us in the course of one or more charged encounters and
thereby reveal us to ourselves—in spite of the disappointments recorded
by countless travelers and writers. Although even Kapuscinski, the most
ardent and optimistic of travelers, notes that conditions in one place or
another may prevent encounter of a meaningful kind—as where persons
have little access to sources of information and believe, of necessity, only
what they are told by their handlers or overlords.

But often the other is not remote from us. Often the other who is
central to our experience of otherness is someone near, a person we have
known or loved, perhaps a parent or grandparent who has suddenly
moved into the country of the waiting-for-imminent-death and is thus
no longer interested in us and our future or, for that matter, the future of
the planet. One who has become immersed in a perspective not accessible to us and determined to remain so. Or it is the husband or wife who
has fallen totally, unaccountably out of love with you and can find not
one memory of your long years together that does not now seem disappointing, in spite of what you had thought an entirely satisfactory time
and an unwavering commitment unto death. These are, to be sure, com-
monplaces, and it may well confuse our discussion of the other to include
within this framework what would then be experiences so universal as to
encompass, potentially, pretty much everything.

And yet I want, in closing these reflections, to insist that the other is always remote from us in at least one sense that matters. The other is far enough removed from what we take to be usual or comprehensible as to provoke us to consider—however reluctantly—who we are. Thus the other may well prove to be someone I thought I knew who turned out to be radically different and thereby managed to call into question my own sense of what was real and possible. Or the other may be a stranger conducting his life according to precepts and customs that seem to me astonishing, or appalling, which may in turn call into question everything I thought was sensible and true—about relations between men and women, or the proper raising of children, or courtesy, or the recourse to violence. Of course we have reason to hope that the encounter with the other will move us to considering, compromising, assessing, perhaps revaluating. Otherwise we may be provoked simply to turn away, as with disgust or, convulsively, thoughtlessly, to strike out, as with a cleansing or murderous fury. In *The Shadow of the Sun*, Kapuscinski's book on Africa, he notes that "our contemporary suspicion of and antipathy for the Other, the Stranger, goes back to the fear our tribal ancestors felt toward the Outsider, seeing him as the carrier of evil, the source of misfortune." But such a formula, however suggestive, really tells us little about the actual encounters and antipathies most of us are likely to experience. It also assumes what the book as a whole, in great and patient detail, largely contradicts, namely, that our difficulties with the other have mainly or exclusively to do with "suspicion" and the antipathy bred by suspicion.

In fact, the other, in being himself, will often seem compelling and inspire in us not a desire to flee or turn away but a desire to look more closely. It is also possible that only in looking closely at the other will we find reason to fear him. Kapuscinski himself records his own intrepid encounters with others who, upon closer acquaintance, turn out to be murderous, not for any ordinary motives he can assign but for no good reasons at all. It is not his own instinctive suspicion and antipathy that create a fear of the other but the sheer unfocused malevolence of persons—the particular instance here is narrated in Kapuscinski's journalism on Liberia—"who do not know what they are doing," who are "unable to cope with anything." The tens of thousands of ordinary Liberians who flocked to bars and other locations in Monrovia to watch, over and over again, the two-hour-long videotape of the gruesome torture of President Doe in 1990 became for the journalist a multitude of fearful others because of what they revealed themselves to be—brutal, bloodthirsty, easily whipped into a barbarous frenzy—not because they conformed to some idea of the other Kapuscinski imposed on them.

My own most significant other—near and remote, thoroughly familiar and largely incomprehensible, loved and feared—happened to be my own mother. She was, in many ways, a character a novelist would have hesitated to invent. Fiercely attentive to me and to my younger sister, she was, at the same time, rarely motherly—which is to say, rarely tender or sympathetic. As a child in elementary school I wondered at what already seemed to me the absence in her of the usual motherly attributes I noticed in the parents of school friends or cousins. Though my working-class father never used foul language and warned us never to "sink so low" as to use derisory epithets for the non-Jews in our Brooklyn neighborhood, Mother often referred to things and even persons as "pieces of shit" or "crap." Often when my father was not around, she would declare to us that "life is shit" and, after throwing a fit, would swear us to secrecy and threaten to murder us should a word of her behavior reach my father. Though she taught us to read and write and administered daily after-school lessons that served us well, she avowed no genuine interest in anything—not in the work we were assigned at school nor in the news of the world that my father insisted on discussing with us at dinner each night before heading back to work around the corner in the family store. Quick-witted, occasionally playful, her repartee tended often to insult. Wanting to admire her quickness and to participate in her instinct for fun, I never really understood why her thrusts were so often pointed and venomous.

Though Selma Boyers was in a sense what she herself called "a truth teller," her idea of the truth was that, to be worth taking seriously, it had to be withering. She mistrusted generosity and regarded soft-hearted people as deceitful or, worse, deceived. Though she demanded that we speak respectfully to our elders and treat children our own age with forbearance, she mocked in us anything that seemed to her "idealistic" or "stupid." When my father came home at night from his small corner dry goods store singing the praises of the hardworking black high school or college students he'd hired for part-time work during the Christmas season, she ridiculed his tender sentiments and predicted that the kids would soon be robbing him blind, seeing how easy it was to take him in. When he mentioned that two kids had asked him for help with their homework, which he'd happily offered, staying on after closing time to get the job done, she laughed at his "pretensions" and asked why, if he was so smart, he hadn't gone to college and become a teacher.

Though I knew my mother, of course, and lived in a small apartment with her and my father and sister until I was twenty-one, I never felt that I understood who she was. Improbably, she always seemed to me surprising, even shocking. Who was this person who could be so cruel and cutting? Would anyone who hadn't seen her close-up believe in the existence of such a person? To be sure, she had friends who seemed, more or less, to like her and think well of her, but I learned, as an adult, that many of our family members—aunts and uncles and even her own father—thought her something of a nut, maybe a little mad, driven, potentially dangerous. Living with her over two decades was for me an experience of attritional intimacy. The more I knew her, the less I thought I understood, and the less I felt I could bear.

My mother as significant other was felt to be alien by virtue of qualities that seemed to me unlovely, sometimes ugly. She was determined not to be—not with us at any rate—fastidious or decorous in speech or manner, as if to be so would be somehow to put on airs. She was, at home, frankly coarse, sometimes belligerent, out of control. When angry, she threw things, though careful never to go too far for fear of my father, who was not to learn about the full repertoire of her rages and devices. More than once, when I refused to play along with some scenario she'd devised to alert the neighbors in our apartment building to her distress by sending me around to knock on their doors, she would threaten me and hurl fearful anathemas in my direction before turning to physical violence—hair pulling, school books pulled off bedroom shelves and thrown, a milk bottle or kitchen pot aimed—only two times successfully—at my head.

Selma herself provided all I needed to confirm that she was indeed, so far as I was concerned, an other. She noted, by the time I was in college, that I seemed to her cold and unresponsive. That she couldn't any longer get a rise out of me. What are you afraid of, she would sometimes ask, wanting to provoke me to an altercation—as violent as possible, at least at the level of verbal violence—that I refused absolutely to get into. High and mighty, she would say about what seemed to her my aloof demeanor, my refusal to be prodded or to accept that her insults could be meaningful or hurtful. So strange, I felt. So angry and bitter and determined to be nasty. So fabulously unyielding and unlovely. Here was an other whose language I did not fluently speak, one out of reach of what I took to be reasonable solicitude or correction. The intelligence of this other was unmistakable, as also her considerable reserves of energy, and yet she went on as if driven by forces committed not to intimacy and repair but distance and resentment. Confronted again and again by what were intended to be words of comfort, she would recoil and remind me that we were different. Often I wondered what this flesh of my flesh really wanted me to hear in the words she uttered and the gestures she made, unexpected gusts of generosity undercut by an almost savage enmity. The mix, the alternation, the sheer howling intensity all often seemed rather incredible to me, and though I was always tempted to soothe my doubts by saying, well, she's obviously mad, I found this too a solution impossible to sustain.

After all, this other was a person who shopped, cooked dinner, went to work at an insurance company office in Manhattan, and maintained a network of moderate friendships. She did not raise her voice or spew insults when on the phone with friends or at Sunday afternoon get-togethers with extended-family members. Each morning before work she carefully teased her hair, applied makeup to her face, and dispensed instructions to us about after-school hours. If she was mad, she was selectively so, and thus I thought of her as a person who, though often not in control of her emotions, was in fact responsive to aims and protocols that my sister and I simply had not mastered. At the bottom of everything Selma said and did when she was most herself was what seemed a fixed determination not to be moderate. Moderation was, to her, a manifest of deception, a sign that one wished to curry favor with persons who existed to take you as you were. Boundaries were clearly necessary in one's transactions with outsiders, persons with whom it was necessary to get along in spite of your relative indifference to them and theirs to you. But in your most intimate relations, at home, your responsibility was to transgress boundaries, to affirm that truth alone was essential, that to be anything but frank and coarse and abrasive was to betray your own vital humanity.

In *Travels with Herodotus*, Kapuscinski recounts a tale, quite involved, that bears on an ancient Persian "mind-set that had manifested itself in this culture thousands of years before—namely, that a man whose dignity was undermined, who felt himself humiliated, could free himself from the burning sensation of shame and disgrace only by an act of self-destruction." I imagine that my mother felt herself perpetually scarred and unworthy, and she did clearly behave as if bent on a form of self-destruction that might alone bring to her relief from the "burning sensation" she lived with. Much of the time miserable and angry and exasperated, as she often told us, she indulged tantrums that brought her no relief and alienated her from those who might have helped her. Self-destruction is one way of describing the project of one who strives to make herself frightful or loathsome and thus to drive a wedge between herself and those closest to her. My mother regarded her own lonely, hard-earned status as the one and only truth-teller as preferable to the life of compromise and deceit embraced by everyone else.

At times it was hard not to suppose that she was merely impersonating the figure she had contrived for herself, much in the way I entertained that thought while reading *A Small Place*, confronting an author so unforgiving and relentless, so unwilling to be moderate or reasonable. But then a woman who impersonates a coarse and unlovely and unreasonable person over many years will feel not only that the role becomes her but that she can only imperfectly summon any other mask to wear. When, after thirty years of marriage, my father left my mother, her behavior became ever more erratic and violent. On several occasions in the course of her workday she would stretch out on the floor and refuse to budge, demanding that her son be phoned to come and retrieve her, though when I appeared at the insurance company office, hours later, she would ask, still rigid on the floor, what had taken me so long, and what I was looking at, again "so high and mighty. What," she would go on, "you couldn't be bothered to rush over, not even if—who knew—your own mother might have had a heart attack, maybe smashed her head, still taking your time?" In the car soon after, as I drove her home to Queens, where she and my father had moved when I was a teenager, she would pass a brush though her iron-gray hair, apply fresh lipstick to her mouth, and berate me for looking humiliated in front of her colleagues. "It's good for you," she would say, "to get a little humility for a change. And anyway you don't give a shit for those people any more than I do. I know you. You're all pretend, but like me—this I know for sure—you have a heart of stone."

Did I in fact have a heart of stone? I didn't think so, though the revulsion I felt in my mother's presence often made me feel that I lacked the sentiments appropriate to a son whose mother was perpetually in need of something he could not—would not—provide. If the other is someone whose ways seem alien and yet can somehow seem to show you your own face, then my mother was, unmistakably, my own personal, insurmountable other. She inspired in me the desire always to remain an other to her, never to capitulate to her sense of me as someone with a heart of stone. This was an other, as the poet Randall Jarrell might have had it, for the soul to break its arm on, so impossible did it seem even to attempt to lift it into some semblance of an appealing presence. The other, then, as necessary to one's sense of self, not as a cure for one's own arrogance or ignorance but as an object lesson in what not to do or be or strive for. If the current standard line has it that we become most fully ourselves by acknowledging the many selves (or others) who live within each of us, I would insist that the other is also necessary to us, much of the time, as a valid object of dislike or fear. My aversion to much that my own mother did and said helped me to define how I wished to think of myself and my ambitions. Though I never found it entirely easy to acknowledge how much I feared and disliked my mother, those feelings helped me to clarify my relation to the world. If Mrs. Rutledge introduced me to a species of fellow feeling and discrimination I could aspire to, my mother forced me to exercise, over and over again, that faculty of taste and discrimination. This, I learned increasingly to feel confident in declaring, is mean, this is fine; this coarse and self-indulgent, this properly restrained and eloquent; this poisonous and bigoted, this full of passionate intensity but generous. The other, then, good for many things, but not least for sharpening the sentiment of profound disapproval indispensable not only to judgment but to the pleasure one takes in the good, the beautiful, and the worthy.

[7]

POLITICS AND THE NOVEL

... the political awareness that is not aware, the social
consciousness which hates full consciousness, the moral
earnestness which is moral luxury.

—LIONEL TRILLING

At a public interview I conducted with Nadine Gordimer
more than thirty years ago, she bristled at my use of the
epithet "political novel" to describe her masterwork.
Burger's Daughter was not, Gordimer argued, written to promote
an agenda. It did not subscribe to a particular idea or ideology.
To call it a political novel was to suggest that it had—as Henry
James once put it—"designs" on us, that its author wished to banish incorrect opinions and to install in their place clearly more
beneficial views of politics and society. At their best, Gordimer
contended, novels were not useful. If I admired her novel as much
as I said I did, I would do better to regard it as a free work of the
imagination, an inquiry with no purpose that involved providing
answers to the difficult questions it posed.

Of course I had no intention of reducing Gordimer's book to
a species of blunt propaganda, and I thought of the epithet simply as a shorthand for "a novel invested in politics as a way of
thinking about the fate of society at a particular place and time."
There was a great tradition of political fiction that included classic
works like Stendhal's *The Charterhouse of Parma*, Dostoyevsky's

The Possessed, Conrad's *Nostromo*, and James's *The Princess Casam-assima*. Such novels defined the tradition and suggested that there was really a special kind of work whose interest in politics exceeded any-thing to be found in other novels. But these classic works were also, I thought, so entirely not works of coarse propaganda, so clearly not com-posed with obvious designs upon their reader, that no one would object to the words "political novel" as Gordimer had done.

In the years since my encounter with Gordimer—one of many I have enjoyed over the decades—I have come to feel that the great South Afri-can writer was quite right to take me to task. Though I have written books on the subject and taught graduate seminars on "politics and the novel," I have forsworn the offending epithet. Not to avoid offending my writer friends but to avoid the suggestion that the novels I love are composed to accomplish a narrow, singular purpose. *Burger's Daughter* does not propose an indisputably correct way to deal with, or think about, or over-throw, South African apartheid. It is, at its core, unmistakably an oppo-sitional work, and its heroic characters are willing to sacrifice their lives to the cause of defeating what was for many years the established order in their society. But no reader can suppose for a moment that the goal of the novel is principally to find favor with readers by upholding a virtuous position few of them would be inclined to reject. What matters to readers of such a novel is not a stance or a view but a complex way of thinking and feeling about the relation of the individual and society. Like other great writers compelled to engage with political issues, Gordimer operates from an understanding that politics is not everything and that conflicts apparently political in nature often issue from sources far removed from strictly political ends or calculations. Far more important than politics in *Burger's Daughter* are questions about how a person comes to find her own way in the world and to establish for herself what it means to be a serious person with genuine convictions.

In *Politics and the Novel*, Irving Howe describes his own 1957 book as primarily "a study of the relation between literature and ideas." Through-out that seminal work we find references to "feminist ideas," the "will to power," "existentialism," "liberalism," "anarchism," "romanticism," and "imperialism," among others. Yet in the main Howe does not dwell on these ideas as he grapples with individual actions and characters and

teases out implications. The more he thinks about the ideas associated
with the classic works in the tradition he studies, the more he concedes
that, in successful novels, ideas "are transformed," and that at its best
"the political novel generates such intense heat that the ideas it appro-
priates are melted into its movement and fused with the emotions of its
characters." In this sense, we might also observe that in such works ideas
are rarely accorded the formality we associate with system. Exceptions—
Arthur Koestler's *Darkness at Noon* is one obvious example—of course
spring to mind. But in James and Conrad and Stendhal and Dostoyevsky
we find that the ideas are constantly changing shape as the novels wind
and unfold. Alternatives are posed not as fixed positions but as possibilities not fully understood, whatever the actual consequences they may
portend. The Italian writer Natalia Ginzburg had opinions about femi-
nism that she articulated in her essays and newspaper columns, but when
she wrote about the lives of women in her novels, she was clearly not
interested in staking out a position. When her primary male character
in the novel *All Our Yesterdays* tells the woman he has just married that
she conducts herself "like an insect," the author is not thereby mounting
an attack on patriarchy or inviting her reader to deplore the tyranny of
men. You do not read Ginzburg's novel for edification or instruction, as if
it were in thrall to a single overmastering idea. The wife in the novel does
in fact behave somewhat "like an insect" and does somewhat deserve the
insult delivered by her husband, who wishes not to lord it over her but
to rouse her to think better of herself and behave accordingly. Feminist
ideas do surely inform the tensions at play in Ginzburg's novel, but it
does not exist to assert those ideas, and the novel is permitted to develop
in ways that seem to us surprising, far removed from any standard ideological trajectory.

In some novels, no doubt, the informing ideas seem often to control the
narrative to a much greater degree. The characters in Koestler's famous
novel debate with one another as if the ideas in dispute were real, as real
as the social forces that drive characters into conflict and cause enormous
suffering. This is true as well in a very different work like Malraux's *Man's
Fate* where ideas—terrorism, the will to power, quietism—are made to
seem coherent, have at least the semblance of formal systems capable of
inspiring belief or adherence. Yet even in such novels ideology will seem

to us to matter less than it does to its true believers. Ideas that can seem so substantial to an activist or an ideologue do not in fact account for everything in such novels, whose characters exist not merely as embodiments of the ideas to which they subscribe but as odd configurations of will and weakness and potentiality.

When I teach Turgenev's novel *Fathers and Sons*, I am always moved by the disputes that unfold among my students. After all, this is a novel unmistakably engaged with big-ticket ideas, especially the opposition between "nihilism" and "liberalism." Characters talk about such ideas—though not obsessively—as if they were real to them, and as if it were possible to declare for the one rather than the other and to conduct oneself accordingly. And yet my students are never quite sure what Turgenev makes of the collision between such ideas. Does he love his nihilist character Bazarov as much as he might? Does he not make his sweet-tempered, mild-mannered liberals comparatively weak and thereby signal his affiliation with the more forceful Bazarov, who may be deluded on important matters but has more life in him, more energy and force, than the others? When Turgenev has Bazarov call himself a "harmless person" at an uncharacteristically vulnerable moment, does he not expect his reader to defend the character against his own rueful self-indictment? In following out such questions, I find that students are at once exasperated and thrilled to discover that there is no reliable way to resolve them. The relevant political issues in Turgenev's novel are by no means obscure. The informing ideas are spelled out, and characters, when pressed, openly acknowledge their affiliation with those ideas. And yet the novel clearly courts irresolution and misgiving. Though it alludes to a political ferment in the society that may well have to do with movements and policies, the choices available to characters within the framework of the novel have little to do with parties they might join or petitions they might sign. As is so often the case in such works, even ideas that carry distinguishing labels—nihilism, for one obvious example—really exist for us primarily as reflections of temperament and inclination, and it is not easy to be for or against a temperament.

Of course we do not require that novels dealing with politics refuse to make up their minds about anything. No one doubts that in *The Possessed* Dostoyevsky mounts a savage attack on the political radicalism to which he himself had once subscribed. James's portrait of the princess in his 1885 novel is indisputably intended to reveal the false consciousness and posturing associated with radical chic, long before that term came into use nearly a century later. Even in Turgenev there is no question that the liberalism on offer, however gentle and humane, is ineffectual, hopeless, and that Bazarov's nihilism is at most a compelling half-baked idea, a mere rejectionist reflex with no prospect of altering society or mobilizing a mass movement. Novelists can see things as they are even when they are consumed with ambivalence.

For a reader, of course, what will matter more than anything else in the reading of novels—especially those that purport to engage with politics and ideas—is what Natalia Ginzburg called the "spiritual attitude" discernible in the work. What is a spiritual attitude? It exists for a reader as the sign, or token, of the seriousness with which ideas are entertained. Novels in which politics play a central role purport at least to represent reality in a way that will seem plausible to an adult intelligence. And yet often the spiritual attitude underwriting such works is deficient, portrayals of reality flagrantly one-dimensional, ideas taken up as if they were merely tools or weapons with which to impress readers and thereby to evade the difficult questions implied or invoked. Some years ago, in a review of Phillip Roth's novel *American Pastoral*, I argued that Roth had not done what was necessary to get inside the idea of political radicalism. Instead he had created, as an expression of "the indigenous American berserk," a pathetic, twisted, angry young leftist who was made to exemplify the primary thrust of the 1960s New Left. An extremist with some plausible relation to actually existing elements in the counterculture of the period, Roth's Merry Levov could seem genuinely terrifying. But she was, at the same time, an undifferentiated cartoon of adolescent rebellion, and her creator had made no effort to accord to her or her associates the benefit of any doubt, to accord to anyone associated with the New Left even a modicum of respect for their idealism and their opposition to an established order that had given us the Vietnam War. The spiritual attitude exhibited in such a novel is thus deficient in the sense that it does not labor to resist the reduction of reality to caricature. Roth offers no sign whatever that he entertained misgivings about the easy reduction of the radical left in the 1960s to lunacy and puerility. The one-dimensionality of the political in Roth's novel is readily grasped when it is placed alongside a novel like Mario Vargas Llosa's *The Real Life of Alejandro Mayta*, where the youthful revolutionary Mayta, fond and foolish and in many ways misguided, is also granted a dignified passion for justice. Vargas Llosa operates, throughout the novel, in good faith, dramatizing the ambivalences that frustrate the efforts of a narrator—a narrator very much like the author himself—to put definitively behind him his own youthful infatuation with leftist ideas.

Michael Ondaatje's novel *Anil's Ghost* is set in 1990s Sri Lanka during a time of civil war, when the order of the day was atrocity and the violence could seem random, disconnected from any prospect of meaning or purpose. Though the novel's outsider protagonist wishes to believe that there is a difference between clean hands and dirty hands, she learns that there is not much to differentiate one political faction from the other—not in ethical terms, at any rate. Ondaatje moves us across the terrain of the war he depicts with a wary, calculating delicacy, identifying isolated moments of grace that might almost provide a foundation for hope. But he refuses to impose on any episode or stray nobility an extravagant symbolic or symptomatic importance. When he introduces an ostensibly promising idea, as he does when he quotes a passage from the poet Robert Duncan ("the drama of our time is the coming of all men into one fate"), he alerts us, quietly, to the fact that this is not much more than wishful thinking, one of those ideas we indulge to pretend that we have mastered the chaos around us. Other ideas in the novel ("the reason for war was war") are likewise permitted to circulate while remaining eminently resistible, at most a reflection of someone's need to think them. The spiritual attitude governing such a work is measured by its steady resistance to all simplifying formulas and caricatures.

Late in V. S. Naipaul's *Half a Life*, we read that one character "had been given an idea of the uncertain ways of power." With this idea the man comes to know things he had not grasped before. That is what we are told. But Naipaul wants to do more than register a momentous awakening in the life of a minor character, wants in fact to examine what is sometimes called false consciousness, as if this were a temptation to which any one of us might succumb. Naipaul's character is by no means a stupid man. A landowner in an African colonial outpost, he had gone about for many years predicting, to anyone who would listen, the "calamity to come, something that would sweep away the life of the colony, sweep away all his world." He had known, in other words, for a very long time, the uncertain ways of power but had carried that knowledge only in the way that one carries a vague but oddly compelling idea that has no determinate shape and no trail of sharply imagined consequences. "A man who lived easily with that idea (and liked to frighten people with it)," Naipaul writes, should not have been suddenly impressed, amazed, undone by the actual eruption into his life of the thing itself, the raw demonstration of power and its "uncertain ways." But he is amazed and undone. And thus we are asked to observe that the philosophical view the character had long trumpeted was "a sham," an "abstraction," "a way of self-absolution" in the sense that the holding of the idea required no intellectual exertion, no resistance. Like the ideas so often held in works of political fiction, the idea that gripped Naipaul's character had been held in a fundamentally unserious way, and it is one great burden of Naipaul's novel to examine the difference between a serious and a fraudulent, spiritually deficient way of engaging reality.

Such things are not always easy to sort out in the case of a particular novel. A few years ago Christopher Hitchens took Orhan Pamuk to task for his failure to depict political Islam as it was, in a novel that purported at least to do just that. Why, Hitchens asked, would Pamuk, in his novel *Snow*, present fanatics "in a favorable or lenient light"? Why portray young girls "who immolate themselves for the right to wear head-covering" as the victims not of their Islamist imams and devout, coercive parents but of "the pitiless [secular] state" with its empty Westernizing ambitions? Why in the novel is so much sympathy given to characters who are consumed with ressentiment directed at "European ways"? Grant that Pamuk is somewhat accurate in his depiction of the secular regime long dominant in Turkey, which imposed "a uniform national identity" on the country, "where ethnic and religious variety was heavily repressed." Even so, Hitchens argues, Pamuk as novelist is less than forthright and courageous in handling his Islamist characters, refusing to draw the obvious conclusions to which his own novelistic material should have directed him.

Pamuk's novel is built around a poet named Ka, who has "no interest in politics" (Pamuk has occasionally said much the same thing), and it is part of the business of the novel to represent things as such a character would see them. But Ka is a determined innocent who refuses much of the time to acknowledge what he sees. The air he breathes is suffused with what Hitchens calls "passivity and fatalism." As a sensitive and generous soul who clings to his own innocence, such as it is, Ka wants to believe that at bottom political Islam is simply a protest against meaninglessness. The so-called Party of God in the novel may look as if it is determined to punish infidels and to be vigilant against the tiniest of infractions, and still the energy of the novel is largely devoted to Ka's misgivings about his own mild atheism and free-thinking. Readers like Hitchens demand from Pamuk not a tract but a focused interrogation of a religious movement overwhelmingly dominated by provincial and reactionary sentiments and determined—even on the evidence of the novel itself—to win the war against modernity and multiculturalism. On this reading, Pamuk as novelist is far too invested in the benign, dreamy, generous perspective of his poet character, and the novel thus fails to engage adequately with the ideas embraced by proponents of political Islam.

Though I am taken with Hitchens's strenuously argued—and deeply informed—reading of *Snow*, I find it not, in the end, fully persuasive. It is not timidity that I see in Pamuk's identification with Ka's dreamy and irresolute perspective. The very fabric of Pamuk's writing in *Snow* is such as to undermine polemic. Even where characters are made to declare for this or that position, the movement of the novel as a whole tends toward diffidence and doubt. The love interest at the center of the novel, along with the local intrigue and the occasional passages of casual but gorgeous word-painting, make us feel that *Snow* is anything but a novel of ideas. The handling of loaded issues—the ongoing heard-scarf controversy, the suicides of devout young girls, the violent threats to tolerance and diversity—is such as to make all such matters subordinate to larger and perhaps deeper issues. Politics is at the center of the novel, and yet politics takes a back seat to other concerns. A character named Blue has much to say about the "degradation" of Muslims by "Western eyes." At one point he publicly threatens to murder a television host who has uttered "inappropriate" remarks about Mohammed. And yet what matters most, in our sense of this figure, is Ka's observation that next to Blue he cannot but feel "ordinary and superficial." A Western, secular reader may not like or approve of that sentiment—I'm with Hitchens there—but no reader of the novel will deny that it is fully compatible with the dominant tone and thrust of the book.

As for the other charge, or objection, that Pamuk should not have been so generous to political Islam—not when he observes, in the novel itself, what it entails—I can only say that the instinct to generosity is matched by another, contradictory impulse. Call it the impulse to satire, or farce. Hard not to regard much that passes for earnest Islamic conviction in the novel as preposterous. Hard not to feel that Pamuk has deliberately made it seem so. The novel thus portrays fanaticism as awful and comical. So bizarre are the convictions and rages and stratagems of the Islamist fanatics that we cannot but regard them as part of a highly stylized extravaganza, a sort of wild opera buffa. The devoutness that can prompt the actions of adolescent suicides seems at once terrifying and moving and also terminally infantile. To feel "ordinary and superficial" next to a devout fanatic willing to die for his beliefs is understandable, but the novel also incites wonder at ostensibly reasonable adult figures who can get worked up about the virginity of unmarried adolescents and think it a good idea to have Islamic thought squads interrogate people like Ka about their atheism.

In the end, Hitchens's objection to *Snow* may be said to turn on his suspicion about the author's spiritual attitude. Is Pamuk honest in his novel? Does he allow himself to reveal and engage with the relevant political implications? Here it is necessary to observe that Pamuk relies, legitimately, on the complicity of his readers. He assumes that we are equipped—that the novel equips us—to fill in what is not in so many words spelled out. And when we think about the ideas that revolve more or less consistently in the narrative, we do so in the spirit of the work itself. We are moved, steadily, to supply the sense that much that passes for ideas in the world Pamuk evokes is nonsense, but that it is important nonsense. Even terrible and nonsensical ideas attract adherents in the world of Pamuk's novels, and there is not much that persons who are not themselves inclined to fanaticism can do but deplore the ideas and consider how impotent they are to stem the tide of ignorance. The likably skeptical Ka belongs in every way to the spirit of the novel, which is essentially generous, though at bottom generosity too is consigned to ineffectuality in this realm. To complain about such a work that it does not call things by their rightful names is to miss the mood of the thing and to overlook the reader's steady enlistment in that mood, a mood that resigns us to the fact that there is everything to worry about and deplore and nothing to be done. Can that mood successfully drive such a work and make its ideas seem to have been responsibly engaged? Contra Hitchens, I would say that *Snow* manages perfectly to accomplish the feat.

Of course there are no decisive conclusions to be drawn from what I have said here about the general relation between politics and the novel. Readers inevitably bring to works of fiction built around issues their own demands for ideological correctness and relevance. And writers, for their part, strive to shape responses to their fiction, sometimes by giving interviews that express their "real" views on questions handled less explicitly in the fiction. Pamuk surprised no one when he admitted that he routinely tries "to determine . . . how my books should be understood and read." But most novelists also freely concede that their take on issues and ideas in fiction is richer, more complex, and thus truer than anything they can say outside the framework of their novels. The novel as a form allows a good writer with views to resist the temptation to simply and straightforwardly promote them. Bad or lesser writers are unable to resist that temptation. Likewise, readers who are unable to read without demanding a comforting echo of their own beliefs will have no real feeling for the rigors and inflections of serious fiction. Politics, in novels we can admire, must always pit ideas against the world as it exists, or might conceivably exist, and allow, at every turn for contradiction and irresolution. Irving Howe got it right when he spoke of "the vast respect which the great novelist is ready to offer to the whole idea of *opposition*, the opposition he needs to allow for in his book against his own predispositions and yearnings and fantasies." To think of politics and the novel without bearing in mind that commitment to "opposition" is to miss more or less entirely what is central to our great and familiar subject.

[8]

REALISM

The things of everyday must be lifted out of the realm
of the self-evident.

—HERBERT READ

I want you to understand the archaeological surround
of a fact.

—MICHAEL ONDAATJE

Not long ago I had a call from an undergraduate student
eager to interview me at length about the 1960s. She had
heard from a younger faculty member in another department that I was a "veteran" of the antiwar movement, a conscientious objector, and an unrepentant "leftist." I had even published
my angry opposition to the Vietnam War in articles and reviews
and for good measure continued to teach a popular course in
"Politics and the Novel," the subject of two books I had written. I
could provide a "living voice" of "radicalism" and yet speak with
some presumed "realism" about the actual consequences of the
positions I had taken forty or more years earlier.

About my own youthful radicalism I could speak—did
speak—with genuine authority. I remembered, vividly, what it
was like to be perpetually angry. I recalled the sectarian disputes
that animated my encounters with friends and family members,
and for good measure I could explain the difference between
proponents of violence and proponents of peaceful dissent—like

myself—whose views were shaped by older members of the democratic
Left like the critic Irving Howe, who became a mentor and a friend.
I detailed the stages of my growing radicalism, my refusal to show up for
a draft board physical at the height of the war, my stated willingness to
go to prison rather than be drafted, my involvement with antiwar groups
in New York City.

But my primary commitment, I discovered, in speaking to a student
forty years after my radical seed-time, was to reality itself. In attempting
to honor the truth, in hoping to tell, for the student's sake and my own,
precisely what happened, I acknowledged the extent to which I had
become—dreaded word—a realist. I was, from the moment I mailed
my letter of conscientious objection to the draft board, perpetually agi-
tated and afraid. This I reported. I was torn between my own instinct
to flee, if necessary, to safety in Canada or some other country, and
my determination to do the right thing and pay the legal penalty for
my "conscientious" opposition to the laws of my country by going to
prison. Filled with pride at my own noble refusal to yield to the dictates
of the established "reality," I was perpetually astonished at what seemed
to me the palpable idiocy (and ignorance) of many of my comrades
in the antiwar movement. Moved by the liberationist agenda taking
shape in many quarters of the counterculture, I was, at the same time,
appalled at the reckless self-indulgence and cravenness of most of the
young people I ran into at political demonstrations and even in peace
workshops we attended. Satisfied that our mobilizing efforts had driven
Lyndon Johnson from the White House, I was appalled that many on
the American left thought it no big deal if by sitting out the 1968 presi-
dential elections, in "principled" protest against the entire "system," we
would bring to power Richard M. Nixon, who would surely make things
even worse than they were before he took office. Supposing that the
political journalism of the honest reporters who wrote for the young
New York Review of Books—writers like I. F. Stone, Joseph Kraft, and
Andrew Kopkind—would inspire other young people who wished to
understand what had been going on, I was astonished at the posturing
and sloganizing that passed for political discourse in many precincts
of the American Left, where opposition to America's role in Vietnam
was thought to entail support for the other side and the pretense that

war crimes were committed only by U.S. troops, never by the North Vietnamese or the Viet Cong.

In carefully laying out the story for the eager young student, who had by that time read two popular histories of the 1960s, I realized that she had soon become rather disenchanted with my recitation. It did not jibe with the somewhat heroic view of my generation that her young instructor in the college history department had promoted. As a symbol of something selfless and exalted I was not sufficiently inspiring. At one point the student wondered aloud whether my political views had perhaps drastically changed. It seemed to her—in spite of my assurances to the contrary—that I now regretted the "positions" I had taken back then. Did I think, perhaps, that it was simply my having grown "older" that made those actions of the past now seem foolish? Was it not that I did in fact now regard my opposition to the war as foolish? By way of response, I asked the student whether, in acknowledging a divided view of what I had experienced, I had seemed to renounce the convictions I once held. Yes, she said, that was what she had heard. And did what I told you of my own internal divisions and disappointments seem to you unreasonable? Not unreasonable, no, she replied, though she didn't think she agreed with everything I'd said. Fair enough, I went on, but agree or not, you'd say I offered you a realistic assessment of what I saw and felt? Maybe so, she hesitated, but she was not sure she knew what I meant by realistic. And at that I saw the muscles of her forehead rise in protest.

In fact the student's confusion about the meaning of the term "realistic" is common among people of her generation and, increasingly, among older people as well. On the other hand, I now see that my own attraction to a species of realism is not something that I recently picked up but was always an aspect of my youthful radicalism. Where does radicalism begin when it is not a raging fever in the blood? Theories abound: there are those who cannot think without first declaiming a topic sentence and a thesis. In my case the radicalism, never "revolutionary" or inclined to violence, had much to do with "non-identity thinking," a term to be mistrusted, like all theoretical abstractions, but potentially useful in pointing the way to something actual. The term itself belongs to an arsenal of terms developed by the German thinkers of the Frankfurt School in the middle decades of the twentieth century.

Herbert Marcuse, for one, wrote about what he called "the power of negative thinking," and T. W. Adorno, like Marcuse, used the term "negative
dialectic" in building on ideas drawn from both Hegel and Marx. In
essence, this language identifies a refusal to regard "reality" as a given.
The notion that what we see is real and that what we merely imagine is
unreal is what these thinkers most fundamentally dispute. To say that
reality is simply the stone we stub our toe on is to misapprehend the
nature of reality. The thinkers associated with non-identity thinking
sought to reintegrate the finite and the infinite, the actual and the possible, the "objectively" true and the imagined truth. They argued that to
understand reality we must regard the apparently real as not identical
with reality itself. This way of thinking could seem obscure or willful,
but its effectiveness in shaping a powerful critique of every established
political and social order is also indisputable.

If we say, for example, that "realistically speaking" most Americans
are opposed to government interference in the economy and in other
areas of our lives, does this mean that the opposition is "real" and that
the plans most persons think they oppose are the "actual" plans proposed
by proponents of enhanced government intervention? Suppose we say, as
non-identity thinking would have it, that public opposition is only apparent, based as it is on a widespread misunderstanding of the relevant pro-
posals, which is in turn the consequence of lies and distortions contrived
by persons whose interests move them to derail the plans proposed by
a "liberal" president. Thus we conclude that the apparently actual sentiments, assembled and tallied in polling numbers and contained as well
in reports based on anecdotal evidence, are not identical with what the
actual sentiments would be if the several relevant factors were properly
understood. The poll numbers then represent an actual state of affairs
only in a very limited and misleading sense. The actual reality of the situation can only be understood not as indicated by the numbers—not, then,
in terms of the available hard or anecdotal evidence—but in terms of
what the evidence would conceivably be if the situation were reasonably,
rationally altered, so that citizens might then be capable of consulting
their own actual interests rather than responding largely as administered
subjects easily manipulated by the media and other forces beyond their
present understanding or control.

To be sure, in thinking of reality itself in this way, in resorting again and again to what would be the case and what might be the case and thus to what should be the case, we make it very difficult to operate in terms of criteria of truth and falsity. We accept that, in mistrusting (though not necessarily repudiating) what appears to be hard evidence, we must often speculate and suppose. But then this is at the root of most forms of radicalism and remains very much an aspect of a mature relationship to reality. What is real cannot be ascertained simply by opening our eyes and looking. We may do our best to be attentive observers of the available reality and try not to be dismissive of what passes for obvious. We may even acknowledge that even scrupulously fair-minded observers like ourselves will often be deceived or will see principally what we are primed to notice or to take seriously. But we must also accept that in supposing reality often to be other than what is obvious and accredited, we run the risk of presuming what we have little right to presume. Marcuse argued that the satisfaction or happiness experienced by most persons in advanced industrial societies was not true happiness. If they understood their true needs, most of those people would see that their ordinary habits of consumption and gratification were responses to needs manufactured for them by business and the media. In *One-Dimensional Man*, Marcuse wrote that "In the last analysis, the question of what are true and false needs must be answered by the individuals themselves, but only in the last analysis; that is, if and when they are free to give their own answer." The danger in such a formulation should be obvious, for Marcuse here in effect presumes that he and others like him are more apt to be legitimate arbiters of true needs than are merely ordinary persons, who believe— mistakenly in many cases—that they are themselves in touch with their own actual needs and desires. Marcuse's presumption may well put us in mind of those follies to which intellectuals are notoriously susceptible. Mere empty notions floated by persons with too much esteem for their own advanced powers.

And yet. And yet. A realistic assessment of reality would seem to require just that risk of presumption, a willingness to speculate beyond what any available evidence can fully support. This is not, after all, merely a radical proposition but the foundation for any reasonable idea of thinking itself. I may not presume in myself what Marcuse believes about his own powers of discernment, may not quite agree that ordinary persons are not yet "free to give their own answer." I may in fact regard the undulations of mind swollen with thoughts of its own magnificence as essentially comical. All the same, in trying to get at what is real, I am willing to risk the several dangers we have cited. In attempting to reconstruct for a student my experience of the 1960s antiwar movement, I did portray the movement largely in terms of its non-identity with two deeply entrenched views of it: the first, a view entertained by those who recall it with derision and contempt; the second, a view held by those who regard it as an ideal flowering of conviction and altruism. In trying to think against the false idealization of a very complex phenomenon, I imagine what a conceivably honest idealization might look like. When, in my 1997 *New Republic* magazine review of Phillip Roth's novel, *American Pastoral*, I asked whether his caricature of the American Left (young activists psychotic or fanatical) was credible, I argued that in truth it was far too easy and one-dimensional. For it seemed to be inspired by a too ready, too little resisted contempt for those who had been absurdly romanticized in novels and histories of the 1960s. My own memory of the period was rather more generous than Roth's, and yet, as I have indicated, I could not help considering how much the actual diverged from any ideal version of a radical Left I might entertain: a vision of a movement not so very given over to slogans and posturings, not coarse and abusive even in its more confrontational moments, not disposed to lie to itself about its motives or the allies it chose, not willfully blind to historical precedent or to the thought of likely outcomes, not self-righteous.

Yes, of course, I know, and knew then: a radical movement such as no one has ever seen, against which nonetheless I would measure—however improbably—every actual movement or insurgency we can recall or envision. And yes, of course, I can hear the voices of friends, sensible, loyal, ringing in my ears, in my head, declaring more than skepticism about the insipid picture—my own thought-picture—of young activists surging forward without a slogan or an arsenal of abusive epithets or simplifying formulas to enflame them. My very own folly, to imagine such a prospect.

And yet—again *and yet*—this non-identity thinking, this hopelessly speculative resort to a dream of a world or a movement more attractive, call it what you will, has a pedigree that may compel just a bit further

attention. Can there be "realism" in an approach so insistently rooted in
the what-is-not and never-has-been? The John Stuart Mill who wrote in
1869 about "the subjection of women" was, so far as we can now ascertain, entirely realistic and yet visionary in his way of dealing with what
then seemed—surely to his contemporaries—not much of a problem.
He noted, of course, that in 1869 it was plainly impossible for anyone
to know what women were or were not capable of, though just about
everyone else—including most women—thought their inclinations and
competencies quite obvious. They were not, clearly, much interested in
current affairs, as indicated by the fact that few were involved in politics
or journalism. They were not inclined or suited to scholarship, or to science, or to mathematics, or to the demands of logic. They were—so it
seemed—suited to the standard lives most women led. Experience clearly
furnished few exceptions to these observations. All you had to do to know
what women needed and wanted was to take note of the lives they led,
most of them apparently contented, or at least not moved to declare themselves notably unhappy with their lot as women. Did not most women see
themselves primarily as wives and mothers and servants and subordinate beings? Did they not agree to leave the business of business to men?
The evidence was, in every sphere, rather overwhelming, in spite of very
occasional indications to the contrary, and it was reasonable to assess and
plan and predict on the basis of that evidence. It was reasonable, in fact,
to assume that the nature of women could be nicely established, with the
actual, observable nearly universally accepted lives of countless women
as an entirely reliable foundation.

Realism, then, as Mill understood it, required first a realistic assessment
of the social, cultural, political, and economic forces that had together
conspired to make of most women what Mill called "willing slaves." They
had agreed to abide by the protocols and expectations devised for them,
in part by their "masters" but in truth made possible as well by their own
inveterate willingness to go along, to purchase a sweet approval by the
conventional means typically available to them. A so-called realism would
then have seemed, to almost everyone, a perspective eminently sane in the
degree that it assumed nothing not founded in established fact, whereas
for Mill nothing was less promising, less "realistic," than an outlook willingly constrained by established fact. If most people thought women fully

revealed in their natural appetites and capacities by the regime that constrained them, that was for Mill but the starting point for a thoroughgoing
reappraisal of women: of their natures, their capacities, their desires. The
assortments of female forms—sensual or plain, brainy or dull, moving to
and fro in sharp outline or cloudy amber light—seemed to Mill merely
the shadows of what they might be. Their natural endowments, prodigal
or meager, were no more available to their own present understanding
than to the imagination of the men closest to them. Realism was for Mill
a way of acknowledging standard limitations and a strategy for getting
past them. To be a realist was to imagine possibility and, in doing so, to
confront one's own immoderate desires. In Mill's case, those desires had
to do with the intimate companionship of an extraordinary, hard-driving,
strong-willed woman named Harriet Taylor, who embodied for him a
dream, a possibility others could not so much as imagine. Though Mill
was not at all given to mystic flights, his realism drove him to the intuition
that there was a palpable correspondence between the apparently actual
and the figure one might only imagine or posit. He was able to believe
that the reality accredited as such in his culture could best be understood
when it was juxtaposed against the "reality" that did not yet exist.

The critique of the so-called realism associated with Mill and other
liberal, or radical, thinkers is familiar in the writings of numerous conservative thinkers. They argue that reality and dream are by definition
mutually exclusive concepts, and that to speak of a "correspondence" is
to invite confusion and wishful thinking. The enemy of the possible, they
contend, is the impossible or improbable evoked in dreams or fantasies.
Recent history, they remind us, is filled with examples of persons who
thought to realize their own immoderate desires by forcing reality to
conform to their wishes. In politics especially, they say, we see what can
happen when persons without a decent respect for limits, or natural laws,
or the established order, seize power and then stop at nothing to realize
their ambitions. "The glorious and final benevolent utopia" devised by
Karl Marx and other "dreamers," writes Leszek Kolakowski, turned out
to be "a good blueprint for converting human society into a giant concentration camp." If old-style Marxism is by now dead, Kolakowski notes,
the dream of a "final benevolent utopia" entertained almost nowhere, the
"virus" that fed such dreams may simply be "dormant, waiting for the next

opportunity. Dreams about the perfect society belong to the enduring stock of our civilization."

Kolakowski was the most astute and devastating critic of Marxism, and he did cogently anatomize the cruelty, corruption, and intellectual shoddiness of most of the thinkers associated with that tradition. But his attempt to discredit "dreams" and "dreaming" by linking them with the inventors of the Gulag is in some respects misleading. So too is he plainly mistaken in associating the dream of a world more attractive with what he calls "the liberal-evolutionist belief that 'in the last resort' the course of history [is] inevitably for the better." In fact, optimism is by no means entailed in the capacity (and the willingness) to dream, and most of the visionary thinkers who have had instructive things to tell us about the nature of reality have not been tempted to final or utopian solutions. The conservative critique of the realism developed by liberal and radical thinkers has been, for the most part, a paltry and grudging affair. To be sure, as Kolakowski writes, "thanks to the unprecedented speed and diffusion of information, human aspirations throughout the world are increasing faster than the means of satisfying them," and this does more than occasionally lead to "rapidly growing frustration and consequent aggressiveness." But the "aggressiveness" would seem more especially to mark the efforts of conservatives to insist on their own inflexible view of "reality" and to force others to conform to their view of things.

Debates about what is real and what is not continue to stir thinkers in every precinct, in part because it has become increasingly difficult to distinguish between reality as we think we know it and the ten thousand images of "reality" disseminated in the culture every hour. The difficulty has seemed impressive for almost a century. One example: in the 1920s the German satirist Karl Kraus wrote that "In the beginning was the Press and then came the world." He was responding to a growing alarm, a sense that what we call the world is primarily a product of the consciousness (or "information") industry. Another later example: in 1962 the German poet-critic Hans Magnus Enzensberger wrote that "The process is irreversible . . . [the service] essentially the same all over the world, no matter how the industry is operated: under state, public or private management, within a capitalist or a socialist economy, on a profit or non profit basis. The mind industry's main business and concern is not to sell its product:

it is to 'sell' the existing order." Though Mill did not, of course, address a "consciousness industry" or dwell in so many words on the eclipse of the real, he understood that reality is most often grasped only by those alert to the unreality of the established fact. If convention has it that at bottom, in spite of their obvious differences, human beings share a common "human nature" and common desires, the task of realism must be to think against "universality" and to ask what the experience of birth and death and struggle and thinking feels like and amounts to from the perspective of actually different persons, as also from the perspective of the actually different persons they might, under altered circumstances, become.

Realism seeks, as Roland Barthes wrote in *Mythologies*, to avoid the "purely tautological," which is what you get when you rely on so-called "facts of nature, universal facts." Like Mill, Barthes understood that, for so-called "natural facts to accede to a true language, they must be inserted into an order of knowledge," which means postulating that one can transform them, and precisely subject their [apparent] naturalness to our human criticism." Obviously this practice by no means necessarily entails forcing oneself to believe in changes that are unlikely to transpire, or forcing others to accept "for their own good" or "for the sake of the future" what they do not want and cannot bring themselves to believe in. The conservative critique of the realism promoted by Mill and Barthes and other visionary thinkers over the course of the past two centuries fails entirely to take seriously the magnitude of the challenge represented by this realism.

Though realists, at their best, acknowledge limits, they take no pleasure in this. They know that human beings are capricious, that events often occur for no discernible reason. But they do not accept that "man is entirely what befalls him," as Herodotus long ago proposed. Realism need not be humble or long-suffering. Realists despise the limits they feel pressed to acknowledge. The essential mandate for realism, its reason for being, is to think and imagine without supposing that the given reality is all there is. A realism worth our attention can seem insolent. It says, look at the way things are and do not fail to imagine what they might be. It says, do not believe that all things are possible, but do not fail to operate with standards that are immoderate. In the arts, realism at its best confronts the established canons of value with a determination not to be impressed. Though realism is by no means typically revolutionary in its ambitions, it often generates what John Bayley calls "the atmosphere of revolution," an atmosphere tense with the possibility of upheaval in our way of understanding the ways of the world and of art.

Turgenev, in *Fathers and Sons*, does not approve of the nihilist Bazarov, who has nothing but contempt for the old order of his Russian society and nothing hopeful to say about the future. But he sets up the figure in such a way that he must seem a bracing affront to everything settled and comfortable. Everything not associated with Bazarov seems to us unduly mild, timid, sickly, for we look at things with eyes trained in our abrasive encounters with Bazarov. The dream liberated by Turgenev's novel is a dream of a something else for which we have no name or reasonable approximation. Its realism lies in a disciplined refusal to accommodate itself to what seems merely kindly and humane. For Turgenev, the decent and familiar are not—must not be—all there is.

In Coetzee's "Realism," chapter 1 of his *Elizabeth Costello*, Elizabeth's son contends that "my mother has been a man," that she "has also been a dog" and "can think her way . . . into other existences." She is not content to see the world simply as a woman sees it. She is a realist who is not bound by fashionable feminist ideas about "identity." To be sure, Coetzee is somewhat dubious about the "miracle" of imaginative breadth he sponsors in his portrait of the writer and her son. He can laugh at the holy shrines set up to celebrate the writers to whom special powers are imputed. He is enough of a realist in the standard sense to be suspicious about special claims, and he can allow himself the thought that perhaps "*we are not made for revelation.*" At the same time, he allows that we are susceptible now and again to "rapture," "revelation," and extremity of feeling.

But Coetzee mounts his most impressive challenge to a quotidian realism in the novel *Disgrace*. There he gives us a protagonist who seems the perfect realist in the conventional sense, one who renounces high ambition and learns to live very much within his emotional means. Pleased, more or less, with his own mainly moderate appetites, David Lurie has been at best an indifferent husband, a fond but by no means passionately committed father, and a professor who demands and receives rather little from his "postliterate" students. His avidity extends principally to the sexual encounters he enjoys with a paid companion for ninety minutes each week, which produce in him "a ground bass of contentedness." Decidedly a realist if by that we intend a person who knows how to live comfortably with what he has. Though the "indifference" of his students "galls him more than he will admit," he accepts that "he has never been much of a teacher." In sum, he tends to blow neither hot nor cold. He moves in what may be called the middle way, accepting that the world and its creatures—himself included—must be as they are.

But Coetzee's novel will not allow its hero to remain what he has been, insists rather that he be tested and that he thereby be made to imagine—as we must imagine—some alternative dispensation beyond what has seemed to him the fated condition of sensible creatures. What may rightly be called the "miracle" of *Disgrace* is that its hero comes gradually to embrace a view of things that should inspire in someone of his disposition merely contempt and condescension. The plot of the novel is by now so familiar as to require no detailed recounting here. What matters is that Coetzee portrays a man who contends, with enormous aplomb and lucidity, in difficult circumstances, that subjects like the state of one's soul, or the sincerity of one's sentiments, or the depth of one's sense of guilt, cannot be realistically assessed and thus are not really legitimate subjects for discussion. Questions of contrition and repentance belong—so Lurie believes—to a category of concern beyond the competence of reasonable persons determined to live on realistic terms with themselves and others. What is more, the reader of Coetzee's novel cannot but feel that there is a compelling logic in this way of thinking about things. Though Lurie is by no means an exemplary fellow, his realism seems to us, in its lucidity, not tremendously disappointing. Sensible, moderate, is about as much as we can bring ourselves to feel about a fellow who has learned all too well to live within his limitations. Our disappointment in him is made to grow only as we witness his own growing sense of unworthiness.

In fact, the questions that this realist comes to take seriously are apt to seem lethally high-minded and unanswerable, and thus off-limits. Of course the central question has to do with the nature of forgiveness and the meaning of what is absolutely not to be done. But there are others. In what degree are we, as human beings, required to devote ourselves to the amelioration of suffering? Is this not an imperative beyond the charge of ordinary persons, especially those who have learned to live within their own limitations? Is it reasonable to demand that we renounce every privilege and seek reconciliation even with those who are sworn to do us harm?

Such questions bespeak a determination to forgo the satisfactions associated with a clear and apparently reasonable sense of things. Realism of a conventional kind will declare that the guilty must simply be punished, that persons who work hard for their privileges ought to feel free to enjoy them, that reconciliation with persons who are vicious or hostile ought not to be an abiding objective, that the suffering of animals is so different from the suffering of human beings as to warrant no comparison, that to think of oneself as a disgraceful person, a fallen being, is to capitulate to a religious view of our essential nature and to demand of ourselves more than a reasonable portion of guilt and repentance.

Clearly Coetzee's realism turns on the disparity between what is imaginable and what is indisputably real. It does not allow his characters to withdraw from the real life of their time and place or to escape its taint. But they are made to register the fact, as George Lukács once had it in an essay on Tolstoy's realism, that "reality is always different from what human beings dream and hope." Might dream. Might hope. As with Tolstoy, Coetzee's realism permits "the extreme possibilities of a human life" to emerge, fitfully, even reluctantly, though they remain "mere possibilities," neither "abstract" nor "artificial" but "concrete" and "central." A realism that offers the actual and the dream of the actual. The facts of life and a never secure resistance to fact. The world as it is and the world as it might be.

[9]

THE SUBLIME

The undeceived are mistaken.

—JACQUES LACAN

A clear idea is another name for a little idea.

—EDMUND BURKE

The sublime has its acolytes and infatuates, people who live—or think they live—for those moments of surpassing intensity that can make everything, especially the ordinary pleasures, seem paltry and safe. Others mistrust excess and tend to be on guard against anything remotely exaggerated or deliberately heightened, worked up. Such persons regard the sublime as a category of experience open principally to hysterics, or charlatans, or the willfully self-deceived.

And yet we do know—even those of us who belong, like myself, to the party of the wary and mistrustful—that certain moments in our own experience stand out and apart from the run-of-the mill intensities. Sexual transports may well carry us to places beyond anything we can compare with other, more ordinary delights, and yet we don't quite believe, do we, that a pleasure enjoyed two or three or more times each week over the course of many years— with one single partner or with innumerable different partners, in however many thrilling configurations—can quite justify the use of a term long associated with the extreme and unassimilable. Call it oceanic, or mystical, say that never anywhere else in your experience have you felt yourself comparably transformed, or lifted so entirely out of your habitual consciousness of self, and still you may conclude that "the sublime" doesn't really capture what happens to you when you feel the shudder in the loins and the derangement afforded by sexual encounter.

But consider a very different sort of encounter. The setting is a concert hall in Germany in the final year of the Second World War. Though allied bombers are raining destruction on the city, the hall is filled to capacity, and the pianist Walter Gieseking is playing the Waldstein sonata. "Smoke hung in the concert hall and an odor of fire and burst mains blew in through the gilt-and-stucco foyer." All over the city at this time the wailing of sirens and the booming of explosions. People in the hall feel the shaking of the building and sense the imminence of sheer chaos and destruction. Outside "blistered pavements," exploded gardens. And yet for many of those present a sense of drinking deep, of letting go—so the author evoking this nightmare landscape has it, the listeners at the concert rapt, their attention heightened by their fear, which has them in its grip even as they strain to attend to the notes of the music, so that there develops in some of those present a kind of hysteria, the pleasure unspeakably intensified by the thrilling sensation of being at an end, of having denied the authority of what is most obviously real and pressing. Nothing about the experience so undergone belongs to the domain of the ordinary or reasonable. To speak of it in terms of enjoyment, or satisfaction, is to misrepresent it. It is, quite clearly, something else altogether. Not desirable. Certainly not. If sublime, then sublime strictly by virtue of its being unlike anything else, incomparable in its having no relationship to any mundane, merely human appetite.

When I first came upon this episode in George Steiner's little novel *The Portage to San Cristobal of A. H.*, many years ago, I thought it perfectly caught what I wanted to understand about the sublime. I knew, even then, as I know now, that in the main it had nothing to do with me, with who I am and what I hope to experience. Imagining myself into such a moment I can see only the desire to flee, to take shelter, to contact my children so as to ensure their safety. The determination to go on with the musical performance would have seemed to me then bizarre, the inebriated audience members possessed by something almost pathological, the result, perhaps, of their long enlistment in the nightmare of the Hitler years. And yet their willingness to be possessed, their capacity to be thrilled and lifted, if only temporarily, out of any reasonable self-regard would have seemed to me utterly compelling, the sublimity associated with their collective state an awesome spectacle. Nothing wonderful in any of it, nothing admirable. But strange and compelling. A mark of some ordinary human limit surpassed or denied.

Of course we may want to accord to our own, more familiar experiences some special quality that would allow us to suppose that we too, even we, may occasionally surpass what is expected of ourselves. I tell myself that I am open to the sublime and that I have known it here, and here, where it was not expected, in some unaccountable display of courage, or impossible tenderness, or fabulous explosion of rage. And yet most of us must live in the middle way, with the moderate and steady virtues, and traffic not at all, or only very rarely, in the precincts of the sublime. When I read in Keats—is it not sublime?—that the most beautiful thing in the world is the sight of a beautiful woman who is dying, I may swoon at the very notion, or at the poet's way of evoking the twinned impression of longing and loss, and yet know that this conception of beauty is not for me.

So that those of us who are reluctant to admit to an appetite for extremity—or a susceptibility to hysteria—often look for ways to domesticate the sublime, to bring it home, though home is not its proper habitation. As it happens, I often find myself thinking about the sublime during long periods when I live in Italy, where the beauty on offer is so pervasive, the senses so unusually alerted to its presence, that I might almost be forgiven for supposing that I have become another being, less moderate in his appetites, less willing to tolerate what passes for acceptable elsewhere. Still, the beauty on offer is not characteristically an instance of the sublime. More to the point, you do not feel yourself suddenly thrust into contact with the divine or transcendent, however much you may wish to signal the extremity of your pleasure by resorting to words of that nature. The frescos in a Florentine church do not affright and overwhelm. The rows of resplendent palazzos lining the Grand Canal in Venice are sumptuous and reassuring, declaring that the past lives on and is good, if only you know where to look. Even at night, perfectly lit and without the hordes sporting cameras and guidebooks, the gaudy Roman piazzas declare that the fabulous and excessive can be simply enjoyed. Nothing, really, in an experience of Italian sights and landscapes to decisively undo an otherwise secure self-possession.

More promising, in fact, for these purposes, to think of things Italian in another way entirely. A way available only to those who have had a love affair with a place, and a people, while suffering over many years its absurdities and contradictions. The stuff, it may be, of comic novels and oft-told travelers' tales, but promising nonetheless, however improbable. Improbable how? In seeming too mild, too pedestrian to furnish an experience of the sublime, which is perhaps best understood as an aesthetic category and not confused with anything else. Though who would not wish to penetrate to the heart of a venerable idea by taking hold of it in one's own way? To undertake to domesticate something in its nature rare and vertiginous is, no doubt about it, to risk losing it altogether. And yet I want to try, and to say that to sustain a love for Italy and Italians, over many years, is to find oneself oddly, incredibly, in touch with the sublime. To try. To test a somewhat absurd proposition. To see, in effect, whether the sublime, so apprehended, will continue to seem an actual something to which we might have access.

* * *

A small museum in Rome. Not much to look at, but with one or two surprisingly first-rate things in a temporary exhibition. On one handsome wooden door the words "sempre chiusa" (always closed) carefully hand-written on a shabby sheet of note paper. Why always closed, I ask the attendant seated just to the left of the door. It's not actually closed all the time, I'm told. The room in there has some interesting things. Like what, I ask. You'll have to come back and see it some other time for yourself. But if it's always closed, how will I know when to come back, or if I want to come back? That's a problem, replies the attendant, who then turns back to the newspaper she was reading before she was so rudely interrupted. As I walk away, defeated, I note that where the attendant is seated nothing is hung, so that she has nothing to watch over or guard against, the corridor stretching perhaps ten feet before her and giving onto a dark, shallow stairwell.

* * *

A university building in Urbino where my wife and I go each day to use our laptops, our apartment Internet service frustratingly intermittent at best. We go at first to the administrative offices to obtain permission and are told we need nothing official. Is there a code we'll need to gain access to the service in the building? Certo, of course. And what would that be? That I can't tell you. Why not? We don't just give out the code to anyone who comes by to ask for it. And may we then pay for the service for the week we'll be living here in town? No need to pay, our friendly administrator declares, though I can't give you that code. So then you don't want us using our laptops in the building? I didn't say that, the man croons, and we are always friendly and welcoming to visitors. And how then would we obtain the code we'll need? Why not just ask one of the students you pass in the hallways? Which of course we do, succeeding with the first student we meet, a young man, age twenty-three, from the Veneto region, eager to help us out, and to direct us to the "best place in the university to use the Internet," set up in room 327, on an upper floor, "with a wonderful view of Urbino from the terrace outside." And the best way to get up to that room? You should take the elevator just around the corner, I'll lead you there before I run to my class. Lovely. The elevator indeed just around the corner. As we approach, several students getting out and others about to go in. Attached to the elevator door a metal plaque bearing the engraved inscription: "macchinario di ascensore pericolo" (dangerous elevator).

* * *

A large post office in Florence. Each of the windows clearly marked. One for the payment of bills, a second for the mailing of packages, another for "francobolli," or stamps. I line up for the francobolli, soon exchange pleasantries with a well-dressed young man standing cheerfully behind me, and move in ten minutes or so to the counter. I ask for a dozen 1.80 euro stamps for mailing postcards to the United States. Sorry, we're out of those. No problem, why not then a dozen for one euro and another dozen for .80? Sorry, out of those as well. Oh. Well, then, what denomination of stamps do you have? A blank stare across the counter. Followed by a perfunctory flipping of pages in an oversize stamp album. And then a heartfelt, "Mi dispiace," I'm sorry, but I have no stamps. But why, then, are you open at the window marked "francobolli"? Look, he says, an exasperated expression lighting his features, in this country, if you want stamps, you go to a "tabacaio" (that is, a store that sells cigarettes). Yes, I say, I know that sometimes you can get stamps at the tabacaio, though the man there usually tells you he has none when you ask, but here I am at the post office, and I've been standing in line, and you tell me that you have no stamps. "Dificile, le," my postal clerk informs me. "I can see that you're a difficult fellow."

✳ ✳ ✳

A dark autumn afternoon in Milan, strolling around a bit after several hours in the Brera, planning a long walk to our hotel, when it begins to rain, so that we decide to take a bus, though it is rush hour, and crowds are queuing up everywhere you look. Soon we are on the bus we need, standing body to body with others mainly on their way home from work. Only six or seven minutes into our trip the bus stops, the driver announcing that a "schopero" or strike has been called, so that everyone must get off at once. Where to go, what to do? No cab stand in sight. The rain now growing almost torrential. Hundreds of stranded passengers milling about, filling the sidewalks. Angry talk, raised voices. An entirely common occurrence, it turns out, in cities like Milan and Rome. No particular set of goals or demands associated with the decision to strike. Nothing to win from the working people who take buses each day in rush hour to and from work. Nothing really to be said or done. Cowering against the steady rain under our small umbrella, we consult our map of the city and soon set off on foot to find our hotel, the chaos behind us on the packed sidewalks a vivid token of something we have long known.

✳ ✳ ✳

A one-bedroom apartment in Florence, a half block from the Pitti Palace. Rented for six autumn weeks. A dour, impressively solid stone palazzo. Tall ceilings, ancient exposed beams, rough tile floors. A large kitchen stove that rests comfortably within a pink brick wall that juts out—just so—in a way that makes it impossible to boil your morning coffee without hitting your head. The furniture, obviously once rather elegant, now shabby, the seat cushions torn or fraying, tables wobbly, lamps falling apart when you try to move them an inch or two. The shower curtain five inches too short, so that when you run the water the bathroom floor is instantly flooded. Familiar, all over Italy, even in high-end apartments—like this one— sporting the standard amenities and air conditioning. Everything need- ing, obviously, to be replaced, though providing what is casually referred to as "atmosphere." The building itself—Palazzo Belfiore—in this case too good for such trappings. We phone the manager for an extra lamp, a bet- ter expresso pot, perhaps another small desk that won't collapse with the weight of a laptop and a few books. And she complies, friendly, solicitous, apologetic about the missing floor tiles in the kitchen and the toilet seat that won't stay put when in use. But remember, she says, placing a deft and reassuring hand on my arm, Florence is an ancient city, and in an ancient city everything is old.

✳ ✳ ✳

A late October morning in Rome. We make our way to the information office near our apartment in Trastevere, where we are given a small bro- chure about the Museum of Modern Art located on the other side of the city and then a printed sheet containing bus routes. The attendant is help- ful and entirely pleasant. We check everything with her before leaving the office—the bus we are to take at which corner, the opening and closing hours of the museum, the days of the week it is closed, the schedule of feast days in the calendar year when special arrangements are made. Nothing to worry over or fear, so that we set out with perfect confidence, catch a bus right away, and even find seats for what should be a forty-five minute ride. Only to be told, about halfway through the journey, to get off the bus and wait for the next one. No explanation. The bus we took will not go all the way along its accustomed route. Not right now. Not my decision, says the driver. But the same number bus will be along before very long. As in fact it is. Only a half hour wait at the god-forsaken spot somewhere in the city. But relief at the very sight of the thing swinging into view and picking us up. And again two seats. And before long the museum itself, a large, dour structure, unmistakable there in the bright noontime light. The approach on foot from the bus stop across the way uneventful, the guard planted in front of his tidy booth with a welcoming smile on his face. Is this where we buy the tickets? No, you buy them inside, when the museum is open, but today the museum is closed. But it can't be closed, my wife says, whipping out her museum brochure and pointing to where it says that this museum is open on Tuesdays. That's correct, says the nice man, but you see, yesterday was a feast day, and on feast days the museum is usually closed, though on this one occasion the museum decided anyway to stay open, and because of that, the museum had to be closed today. Someone should have told you. But why then are you here, my wife asks. I'm always here, he says. And is there any way, I suddenly ask, that I can find a bathroom somehow before we set out again on the bus? As you can see, I'm a man of a certain age, and I need a bathroom. Oh of course, says our companion. You can just go around the side of the building, that way, and down the stairs, and there you will find the café, where there are toilets you can use. You can even have something to eat down there. But I thought you said the museum was closed, my wife says. It is, says the man, but not the café. In the café the employees weren't told that the museum would be open yesterday, and so they didn't come to work. So today they are working. Even though today no one is there at the museum to eat at the café? But now they will be happy to see you, says our friend.

✳ ✳ ✳

The university in Bergamo. I am there to lecture on "Realism" to students and faculty in the division of English and American studies. The lecture is slated to begin at 4.30 and to extend until 6.00, leaving ample time for questions and discussion. When I enter the lecture hall I see that it is nearly filled to capacity. Before I reach the lectern up front several faculty members come up and shake my hand, offer welcome, tell me how much they have looked forward to my talk, and apologize for having to leave at 5 PM, in time to catch a train to Milan, where most faculty and students live. And in fact, at just past 5, there is a mass exodus, leaving about forty people in the lecture hall. At dinner that night I ask my hosts about this arrangement, and learn that all lectures at the university are scheduled at

the same hour. Likewise many classes on other weekdays, when students
routinely rise and leave just as discussion has begun to build. I say that
this seems to me ridiculous. A problem, I go on, that should be easy to fix.
But that's the way things are done in Italy, I'm told. And anyway many of
our students almost never come to class at all. And you don't mind this, I
offer, and don't mind when students get up and walk out on your lectures?
We do things differently here, I'm told.

* * *

Of course, as someone who has spent several years of his life in Italy, I
can go on with such stories, though by now a reader will naturally wonder what anecdotes of this sort can possibly have to do with the sublime. Taken one at a time, in fact, they contribute nothing whatever to
an understanding of the subject. But in the aggregate they seem to me to
constitute something else. What to call it? Try, I tell myself, to think of
how your love of something—a place, a people, a set of practices or customs, an atmosphere—may so far exceed what is reasonable or deserved
as to have you wondering what could conceivably be the basis of your own
outsize sentiment. Ask for some plausible fit between the bewildering,
exasperating features of the thing you adore and the unshakable intensity
of your affection and you may understand at once that you are in the grip
of something you can hardly begin to communicate to anyone not possessed by a confounding and yet indisputable emotion.

In truth, the intensity of my feeling for things Italian has much to do
with my sense that Italy is not at all easy to love, that it requires of me
something I am not routinely equipped for, which is the renunciation of
my usual commitment to the reasonable. If I ask why I am thrilled by the
persisting evidence of the inchoate and absurd in virtually every aspect of
Italian life, I can only think that I am in thrall to some life force wonderful
because so entirely divorced from mundane practicality or proportion.
Again, taken in isolation, each particular token of idiocy or absurdity is
merely what it is. That is to say, each particular, isolated from all of the
other comparable experiences or features you can assemble, doesn't signify a thing. But put these tokens together and you have, I think, a spectacle in its way wondrous to behold, and perhaps thrilling in the manner

of things that strike a beholder with awe and produce an uncommon, nearly vertiginous sensation.

Of course the impulse to assemble a veritable dossier of tales that will stand as anecdotal evidence of something so rare as the sublime is clearly a dubious undertaking. For the tales themselves revolve around experiences that can only seem very small, even trivial, by no means what is typically associated with the tradition of the sublime in art and literature. The sublime, after all, has long had its place in academic histories of sensibility. Scholars note that over the centuries it has attracted the attention of major thinkers, from Longinus to Edmund Burke. Though the taste for the sublime is no longer very much with us, new works do now and then emerge whose mood or accent bespeaks a renewal of a peculiar urgency most of us find outsize, or hysterical, or overweening. Thus the urge to bring the sublime down to size, as it were, to make it an aspect of what may look like ordinary life, though in its nature the sublime has always been associated with the eclipse of ordinary semblance and emotion. In the eighteenth century Joseph Addison wrote that it had principally to do with "wide and undetermined prospects," with "speculations of eternity and infinity," with wildness and the incommensurable. Wordsworth, in *The Prelude*, celebrated the mind responsive "to something evermore about to be," to the "elevated" and "divine." He was certain, in thinking about the sublime, only that it acted on a properly responsive intelligence in a distinctive and extraordinary way. He believed, with Burke, that you would know yourself to be in the grip of the sublime in the degree that you were amazed at your experience, and confounded. Nothing moderate or modest in the precinct of the sublime.

Other writers, from D. H. Lawrence to William Blake, have been no less attracted to the sublime as a category of experience wonderful and extravagant. Even Milton was said, as by one of his best critics, to supply us "with examples of the image at the point of dissolution—in effect, transcending itself." Again and again devotees have hoped to move on the threshold of a new awakening or conflagration of feeling, to join what Blake called "the religious" and the "voluptuous." Nor was the culmination to be associated with the merely beautiful, for the beautiful was characteristically to be found in tokens of unity, harmony, proportion, symmetry, order, limitation, and restraint. By contrast, the sublime strove to exceed confinement, convention, and closure. It promised, or seemed to promise, a something more ever to be unfolded, an accession of feeling potent because in no way associated with the mild gratifications of garden-variety reason or meaning.

The dangers attendant on too habitual an indulgence of the sublime are obvious. The conditioned yearning for the absolute or out-of-reach may degenerate into a hysterical overreaching. Exacerbations of feeling may be fueled by hyperbole and empty histrionics. An insistence on the high or noble may devolve into posturing and an easy disparagement of ordinary experience. Intensity may be cultivated for its own sake rather than for the sake of any worthy objective that might plausibly incite a genuine hope or passion. In spite of the theological or metaphysical noises emitted in the precincts of the sublime, the "transcendent" evoked in much of the art and literature consigned to this category can seem little more than a vague ether impervious to genuine feeling and without significant content.

Inevitably, many artists and writers seduced by the lure of the sublime have been reluctant, tentative. They have wished to pass beyond the merely intelligible and proportionate without capitulating entirely to chaos or delirium. Drawn to risk and extravagance, the best of them have feared that estrangement and *terribilita* may become easy, comfortable, the recourse to the elevated and divine a practiced way of saying no to quotidian sentiments and moving on the edge of one or another conventional abyss or promontory with no genuine sense of risk.

Not to have known this sort of reluctance and misgiving is not, I suppose, to have seriously confronted the sublime. On the other hand, too ready a disposition to resist extremity, to associate the yearning for transcendence with hysteria or self-deception, is also a way of armoring oneself against the very possibility of disorientation and the terror it can bring. More than occasionally, in my own work, I detect an inveterate recoil from reaches of feeling that have seemed to me exaggerated. My tolerance for sensory derangement characteristically extends only to work in which there is some discernible measure of detachment, in which the sublime, insofar as it can be detected at all, is understood to be a sign or a symptom of something else. Thus *Death in Venice* has always seemed to me an exemplary work, an anatomy of a condition that evokes extremity without yielding to it utterly. Just so, I tolerate mysticism only where the form of a work—its very feeling and texture—is meditative, or where the obsession with transcendence is matched by an encroaching disappointment or disillusion. I cannot feel, with Phillip Lopate, that a film like Robert Bresson's *Diary of a Country Priest* ought somehow to change my life, but I can allow such a film to put me in contact, as Lopate says, "with a habit of mind that I may as well call spiritual." Such works, Lopate goes on, "those with austere aesthetic means" and "a mature acceptance of suffering as fate," can allow a responsive viewer "room for meditation." They are, to be sure, in the casual sense of the term, "sublimely orchestrated disenchantments," but they breathe an air of "calm" and of "dailiness" that sets them apart from the convulsive or ecstatic—apart, that is, from the sublime. Films by Bresson, or by Yasujiro Ozu, are "transcendental works," but they do not substantially challenge or alter the resistance of a viewer, like myself, to the sublime. Not, surely, if it is understood in Burke's terms as an experience of terror that "robs the mind of all its powers of acting and reasoning." No, I say. The sublime cannot often be for the likes of me. Not, again, unless I allow myself to think it compatible with experiences decidedly modest rather than convulsive, experiences recounted in such a way as to make me think myself improbably robbed of my own habitual habits of reasoning by sentiments strange and incomprehensible even to me.

I am by no means alone among contemporary writers in seeking a connection to the sublime without granting to it quite the dominion envisioned by inebriates. Of those who have ventured into this territory, the most audacious (and also, oddly, the most modest) has been the great Polish writer Adam Zagajewski. In his book *A Defense of Ardor*, he assures us that when he thinks of ardor he has in mind simply surprise, illumination, occasional updrafts of revelation. Such qualities he takes to be largely absent from the art of the present moment. Not much ardor, he complains. Not much of what he calls openness. Openness to what exactly? To the possibility at least of the sublime. Or, put another way, openness to disappointment with the "shabby" aspects of our common situation, which our poets might be expected to acknowledge and repudiate. For our accredited ways of dealing with reality do very much seem to the poet to deserve the epithet "shabby," or low. You detect it, he believes, in the note of irony you hear in much of our advanced art, a note that marks the impoverishment of the poetic imagination itself. Though we may not miss, or feel we miss, the accent of the sublime as understood by Burke or others in the past who staked a claim to it, we do miss, or ought to miss, an accent of striving or note of visionary ambition that would bespeak some familiarity with an idea of the sublime. And if we have learned to do without that striving or ambition—so Zagajewski contends—then we must find a way somehow to reconceive or reinvent it.

Of course it is possible, we think, that Zagajewski is after something here that might better be accommodated under some other rubric. But then he is a thoughtful person and a great poet, and one wants to accord to him the benefit of every doubt, so that we are willing—I am willing— to slow down for a while and to ask, first, what the poet intends when he speaks of the shabby and ironic—what, in effect, fuels his complaint. Thus: "Writing and thinking," Zagajewski tells us, "in recent years have come to seem meager, grey, anemic; the poetry produced, even by our most accomplished writers, reveals the overwhelming predominance of a low style, tepid, ironic, conversational." Rarely does the poet find what he wants, which is some mark at least of a "high style": "powerful expressions of the inner life" that are unapologetically visionary, burning with what Walter Pater once famously called a "hard gemlike flame."

Nothing of that gemlike flame, surely, in my own efforts to come at the sublime by way of the anecdotal, Italian hours recounted so as to suggest that there may be within the tiny and quotidian some prospect of a thrill- ing repudiation of ordinary semblance or expectation. Too much—surely Zagajewski would contend—of the "meager, grey, anemic" in my telling. Too much of the conversational and ironic. Not enough "inner life." No "visionary" ambition.

And yet there is nothing programmatic in Zagajewski's summons. He wants, he says, *not* pomp, *not* dogma, *not* some "high-brow mania for tragedy," or an appetite for "drap[ing yourself] in ancient tunics," but an improbably modest version of the sublime. The poet wants, he declares, "merely a metaphysical shudder, an astonishment, an illumination, a sense of proximity to what cannot be put into words." The sublime must accord- ingly be understood *not* as a series of lofty rhetorical gestures presuming to express or encompass a metaphysical truth but as a flash of illumina- tion, suggesting that there is something we would *wish* to encompass if we could. The emphasis here is on the striving, the struggle, the incompletion of a task that will seem essential to human beings who are not at ease in the mundane world that they occupy—or not completely at ease. To be open to the possibility of the sublime, Zagajewski contends, inevitably "involves a certain discomfort with contemporary society." Not a scornful or dismissive discomfort but—the indefinite is an entirely characteristic mode for this poet—a "certain" discomfort, not perhaps entirely to be put into words, but yes, a discomfort that is actual, more or less discernible, a discomfort that will stir us at least to ask what we miss in our lives, what our hunger for further illumination requires of us.

Discomfort, of course, comes in many different shapes and degrees. Most people who are ill at ease in their ordinary lives devoutly wish that they were not. No doubt some people—not necessarily the best of us—are unhappy principally because their lives require of them only the low-grade faculties of caution, prudence, and restraint. But even those who rail against complacency and long for something large and demanding to test themselves against typically cling to their own familiar, ostensibly advanced assumptions. Such persons—including most contemporary poets and intellectuals—are especially suspicious of overt expressions of sublimity and offended by the banal rhetoric of spirituality favored by the saved, those simple souls who suppose that their creeds and churches have something important to tell them about the true and the holy.

Zagajewski is as offended by empty pieties as are other cosmopolitan intellectuals. He wants the sublime without the phony rhetoric of sublimity. He invokes an idea of transcendence, the metaphysical, the mystical, without a commitment to any principle or system that might underwrite a way to reach it. He wants yearning and illumination without illusion or hysteria, and he appears not to believe that he has any obligation to speak about the content of the illumination he seeks. He has an appetite for strangeness, intensity, and revelation but has no feeling for revealed truths, which seem to him narrow and delusional. Nostalgic for a dispensation beyond irony and whim, he is rightly scornful of fake elevation and very much at home in his own ironic declensions.

Over the past century, many writers and thinkers have bemoaned the state of things in the fallen world and sought to inspire a renewal of the sacred. Octavio Paz, for one, very much a modernist writer and an unabashed celebrant of modernist art, nonetheless lamented the spiritual impoverishment of modernity and sought a way out of the "individualistic and sterile." Saul Bellow hammered, again and again, at the paltry circumscriptions and "minor neurotic trifling aims" to which modernity itself consigned us, and often his novelistic characters were made to declare that the "inability to explain is no ground for disbelief." The sublime in Bellow is reflected in the intuition that "the sense of God persists," even in those who "could wish that it did not persist." Knowledge, essential knowledge, is not what is "flatly" known, Bellow often suggested, but simply what, "in his inmost heart, each man knows." For Bellow, as for Zagajewski and others ill at ease in the Zion of the modern world, knowledge demands imagination rather than faith, a willingness to suffer with unsatisfied longing rather than a determination to relax into the embrace of a comforting certitude.

Considered in this way, the prospect set out by writers like Bellow and Zagajewski is extraordinarily attractive. They ratify resistance to the materialistic-therapeutic-accommodationist reality principle without buying into the simplicities embraced by the faithful. If resistance in such writers seems not much more than a tolerable discomfort, they remain ever watchful for some sign of a new way, even if the new way amounts at best to a brief upsurge of feeling, a sudden surge of optimism that will briefly release them from the wary and conditional. We are drawn to the insistence of writers like Bellow and Zagajewski that there are "higher" things to which we are summoned, drawn precisely because these writers are so clearly in doubt about those "higher" things. Zagajewski is a poet we can love because he demands that poetry "tell us what darkness is," while positioning himself uncomfortably between disillusionment and desire, sobriety and wonder. We take him seriously because for him "revelation / flickers and dies," because he is consistently vulnerable to disappointment.

No less might be said of other writers who, though they have their feet firmly planted in the actual, also have their own characteristic ways of bearing witness to the felt tension between the unsayable and the familiar. The great American poet Robert Pinsky is no exception, and his way, in many respects, might well be described in the very terms he has used for Zagajewski, terms like "shrewd, clear, passionate" but also "wonderful." To move through Pinsky's work is to hear a steady alternation, as from high to low, from "faint quavers of music" to "dreamy forgotten divinity," from stabs of wit to sighs of grieving. This, we feel, is a poet of earth and flesh and bone who yet is perpetually alert to what he calls "seizures/Of hopelessness" and "immortal longings."

In a poem called "Work Song," Pinsky offers some of the prose virtues for which he early attracted attention. He speaks as a man thoroughly at ease with all manner of things, from baseball to Beowulf, from games to the standard "difficulties" bemoaned by married couples. He speaks, in fact, in the voice of a poet who might well seem, in Zagajewski's terms, more comfortably invested in the shabby than in the sublime, a poet often ironic, irreverent, and poised to remark our common susceptibility to illusion.

But let us have a look at "Work Song":

> Fascination that dries the sap out of Yeats's veins
> And rends spontaneous joy out of his heart, with Art—
> Art, not "dolts" or "management of men" the difficulty
> Craved and admired more than pleasure more
> Than accomplishment certainly more than Eden.
> Heroic fascination of an overwhelming difficulty:
> Joan of Arc tortured to death by clergymen
> Her failure incidental as Jackie Robinson's engaging
> At one and the same time two worthy difficulties.
> Other athletes succeed in getting rich and in attained
> Leisure seek out even in Eden or Gomorrah the green
> Fields of the idiocy Golf because it is reliably difficult.
> Old joke *It has to be hard to be good.* Manipulable
> Light of the Xbox for all its eviscerations or hoops
> Like chess a grid of exploits adequately difficult.
> Music is difficult poetry is difficult Odysseus most
> Interesting of the Greeks fails to get his companions home
> But he does engage many an interesting difficulty.
> Love also is difficult as in "Adam's Curse" at the end
> Like at the Odyssey's outset failure as it emerges
> Like the hollow moon the couple is having Difficulties.
> Even the infant sated by the breast turns eagerly
> Irritable to its measureless impossible chore like Beowulf
> Down to the darkness with his old comrade the monster.

It is a poem centrally preoccupied with "difficulty," here conceived as "overwhelming" or "worthy," "reliable" or "adequate," "interesting" or "craved and admired." It moves from the difficulty associated with the visions of Joan of Arc to the difficult feats associated with Jackie Robinson, who aspired to steal home plate and, at the same time, to alter a nation's view of race. The mode of the poem is inspired juxtaposition and discontinuity, its music now elevated ("And rends spontaneous joy out of his heart") and suddenly prosaic ("But he does engage many an interesting difficulty").

In fact, the poem's commitment to the sudden and transitory, its essential changeableness, tethers it to the here and now of the poet's mercurial consciousness. We are challenged by the velocity of the poet's starts and swerves, the flickerings of the half-light he briefly casts on each particular he summons. His attention seems to us at once fierce and feckless, the prospect of revelation radically unstable, more an instinct than a promise. This, we feel, is a poetry of slippages and equivocations, yet it seems as well a poetry of ardor and inspired cunning. Nothing gray or anemic in Pinsky, nothing tepid or blandly conversational. Neither is there the fear of sentimentality or intensity that often marks the work of poets haunted by the sense that the fall into the quotidian is all we know. Pinsky may believe, with Zagajewski, that "the climate for lyric poetry has become increasingly inhospitable," as Walter Benjamin had it many years ago, but he writes as if that were not necessarily so. There is no surrender to the slender facts of life in Pinsky.

Would Zagajewski agree to speak of ardor in a poem like "Work Song"? There is no panting after the transcendental in Pinsky, no obviously visionary reach. Certainly there is no intimation of a presiding presence that might banish contradiction and remove the speaker from his habitation in the here and now. In fact, if there is anything we might speak of as a gesturing in the direction of the unsayable and essential, it is the poem's restless engagement with the idea of difficulty itself. Difficulty is the "measureless impossible" something toward which this poet irritably, anxiously yearns, difficulty this poet's way of thinking beyond limitation, comfort, presentness. Pinsky's nearest approximation to the sublime is glimpsed in the implied image of the great Robinson improbably stealing home or in the infinitely insatiable, questing infant confronting its "measureless" developmental task. It is felt in the poem's refusal to yield decisively to the ironic, deliberately cultivated intrusions of prosaic language that now and again erupt into the discourse of the poem.

Is any of this commensurate with what Zagajewski calls "a metaphysical shudder, an astonishment, an illumination, a sense of proximity to what cannot be put into words"? There is, in Pinsky, an aura of restless dissatisfaction, though not a dissatisfaction with anything so definite and yet vague as "contemporary society." Dissatisfaction in Pinsky has more to do with the sense that there are always losses and disappointments to contend with, and that the smaller pleasures and gratifications we devise for ourselves are not really, or not alone, what we are after. If this is "illumination," it is of the kind that we acknowledge when we say that one thing does not inevitably or logically follow another, that words themselves are slippery, that meaning is always darting out of reach, even when it seems briefly palpable and reassuring.

In truth, the "metaphysical shudder" provided by Pinsky's poem likewise has everything to do with its embodied embrace of difficulty, its peculiar way of seeming more than a little unaccommodating while yet setting before us a consciousness whose fits and starts and moods and severities are very human. Pinsky refuses to wear the unfathomable on his sleeve while nimbly, playfully, earnestly, devoutly working at the stuff of the common experience with a view to arriving at something he knows to be of potentially great importance without knowing quite what to call it. He is, in the best sense of a much-abused term, a realist who does not suppose that what is seen is all there is, or that a poet's use of words like "soul" or "spirit" or "mystery" can automatically validate an intimate acquaintance with revelation or the sublime.

In making his sometimes bewildering case for ardor and sublimity, Zagajewski targets an essay by the philosopher Tzvetan Todorov entitled "In Praise of the Quotidian," "a discussion of several paintings from the golden age of Dutch painting." This essay, the poet says, praises the work of Vermeer, De Hooch, and others for seeing to it, as Todorov asserts, that "the world's reality will not go unremarked." Rightly Todorov admires the mundane "poetry of dim [or bright] interiors," the willingness to disclose "the delicate being of things." All, so far as it goes, well and good. But what the poet takes to be unfortunate is the normative or "programmatic" aspect of Todorov's essay, his attempt to confer "special ontological status upon the quotidian," to view the Dutch paintings as a summons to live in the present moment, to root ourselves in reality. This, in Zagajewski's view, is a programmatic "reduction of reality," a "contraction of human life," a "dangerous"—that is the poet's word, not mine— program of resistance to the fantastic, the utopian, the saintly, and the heroic. And indeed, Todorov does in fact claim that "there is no place" in the Dutch paintings he admires "for heroes and saints." Like others who escaped from the several paradisal regimes of Eastern European communism, Todorov would seem to have had a bellyful of mystification and delusion, and he is thus very much at home in the relatively illusionless universe of the Dutch paintings he admires. This our poet takes to be a "complete" repudiation of the sublime, and worse, "a breach of faith," a refusal of the thinker to "open himself to the world beyond" his own very limited purview.

Very strong language indeed. Breach of faith. Treason of the clerks. Todorov does not apparently acknowledge—or not sufficiently—that the refusal of the Dutch masterpieces to celebrate what Zagajewski calls "final things," "mystery," "the spiritual realm," is a mark of their great limitation. He does not, apparently, as the poet would have him do, acknowledge that his own deep investment in these paintings is a mark of his own spiritual failure. We are, to be sure, as the poet says, each of us "stuck in this world up to [our] knees, even [our] waist." But how can we not lament this fact and look to other realms where the spirit longs to be? The "high style," as Zagajewski proposes, "grows from a ceaseless dialogue between two spheres," and if we find no trace of that dialogue in the Dutch paintings, that is a misfortune, and the viewer who sees in those works merely a magnificent ratification of our own shabby resignation to the ordinary has surely betrayed the "clerk's duty to open himself to the world beyond clerkdom."

But of course Todorov never proposes that we should admire exclusively the art of those Dutch painters, and neither does he suggest that those artists, in their commitment to the ordinary, have no prospect of delivering at the same time some aspect of the "enigmatic," the "potential," the not-quite-there, what might even be called the absent cause of the physical world that is so sharply and beautifully represented. I am especially puzzled by the poet's insistence that in Todorov we find a "breach of faith" when he quotes from Todorov's text a passage on a painting by Pieter de Hooch: "The girl is not looking at anything," Todorov writes; "she turns her eyes toward the emptiness outside, smitten by a spell that has stolen her away from the real world. The whole of life, the infinity of the universe, drives her on."

The poet regards the passage as "one of my favorites," sees in it "a way to revise Todorov's narrow program." But there is, I think, no need for the poet or for us to revise anything. For Todorov's program is quite clearly not at all narrow. He observes that in the Dutch paintings he studies, there is no representation of anything outside the real world that is ostensibly represented. But that does not prevent persons depicted in those paintings from looking toward something, or nothing, outside or beyond what their eyes can see. They are, like us and like all who look at the paintings, potentially susceptible to spells and seizures of inspiration. They are open, as we are, or may be, open to the impression that there is a "whole of life" beyond what is immediately apparent to us when we move our eyes over the surfaces of the material universe. The program, as the poet calls it, is not narrow when it acknowledges that what is out there may be (or may seem to us) an emptiness. That may well be what we confront when we sense that there is something beyond the objects we take in with our eyes. The impression that there is an "emptiness," not a fullness or a wholeness, out there, is an aspect of a vulnerability to reality that Todorov honors in his celebration of Dutch painting. That is after all what we typically honor in realism: the impression, not only that there are things, objects, solidity, but that there is more, a "more" we can find only when we venture out beyond what we can see, not always or predominantly spiritual sustenance or metaphysical comfort but absence, emptiness. To discover the one rather than the other is not to be narrow so long as the artist has ventured out and has honestly looked, or sought, or permitted us to look and seek.

The poet wants more, of course. He wants tokens of what he calls "an unflagging drive to seek out something higher." And so the question we must ask is what might persuade us that there are, in the Dutch paintings and in the poetry of Zagajewski's contemporaries, adequate tokens of that "unflagging drive." The mere presence in a poem of irony, which the poet himself considers a valuable component of the poetic sensibility, cannot tell us that the poem lacks the necessary drive. So long as the irony is not informed by *ressentiment*, that is, by a settled contempt for all things higher, more ambitious, more spiritual than itself, it remains promising. So long as the irony in a poem does not come through as a "bitter," "mocking," "misanthropic" dismissiveness, we are not necessarily put off the scent of the something higher Zagajewski demands.

Of course the Dutch paintings celebrated by Todorov are not characteristically informed by irony, and it is fair to say that the irony on display in the poetry of writers like Pinsky is never bitter or misanthropic. All the same, so far as we can tell, Zagajewski is in search of something he rarely finds nowadays and is troubled both by the shadow of doubt and by the flat accent of resignation whenever he confronts them. Presumably he wants, like others committed to the idea of the sublime, an expression of attachment that is not simply inferred or inferable but more durably and discernibly imprinted on the surfaces of a work than is nowadays common. He fears the corrosive effects of irony and colloquialism, signs—so he believes—not of modesty but of a contempt for the ecstatic.

In fact, the word "infer" seems to me to designate what is oddly lacking in Zagajewski's aesthetics. Though he wishes to see in a work he admires what cannot be put into words, he insists in effect that what cannot be put into words be nonetheless palpable, embodied, there. He is suspicious of paintings that summon us to live in the present moment because they do not clearly, unmistakably summon us to live in some other moment outside of quotidian time. The poet is unwilling to yield to works whose invitation to the sublime, to the ideal, is merely inferable. He mistrusts mere inference and is reluctant to credit the authority of works that seem reluctant to spell out their own impatience with the things of this world.

Zagajewski's is by no means a new set of aesthetic demands, though the case has never been more attractively set out. In "The Poetry of Barbarism," an essay originally published in 1900, the philosopher George Santayana launched a venomous attack on the poets Walt Whitman and Robert Browning. Santayana conceded that Browning could be a vivid and occasionally thrilling writer, but his superficial virtues were offset by his failure to provide what Santayana calls a "total vision," a "whole reality," a "sane and steady idealization." "Our poets," Santayana claims, a hundred years before Zagajewski targeted shabbiness, "are things of shreds and patches," with an appetite only for the "negative and partial," for a "blind and miscellaneous vehemence." We reject the works of "barbarians" because they do not "subordinate" the passion or sentiment expressed in their poems "to a clear thought." "The barbarian," Santayana contends, issues so many "barbaric yawps," which are "aimless in their vehemence," and "regards his passions as their own excuse for being." His speakers are said to betray an unfortunate "realism": they are "like men and women in actual life," alas, "always displaying traits of character and never attaining character as a whole." The worst things that can be said of these barbarians are, first, that the crudities and limitations of their speakers are not renounced by the poets but implicitly adopted by them as expressing their own limited capacities as human beings; and second, that the poems are at best "little torsos made broken so as to stimulate the reader to the restoration of their missing legs and arms."

Here we come again to the heart of the matter, as Zagajewski would seem to regard it. Poetry or painting that is rooted in the quotidian, he suggests, is implicitly committed to the quotidian and nothing else. Work that does not ultimately struggle against the earthbound sentiments on which it lavishes its attention is obviously content with the earthbound and has no capacity to stimulate in a reader or viewer the thought of alternative, higher possibilities. A work, so Zagajewski would seem to suggest, like Browning's poem "Soliloquy in the Spanish Cloister" (a poem Zagajewski nowhere mentions), which sets before us a brutish and resentful speaker, cannot legitimately expect a reader to infer from the vehement awfulness of the utterances expressed that Browning is not himself attracted to those utterances and expects the reader, in fact, on the basis of what is given, to attempt the "restoration of missing arms and legs," that is, to imagine the range of corrective sentiments—charitableness, scruple, compassion—that are missing from the utterances of the degraded speaker.

Inference, then, as we have suggested, is the name of the element that is oddly slighted and resisted in Zagajewski's aesthetics. When it comes to the sublime, the ideal, the higher things, his aesthetics demands a degree of explicitness, embodiment, and certainty that many of our best poets and artists do not provide. This requirement seems odd because in his own poetry the Polish master's stance is decidedly moderate, his aspirations to the higher things often relying quite considerably on the reader's willingness to infer. In fact, Zagajewski is famously reluctant to claim too much for our powers of spiritual affirmation and embodiment, believing that modesty, implicitness, and obliquity are better suited to the temper of an ironic, skeptical age than the sort of forthright, steady, unabashed idealization that Santayana championed. You read Zagajewski's poetry and then turn to the aesthetic demands formulated in the essays and you cannot but wonder, more than a little, how those demands can seem so essential to a great writer who operates very often as if a "summer morning's mildness" were the best thing in the world, and hope for anything better or higher were pretty much dead and forgotten. Usually, this poet memorably tells us, when we try to take hold of "precious thoughts," we "catch just / scraps," and all of us learn as we must that the trees express "nothing / but a green, indifferent perfection." Why a poet of such exquisite modesty should, in his essays on art and poetry, express such dissatisfaction with the so-called shabbiness even of the great Dutch painters, and suggest that our poetry too is somehow meager and impoverished, is one of those mysteries that Zagajewski's poems themselves may assist us to understand, though not nearly as well as we might wish.

Consider that in Zagajewski we find, here and there, poems whose gestures in the direction of the metaphysical are transparently inadequate. In "On Swimming," he concludes with the lines, "Swimming is like prayer: / palms join and part, / join and part, / almost without end." Reading such lines, I am tempted to say, simply, no, swimming is not "like prayer," and that really, to suggest that it is, is to declare, flatly, sweetly, what the poem has not earned. What we have in Zagajewski's poem, in other words, is merely the will to assert something that is not felt. Call it a small sample of the sentimentality that the urge toward sublimity in Zagajewski may occasionally, very occasionally, yield.

Or consider how, in the poem called "Holy Saturday in Paris," the poet evokes a day of "spring rain," insinuating into his abbreviated impression a number of telling, pointedly deliberate particulars: the day is a "feast day"; the speaker's companion wishes to go "where monks sing"; someone is said to have seen "the earth split open." In short, the poem furnishes what might conceivably justify the use of the word "Holy" in the title Zagajewski has assigned to it. We do not know, of course, whether there is in fact anything that deserves the epithet "holy" in this Saturday, or that the relevant signs are not assembled to confer on the day the mere appearance of a dimension that can serve to stir up certain feelings in the vulnerable poet. But we do note that the speaker in the poem shares with us the standard skepticism so familiar to our kind, observing, as he does, the "two-headed doubts, / slim as antelopes," that "barricade the damp street." That note, that mysterious, delicate turn to the slim, unfathomable antelopes, is in some ways the most appealing accent in the poem, the doubts invoked in their own way doubtful, full of wonder, pointing to who knows what horizon of possibility.

But then, at once, the poet, in his final line, cancels that delicacy of impression with the words "Lord, why did you die?" as if aware that his own intimations of holiness were obviously insufficient, concluding that he is not the man to provide what is wanted. Modesty and a certain quiet desperation are the hallmarks of this earnest grappling with the will-to-holiness, a will that such a poet cannot sustain. It is the silence, or absence, of God the poet acknowledges in that final line, thus acknowledging as well that the best he can do is to stammer, beautifully, a few occasional words to the effect that he misses something he lacks. The poet thus turns to standard terms derived from the discourse of religion only because they serve most poignantly to signal both his desire and his disappointment.

Zagajewski's repudiation of the shabby, his feeling that poetry in our time is without the kind of ardor he values, would seem, then, in many ways, to have a source in his own work. His critique of Todorov and of the poets reads, in this sense, like an expression of his own bad conscience. He wishes, as a poet, to do what he cannot do. He wills what cannot be willed and demands of others what he demands of himself but is unable to summon up. He too is a man of shreds and patches, whose work typically offers the fragmentary and partial. He admires conviction, the openness to higher things, but he finds, again and again, that he cannot be what he most admires, cannot identify in art an adequate substitute for lost faith or generate unequivocally "powerful expressions of the inner life" focused on the sublime. His burden is to write in a minor key, and though he has managed to persuade some readers—like the poet Edward Hirsch—that he is "a celebrant in search of the divine, the unchanging, the absolute," he is best described not as a celebrant but as a perpetual seeker after qualities he does not quite believe in. Indeed, we might well say that, in his criticism at least, Zagajewski doth protest too much, that his assertions have about them the somewhat hollow ring we pick up when a speaker doubts what he clearly intends to say with perfect confidence.

To be sure, one of the most likable things about Zagajewski's poetry is its modesty. It is just like him to promulgate in his poems what he calls "a mysticism for beginners," and the original dust jacket of the volume of that name rightly cites "the gentle meditative authority of Zagajewski's voice." But of course the word "authority" there derives from the impression we have that this poet refuses ever to speak with perfect self-confidence or systematic certainty. The authority we grant to him has to do with his diffidence about ultimate things, his willingness to live with enigma and doubt. The authority Zagajewski earns in his poems is not a reflection of his having arrived at any particular destination. He does not speak to us as one of the saved but as one who is uneasy before "the river of Never" and attuned to disillusion.

At his best, which is most often, Zagajewski is not a celebrant of higher things, whatever those may be. He is a worldly poet, open to small pleasures, transitory impressions, sly indirections, "cryptic greetings." In a poem called "Dutch Painters," far and away the most polemical of his poems, he complains that "There's no mystery here, just blue sky, / restless and hospitable," but his poems typically give us precisely that: a restless rumination on reality that seems to us hospitable because the poet knows so well how to deal with what is dealt and how not to demand what is in any case not forthcoming.

Which leaves us where in the matter of the sublime? Banality, no doubt, in the plain acknowledgment that each of us is susceptible or resistant in different degrees. I myself have known those whose brains worked at a temperature clearly different from mine. Persons whose dreams seem to them fabulous and moving, whose least experiences they describe as if they were the stuff of legend, for whom revelation is always near and each discovery is pregnant with the extravagance of ultimate or shattering insight. People for whom small signs may be taken for wonders. To such persons the sublime must seem—must be—an ether clearly fit for the likes of them to breathe. An ether not, then, congenial to others more inclined to doubt and indirection. I knew a man once who said to me, in all earnestness, "I like a woman to look tragic," to which I could only respond, "Do you know how funny that is?" Nothing there, I thought, that a good therapist wouldn't know how to take to pieces.

At a funeral not long ago I observed a man whose display of bereavement seemed to me magnificent, the proceedings clearly an occasion for a towering expression of unappeasable grief, the mourner himself thrilled by the extremity of his own inconsolable suffering. Enviable, I thought, this man who had found his vocation and thus his way to a sublimity probably not otherwise available to him. Then I recalled my own earlier bereavements and relived—though I had long forbidden myself to revisit them—the losses that had once left me desolate and, for a time at least, inconsolable. And I recalled as well that my own displays of bereavement on more than one occasion would have seemed, to a detached observer inclined to condescension, theatrical and extravagant and might well have provoked in that onlooker the callow observation—my own callow observation—that only thus could a person like me taste a sublimity beyond decorum, restraint, or proportion. A sublimity of suffering indulged, voluptuous.

Now, as I think of that brief accession, the notion of a sublimity of unappeasable suffering beyond restraint, I note that it has very little in common with that other species of sublimity I sought earlier to portray in my abbreviated tales from Italian life. And not much more in common with some of the classic instances cited in the standard sources. It may be that any effort to think "the sublime" outside the framework of art and literature and music is inevitably doomed to failure. The extremity of emotion associated with actual, unbearably painful loss is finally not best understood with the assistance or "clarification" of an essentially aesthetic concept. Just so, the thrill, or pleasure, or exhilaration afforded by long acquaintance with a place that has little apparent or reasonable claim on your loyalty is not adequately explainable by recourse to "the sublime." Alas my own somewhat desperate insistence on extending "the sublime" to accommodate experiences better grasped in other ways—so like the stubborn insistence of Zagajewski and other writers of my generation—bespeaks the fact that certain ideas, however compelling, are no longer fully accessible to us. In this case it is tempting to say that the advancing inaccessibility of a sentiment like "the sublime" is a sign of a certain emotional or intellectual impoverishment we can do little to reverse. But I prefer to believe that the sublime exists for us still as a sort of marker, or instigation, assisting us to weigh the gains and losses entailed in the emotional culture we have inherited. This is by no means an adequate consolation for the sense that we have definitively lost touch with something precious. But then it is never possible to predict with confidence the rise and fall of an idea. And as I look around at what often passes for sublimity in contemporary culture, I cannot think that it is altogether a bad thing to do without it.

[10]

PSYCHOANALYSIS

For us, science is a refuge from uncertainties, promising—
and in some measure delivering—the miracle of freedom
from thought.

—JOHN GRAY

Psychoanalysis is that illness for which it regards itself as
the cure.

—KARL KRAUS

The sociologist Philip Rieff, perhaps the most brilliant critic
of the psychoanalytic tradition, often derided what he
called mediums "fit only for messages." Is psychoanalysis one such medium? Surely it can seem so. In attempting to
explain a multitude of complex, often unfathomable sentiments,
contradictions, and impulses by resorting to keywords and cat-
egories, psychoanalysts have often presumed to banish mystery
and to reduce experience to formula. The mind, said Rieff, "begs
to be violated by ideas," and surely he was thinking not only of
minds in general, but of therapists who have made that species
of violation especially tempting for their patients. In offering up
a standard assortment of apparently decisive and unimpeachable
ideas, many analysts have, for generations, provided messages
that seem to numerous human beings consoling precisely in
their apparent ability to make everything seem comprehensible,
or nearly so.

Consider, for example, the notion that sexuality is central to human development. Has this notion not become a commonplace in Western culture? Does it not presume to account for a great many things, some of which have little to do with sexuality? And is this notion not at the root of what Leslie H. Farber once called "the aha phenomenon," which routinely occurs whenever a therapist encourages a patient to accept a definitive-sounding "explanation" that is presumed to settle questions about the ostensibly "true" origins of an impulse? When Freud offered his patient Dora an explanation of her condition that made sexuality central to her problems, was the message thereby conveyed not intended to consign to virtual irrelevance other compelling features of her experience, especially those about which she herself felt some conviction? And was not Dora's potential understanding of her own condition not thereby somewhat diminished in spite of the apparent expansion of her understanding achieved by Freud's unanswerable interpretation of her condition?

The mind that begs to be violated by ideas is a vulnerable mind, a mind eager for resolution, exhausted or confounded by the doubt or misgiving it has had to entertain. Of course there are analysts who are not as inclined as others in their profession to explain away or otherwise banish confusion, and many contemporary analysts assert that "truth" is constructed and is never incontrovertible. Just so, many analysts scoff at the idea that sexuality is inevitably at the core of human motivation. And yet it is fair to say that in the main, therapists are in the business of dispensing apparently reliable ideas, or insights, that can assist people to get on with their lives. That is the necessary burden of therapy, its benevolent promise, and, in an odd way, its fatal misfortune. When Rieff wrote that "therapy is that form which degrades all contents," he was contending that the actual "contents" of a patient's experience were reduced in the therapeutic encounter to the status of manipulable material, interpreted and transformed into a symbolically significant symptomatic content compatible with an established therapeutic view of conflict and resolution. Though analysts may well contend that Rieff's sense of things is outdated and "Freudian," and much has changed in the domain of therapy in the past quarter century, my own recent conversations with therapists and their patients persuade me that Rieff's observations remain compelling.

Of course the therapists themselves will point to theoretical advances that give the lie to my impression. Adam Phillips contends that psychoanalysis is not so much a "self-justifying" system but "rather more of a grab-bag of [our] culture and history." Analysts, he says, have looked to creative writers and artists for "the possibility of an eccentric life, a life untrammeled by system or convention," and increasingly, he believes, his colleagues in the profession will come to regard what they say and write not as expressions of the "truth" but as a way of finding out whether or not they can believe it. Phillips concedes, parenthetically, that "it has always been difficult for psychotherapists to avoid putting the answer before the question," but he remains optimistic that they can do better. Yes, to be sure, typically psychoanalytic writing reads like "incantation . . . characterized by the hypnotic repeated use of favorite words such as play, dependence, development, mourning, projective identification, the imaginary, the self, etc.," but there have long been signs of impatience with this state of affairs.

Central to the developments Phillips would wish us to consider is the emphasis placed—by numerous analysts—on "something called 'not-knowing.'" Indeed, Phillips contends, "it has become a virtue in psychoanalysis" for the clinician not to jump "to authoritative conclusions." And what has been the source of this development? The poets, chiefly John Keats in his recommendation of "negative capability," had offered an implicit critique of the will to interpretation and of "the analysts' will-to-intelligibility." Keats, of course, had famously defined negative capability as a condition in which "a man is capable of being in uncertainties, mysteries, doubts without any irritable reaching after fact and reason." For the analyst, Phillips believes, this was an injunction against "the failure to observe," the failure to wait and be patient before committing to interpretation. The analyst is warned against "premature or pre-emptive knowing" or "propagandizing."

At the same time, Phillips concedes, the analyst, "like the so-called patient, is not supposed to not-know forever." Therapy is "indisputably a method for self-knowledge." However diverse the schools of psychoanalysis, each having its own "distinctive version of the self-knowledge story," there will be in each of them a controlled rage to interpret, to unearth a set of meanings that can inform the business of self-discovery.

Thinking about the therapeutic enterprise in this way is encouraging, and no one will doubt that practitioners inclined to operate as Phillips describes will often accomplish wonders for patients in need. The suspension of certainty will be essential if therapists are to benefit their patients. And yet it is not easy to banish the thought that few analysts will find it possible to operate as Phillips believes they should. To read the testimony of contemporary Lacanian analysts—to take but a single notable example—is to note how the insistent privileging of "desire," as an ostensibly constitutive feature of virtually every human transaction, largely incapacitates these analysts from paying plausible attention to other competing factors in the experience of their patients. The degradation of content Rieff noted in earlier psychoanalytic writing remains very much a primary feature of the ongoing therapeutic practice.

It is tempting—certainly for a literary person—to think of literature as a practice radically opposed to the degradation of content. Freud regarded writers like Dostoyevsky and Shakespeare as having understood—without the benefit of Freudian theory—the roots of human behavior, and he celebrated their resistance to simplifying formulas. He made substantial use of the insights he took from such writers, and he was, at his best, a subtle interpreter of conflict and delusion. More, he was not invariably constrained in his thinking by the positivist conception of truth that he championed. Though he inclined to think of religious faith, for example, mainly in terms of the discernible function it served in the lives of believers, and typically reached for terms like "primitive," "fantasy," and "illusion" to describe religious states, he did not repudiate William James's assertion that "no account of the universe in its totality can be final which leaves these other forms of consciousness [such as mysticism] quite disregarded. . . . They forbid a premature [exclusively rationalistic] closing of our accounts with reality." If analysts have often reduced experience to system, Freud and many other analysts were at least alert to the richness of the interior life —James invoked the "many interpenetrating spheres of reality"—and acknowledged the superior ability of the greatest artists to get at the essential features of our experience.

My own limited experience of psychotherapy offers what may be a suggestive opening onto our subject. In 1974 I had separated from my first wife and was preparing to marry a student almost ten years my junior, to

whom I have now been married for forty years. My closest friend at the
time was Farber, author of *The Ways of the Will* and a leading practitioner
of existential psychology. Les was by no means enthusiastic about psychotherapy in general, and his own writing—brisk, anecdotal, searching,
rigorously unsystematic—had little in common with standard psychoanalytic writing. Yet he was insistent that, before going further with my plans
to divorce and remarry, I go into therapy and attempt to get to the bottom
of the feelings that had brought me to this fateful juncture. My cheerful,
unambivalent resistance to this prospect intensified Les's insistence, and
when he told me that he would see to it that I paid only what I could afford
for the therapy, I capitulated, shaking my head at what I took to be my
friend's misguided solicitude.

Though it was not possible for me to enter therapy with the distinguished analyst Les had selected—a man with the improbable name of
Otto Will—I soon settled on a highly recommended, middle-aged clinician well-known to one of Les's colleagues. He was a mild and gracious
man, without manner or eloquence, the sort of man I might well have
invited to play softball or tennis with me on warm weekend mornings
in Saratoga Springs. I could see at once that he was delighted with me,
and I wondered whether I had managed to betray, in our first half-hour
together, some symptom or revealing habit that seemed to him to promise a decisive key to "tendencies" and "problems" of which I was as yet
thoroughly unaware.

In fact, my therapist had known, even before I came through his door,
what he wanted most from me, which was not—or not at first—a key to
my "problems," but a glimpse into the life of my friend Les Farber, about
whom he began to ask me one question after another. Did I think it odd
that my friend would take it upon himself to select a therapist for me?
How had we come to be the closest of friends? Was it true that Les was
married to a former patient? Was he as aloof a father as he was reputed
to be? Had I met, at the Farber apartment, former patients, long-term
inmates at one or another mental institution, and was it true that many
such people were included in the good doctor's intimate circle? How
would I describe Les's interpersonal affect?

As I quickly understood, my new therapist was, had been, a devoted
reader of Les Farber's writings on envy, despair, suicide, anxiety, and will,

and he was eager to learn what he could about the personal life of some-one he deeply admired. The fact that Les was not a man much given to sharing, or discussing, or publishing details of his private life made him seem—certainly to my therapist—fascinating, and no doubt he took my own reluctance to betray anything of Les's private affairs as a mark of the larger pattern of resistance he hoped to break through.

Even when I had made it clear to my inquisitive therapist that he would get very little from me of what he most wanted, he found ways of intro-ducing Les Farber into our sessions. Had I ever discussed "that" memory or episode with Les? When did I first reveal to Les that I was "interested" in a student in one of my classes? Had Les ever told me that my own habits of secrecy and discretion were excessive or at least unusual for a young man just past thirty? Was Les's wife more or less judgmental about what I was doing? I handled these questions and prompts as candidly as I felt I should, and I allowed myself to be amused at my therapist's apparent obsession with Les Farber. Perhaps I had fallen for a carefully orchestrated strategy, and my therapist had brilliantly determined to open me up by overcoming my particular resistance to talking about Les, but that seemed to me no reason to be less than amused each time Les's name came up. And on weekends in New York City, when my wife-to-be and I spent most of our time in the Farber apartment, I made the most of my therapeutic encounters by narrating for Les the latest efforts by my therapist to break through my "resistance" by casually asking me about my friend at the least expected moments. "Have you told him yet that it's getting old?" Les enquired. "I will when it's getting old," I replied. "For the moment it's about the only thing I look forward to in those sessions." "But who's study-ing whom?" Les wondered. "I mean, do you have the impression that he's actually trying to get somewhere with you, apart from your relationship with me?" "Not sure at all about that," I countered.

In fact my therapist did hope to get somewhere with me. Though he was clearly frustrated by my repeated assurances that I had no misgiv-ings about the course I had adopted and no fear that the young woman I intended to marry would soon decide that she had made a dreadful mistake, he allowed me my assurances and soon turned to dream analysis to get us past what was clearly an impasse. The problem here was that I was not much of a dreamer. I rarely had memorable dreams, and I rapidly ran through the few I was able to reconstruct, none of them especially recent. "Are you sure that's all there is?" my therapist asked me, clearly disappointed, a little skeptical. "I told you," I said, "and don't tell me you think I'm holding out on you."

At this point, eight weeks or so into our time together, it occurred to me that this very nice man would dismiss me. We had covered —so it seemed to me—grounds sufficient to establish that I was not in conflict about my choices and that I was aware of the difficulties I would likely have to confront in the years ahead. If my therapist conceded that we had gone on with the so-called therapy long enough, my friend Les would surely accept his verdict, and that would be that.

But before I could bring myself to ask whether we were through, my therapist began to ask me whether I could think of some dreams told to me by others. Perhaps even Les had confided one or two to me in the course of the many hours we had spent together? No, I assured him, so far as I could recall, no one had confided any dreams to me, and I was certain that Les would never be moved to such a confidence, not with me, not with anyone. "Sorry," I said. "For what?" he asked. "For not being more helpful."

"Oh. That's not a problem," he said, smiling. "I mean, you're a literary man, and you know, I've looked up some of your essays, and I know you've thought a lot about dreams. So why don't we just start taking apart some really juicy ones. You know what I mean, like one of Raskolnikov's dreams from *Crime and Punishment*. Did you ever read Moravia's novel *The Conformist*? And then, no reason why not, we can go into film. I read your essay on Bergman's *Persona*, and as you know, there are lots of dreams in *Wild Strawberries* and other Bergman films. That'll keep us going for a long time, don't you think?"

In truth, we did not go on very long with this charming procedure. After helping my therapist to unpack a number of richly loaded dream sequences in Bergman and more than once reminding him that the more obvious among them were the least compelling, I asked, simply, what he hoped to accomplish. Was I bored with this activity? he wanted to know. Yes, frankly, I was bored, and working hard not to feel irritated by what I took to be a waste of time. "You never know," my therapist declared, "what will come of something like this until you've tried it."

"Well," I replied, "I've tried it, and I've concluded that I understand the dreams in Bergman's films all too well. I guess I'm really only interested in dreams that resist me more than some of Bergman's do. I like dreams to be recalcitrant. And that's what I want from art as well, that it not yield entirely to my purposes."

That was the last of my clinical sessions with my therapist. We parted with a handshake and an exchange of jokes, my best and his. In leaving this, my only "extended" therapeutic encounter, which had lasted all of eleven sessions, I found that my misgivings about therapy in general had been confirmed. Theoretically it seemed, to me at least, there was nothing whatever to object to in the prospect of a talking cure. My friend Les had himself modestly recommended good talk, honest talk—what he called "real talk"—as a distinctively human way to work through persistent dilemmas, though he was less than committed to the artificially controlled conditions often devised to govern talk between clinicians and their patients. At the same time, I knew that Les kept much of what he was going through—doubts, fears, depressions, rages—largely to himself and believed in the silent treatment, the conversation the sufferer carries on only with himself, as often the only plausible way to think against one's own will and to avoid "willing what cannot be willed," as he put it. Oddly, for a man who had written an entire book on will and was ever watchful for signs of the disordered will in himself and others, Les had been more than a little willful in his efforts to get me into therapy. After all, he had willed not only that I submit to therapy, but that I think it a good idea, and when, in the wake of my final "clinical" session, I told Les that I had never quite been able to accept that the entire business was anything but hopeless, certainly in my case, he smiled and said, "I know." Just that. "I know." A flash of the apparently imperturbable amenity Les reserved for special occasions, and for the closest of friends, who could be counted on to understand that, when Les said those words, "I know," he knew in fact everything and had, in this instance, indicted himself for willing what could not be willed as surely as I might have indicted him.

Among the many things that Les understood as well as anyone I have ever met is that art and literature, properly regarded, cannot be a forcing ground for ideas. Literature, as he often agreed, is never a medium fit for messages. When my therapist conducted me on a tour of Bergman films with the intention of having me raid them for "insights" or revealing "truths" about myself or "the human condition," he was, in effect, asking me to violate those works by using them to arrive at "conclusions." Of course a very large portion of what passes for narrative fiction and film begs to be violated and exists, in fact, for no reason other than to satisfy our common desire to be comforted by accessible "truths" and appealing "conclusions." But that is not what we want—ought to want—from serious works of art, works created by grown-ups, for grown-ups. And that sense, that there is a difference between one sort of work and another, and that there are radically different ways of approaching a work, is often not at all understood, not by psychoanalysts, and not, increasingly, even by contemporary literary academics. One of the ways of willing what cannot be willed is observed in the effort to read a great film like Bergman's *Persona* or a great novel like *Crime and Punishment* as if there were keys to grasping the singular, not to be controverted, perfectly unanswerable meanings of such works—as if one could come away from them without misgiving, a confirmed message gripped and easily carried in the fist of one's little hand.

Do writers, filmmakers, artists, find anything useful in the domain of psychoanalysis? In a way, of course, the question is answered simply by invoking those famous words of Auden, who spoke of the way that Freud had become "a whole climate of opinion." It is not possible for artists not to be influenced by psychoanalytic concepts, and the influence extends also to those artists and writers who loathe those very concepts and would hope never to be caught making use of them. What writer would not be influenced to some degree by the now very widely assimilated idea of unconscious motivation? Is there an intelligent writer who doesn't accept, with whatever reservations, that the word "transference" does actually refer to something that frequently occurs not only in controlled therapeutic encounters but in other interactions as well?

But though this is not the place for a detailed, wide-ranging analysis of the ways in which psychoanalytic concepts influence the creative process, I can offer a few tentative, further suggestions about this issue. As an occasional writer of fiction, I have the temptation to order my narratives in accordance with one or another premise drawn from the literature of ego psychology. Thus a character who exhibits a variety of more or less coherently interpretable behaviors threatens to become a plausible instance of secondary narcissism. Another makes choices that, while believable for such a character, never really address what he is after and so puts me in mind of those substitute gratifications that point to a standard clinical disorder. A third figure, in yet another short story, enacts procedures that consistently require of him one or another kind of renunciation, so that he comes to seem guilty, repressed, a fellow in need of the proverbial ax to break the frozen sea within him, and thus resembles more than a little a clinical type I have encountered in case studies.

In each of these instances, as in many other narrative instances I might mention, I am confronted with a choice. I do not, in composing my stories, think deliberately, programmatically, about this choice. As I feel my way forward into each story, there are no principles I invoke to guide me. I move, however tentatively, with the sense that there are certain kinds of moves I do not wish to make. I do not wish to make my repressed character into a palpable symbol of the life not lived and to underscore, by contrast, the merits of a liberated existence as an appealing "message" that some reader, thirsty for inebriation, might deliriously carry off. Neither will my plausible "narcissist" be permitted to become a clinical object reducible to a set of symptoms and a suitable diagnosis that will, at the same time, confirm someone's view of contemporary culture and the peculiar character disorders it tends to produce.

I do not know precisely what to call the species of discretion entailed in my inveterate resistance to letting my own creations become objects of use. I am as tempted to interesting ideas as are most other contemporary writers, and like most literary intellectuals, I can speak fluently about internalization and the superego, about displacement and dissociation. But when I am attempting to write a story, I say no, again and again, to anything that might enable confident psychoanalytic interpretation.

Does this—I ask myself—look like a classic case of displacement? Then it must be adjusted so that it looks less so. Is this young woman a plausible instance of the victimization to which women are consigned by "patriarchy"? Then she must be made to seem a less securely plausible instance, less, perhaps, a victim of unseen forces than someone whose victimization has much to do with her own poor choices and her inability to recognize the advantages afforded to her by her native endowments.

Does this man's commitment to duty and sacrifice express a compensatory pattern of behavior inspired by some overmastering sense of guilt? Then the guilt must be made to seem less persistent, the motivation for his behavior more various, less definite.

There is, to be sure, an inevitable relationship between the general and the particular, the eccentric and the symptomatic, in works of literature. A character in a successful novel is always more than one particular person, and a situation is always in some degree a certain kind of situation likely to generate certain kinds of attitudes or behaviors. An unfaithful husband in a novel is not someone who just happens to fall into something. He is substantially if not entirely defined by what he does, and what he does must be made to seem necessary, even in some degree inevitable for someone of his disposition and circumstances. To think about him is to identify a logic that makes him important to us, not as a peculiar person involved in something dangerous or colorful or surprising merely, but as someone who shares with others more or less like him certain tendencies and a suitable fate that must not seem arbitrary.

The line between what is peculiar and yet also, in some degree, representative is not always easy to distinguish, and yet as readers we are alert to that line and to the several ways in which it is drawn and redrawn over the course of a narrative. What is the point at which Gustav von Aschenbach, in Thomas Mann's *Death in Venice*, ceases simply to be an exhausted middle-aged writer seeking temporary refreshment and becomes an emblematic figure of civilization and its discontents, a man whose life has been lived like a closed fist, and who thus invites us to think of him as a man not sufficiently in touch with his own feelings and desires and consequently, as an analyst might well suppose, as a "symptomatic" being ripe for analysis? If Mann was too ready, too eager to invest in his character's unmistakably representative and even emblematic features, I may be unduly resistant to seeing in my own characters such features for fear of compromising the full complexity, variousness, and unknowability of those characters.

It is not possible to declare in general for one or the other emphasis, for each work has its own design and its own peculiar balance of features. That is why writers often worry over such matters, and why contemporary writers often let us in on their travails. Was it a good idea for Vargas

Llosa, in his novel *The Real Life of Alejandro Mayta*, to make his Mayta a homosexual? By doing so, he hoped to suggest one motive for the character's having early become a revolutionary in his native Peru and having felt very much an outsider in a society to which he never really wanted to belong. When, late in the novel, the narrator tells his character about having made him, for purposes of the novel, a homosexual, the character protests, doesn't quite see why it was necessary to portray him and his politics as in any way a reaction-formation stemming from "tendencies." For Vargas Llosa, as for other serious writers, fiction is of course a fabric of lies that aims to tell, or to get at, some aspect of the truth, but it is not clear that the essential truth need have anything to do with a truth conceived as clearly reflecting a psychological condition.

When I wrote a story called "An Excitable Woman," and my sister—a psychotherapist—read it, she recognized at once that the title character was, unmistakably, a portrait of our late mother. Yet my sister protested that the portrait wasn't "fair," and in truth, she was right. It wasn't at all a fair or balanced portrait, leaving out, as it did, a great many features of the person both of us had known, and emphasizing without apology mainly the most unpleasant features of an unusually strident, unhappy, and often belligerent person. But the portrait was also, perhaps, unfair in not allowing the unattractive features of the character to seem the inevitable consequence of a nameable condition that might have exempted her from any imputation of blame. No, my character Rose was built to inspire distaste, and would not be reducible to anything as simple as "paranoia" or "narcissism." She was, she could be made to seem, one of a kind and yet—so I determined—she might also be made to seem familiar, almost a type, a recognizable species of a woman seething bitterly with ressentiment and owing a part of her condition to the fact, yes, that she was a woman and wanted desperately not to be vulnerable in the ways of such a woman. She would be—I would allow her to be—a suitable but by no means easy target for analysis.

The most subversive handling of the relation between literature and psychoanalysis is deliciously embodied in Italo Svevo's novel *Zeno's Conscience*, long known in the United States as *The Confessions of Zeno*. The confessions are written on assignment from a psychoanalyst, whose ostensible goal is to restore the character Zeno to health. Patient and

analyst proceed on the assumption that psychoanalysis can provide coherence, pattern, what the critic Michael Hollington calls "a logical model
of personal development from birth, or even before it, a psychopathol-
ogy of everyday life that outrightly rejects the notion that any aspect of
behavior is accidental or sheerly phenomenal. But the cure goes wrong,"
Hollington goes on; "the psychoanalyst, assuming that all behavior is significant, allows Zeno to write anything about himself, in any order; and
Zeno produces a document, the book itself, which is . . . a text containing
discoveries and interpretations of experience which can exist indepen-
dently of psychoanalysis."

In its way, Svevo's novel is a deeply ironic meditation on the will to
understand and thereby to master the conditions of life. One of its targets is psychoanalysis, a fact signaled from the beginning, when we are
"invited," as Hollington has it, "to see the book [that follows] from a psychoanalytic perspective" in the "witty preface, written by the doctor, asking us to see Zeno's rejection of a cure [which is played out through the
course of the confessions] as a classic case of resistance." As the doctor
writes, anyone "familiar with psychoanalysis will know to what he should
attribute my patient's hostility." But Zeno by no means presents a classic
case of anything. He is in every way a peculiar specimen. Obsessed with
discovering patterns that will steel his resolve to achieve this goal or to
thwart that tendency, he discovers only that "any pattern fits, if you work
hard enough at applying it." He experiments with systems of all sorts,
from patterns involving dates to the initials of names, even the sounds
of words, believing that with their assistance "discords will resolve themselves into harmonies."

Zeno's laughable quest for resolving harmonies is informed by a standard psychoanalytic commitment to solutions. It rests on a belief in the
importance of a fixed perspective, such as that provided by a so-called
science that has its way of assigning particular causes to particular effects
and thereby accounting for what seems confusing. But Svevo's novel
would seem to suggest, as Hollington has it, that such a perspective can
provide at best only a "momentary point of balance." Zeno himself draws
the conclusion, after a great deal of turmoil and self-deception, that "Life
is neither good nor bad; it is original," and Hollington rightly declares
the book "a relativistic novel" that "has no end perspective; it has the

perspective from the middle that informs much Modernist writing."
Psychoanalysis can at best provide what Joyce, in *Ulysses*, calls "a retro-
spective arrangement" that may actually tell us almost nothing about the
internal conflicts and outlying factors that inform the lived reality of any
singular individual. Novels like *Zeno*—ironic, comic, inclined to laugh
away theories of any kind—would seem to ratify the view of a modernist
writer like Thomas Mann, who was drawn to the formal coherence of
psychoanalysis but preferred to it what he called "the really fruitful, the
productive, and hence the artistic principle . . . which we call reserve. . . .
In the intellectual sphere we love it as irony . . . guided as it is by the
surmise that in great matters, matters of humanity, every decision may
prove premature."

In this spirit we note that works of art are frequently designed to mock
interpretation. Often a reader, or the viewer of a painting, is deliberately
tempted—by the apparent signs embedded in a work—to set off in pursuit of meaning. The outrageous juxtapositions, visual puns, and naughty
jokes depicted in a surrealist painting, for example, can seem to portend
revelation only to underline the discovery that no resounding truth or
meaning is on offer. A 2003 painting entitled *Villa* by the Montenegrin
surrealist Voislav Stanic presents, as its literal center, a house, more or less
like any house, beneath a starry night-sky more or less like any other, and
a path in the foreground leading up to the house. There is an unmistakable order, a comeliness in the image, in spite of the figures neatly lined up
along the margins of the path, which seem playful, not especially menacing, though decidedly odd, very deliberately placed as if with an obvious
design on us. Does the bird torso stand for anything, we wonder? Or the
broken torso of a dog? The nearest thing to an ominous detail is a stray
belt curled at the front edge of the sidewalk so that it might well be taken
for a snake. Elsewhere, on the lawn, the human legs beneath a bush seem
not much more than a joke, though with that snake figure, one has to
wonder. The image as a whole is vaguely pregnant without yielding any
aspect of a mystery.

And yet we incline to insist on meaning and revelation even where
there is little to shape our speculation. Stanic's painting thus seems to us to
conceal a "problem" and invites us to unearth the available implications.
Are not one or more figures lined up along the path potentially phallic

objects? Is not the partially lit doorway of the house itself an emblem of erotic promise and inarticulate menace? Such questions impose themselves on us, orchestrated as they are by an artistic intelligence that understands our susceptibility. Yet here all our speculation may well come to seem—like so much psychoanalytic interpretation—a game that everyone can play, and a not especially fruitful game at that. Though Stanic, like other artists of the past century, obviously knows a good deal about symbols and symbolizing, about the unconscious and the vocabularies of meaning derived from psychoanalytic investigation, he is reluctant to invest seriously in those vocabularies. His characteristic manner, in *Villa* as in other paintings, is ironic and teasing. The potential menace inscribed in his works is allowed to remain impenetrable, a fact of life like other facts of life that can point and point without explaining a thing. The dominant sentiment in much of the art produced within the cultures shaped by psychoanalysis is a self-canceling irony. In such work the artist must be willing to commit to something that he himself does not fully understand, however tempted he may be to explanatory principles that promise revelation and the end of uncertainty.

Of course each of the arts must have its own characteristic ways of negotiating the will to interpretation. In literature, especially in narrative fiction, we often find discrete moments in which a narrator or author purports to account for what is unfolding and appeals to our interest in the significance of what would otherwise seem merely an indifferent plot. Often the process of interpretation is staged, so to speak, within the narrative itself, as in novels by Henry James or Proust, where we may find a fictional reader who will seem to operate much as we do when we attempt to decipher material that is or can be opaque. No doubt, when we think of such staged readings, many of us will think first of instances drawn from favorite film narratives, such as Coppola's *The Conversation*, or Antonioni's *Blow-Up*. In *The Conversation*, Coppola's Harry Caul attempts to understand "what really happened" by studying sound tapes that can perhaps take him where he wishes to go. In *Blow-Up*, the photographer-protagonist relies on photographic enlargements to help him reconstruct the stages of a crime he has happened upon. In taking us inside the process of analysis and displaying the gradual precipitation of shape and meaning, such works suggest that interpretation is as much at the heart of literary and cinematic narrative as of rigorous psychoanalytic practice. But what has been called our "compulsion to read" may take us in several very different directions, as we have observed. The correspondence between literary and psychoanalytic procedures may itself be somewhat misleading if we suppose that those procedures are essentially informed by the very same objectives and assumptions.

And with that, I conclude by saying simply that, like other disciplines, psychoanalysis has seemed to me promising and fearful, a temptation and a provocation. To those who have found in therapy some relief from painful emotional conflicts, my own misgivings will seem—should seem—beside the point. But then I have wished merely to offer here an "impression." Is it my impression—I invoke here the language of a prompt I received from the editor of a psychoanalytic journal—that "people are understood more meaningfully and vividly in fiction, poetry, drama, film, and other arts, than when portrayed in psychoanalytic texts?" I have never read a psychoanalytic text that has understood people as "meaningfully and vividly" as *Anna Karenina, A House for Mr. Biswas, All Our Yesterdays, Clear Light of Day, The Charterhouse of Parma*, or *Burger's Daughter*. But that assertion is but the beginning of another, much longer conversation.

[11]

MODERNISM

One must stimulate the curiosity of the public and offer them
the rich reflections that will move their spirits little by little to
the point where they are charmed, but without making them
understand, above all, without understanding.

—GUILLAUME APOLLINAIRE

Thus the new art rages toward a crisis.

—T. W. ADORNO

The word "modernism" no longer calls to mind a simple singular aesthetic or a particular set of ideas. To think about
what it means is to ask "whose modernism?" and "what
kind?" and "when?" Barnett Newman and others of his generation believed that modern art was not about beauty or retinal
gratification, but that was by no means the view of Virginia Woolf
or Henri Matisse. Duchamp regarded the habit of distinguishing
between good and bad taste as ridiculous. But no such animus
inspired the practice of modernist writers and artists like Thomas
Mann or Giorgio Morandi. The poet-critic Randall Jarrell could
praise the modernist poems of William Carlos Williams for their
"freshness and humor" and "fantasy" yet also celebrate the "passion for philosophy" and "order" in the modernist masterpieces
of Wallace Stevens. W. H. Auden saw no reason to refrain from
introducing politics into his work, but other modernist writers
were reluctant—often on principle—to do so.

If "modernism" is not the name of a practice or a set of principles, it also no longer signifies a particular era. In a recent book on modernism, Peter Gay operates on the assumption that nineteenth-century writers like Baudelaire and Dostoyevsky were modernists, and he contends that modernism is a phenomenon that comes and goes, dying out for a time and starting up again, as it did in the middle of the twentieth century with the galvanizing appearance of works by Jackson Pollock, Gunter Grass, and other "modernist" artists. To suppose that modernism was the name of a coherent movement that began and ended in the first forty or fifty years of the past century seems no longer possible for most cultural historians.

Of course the term itself continues to suggest a number of identifiable features, however various the works in which these features are ostensibly embodied. A novel lacking in self-consciousness or in any discernible preoccupation with form would not qualify as a modernist work, even if it appeared in the 1920s or '30s when Joyce, Proust, Faulkner, and others were defining the parameters of modernist fiction. We may admire the work of a painter like Lucien Freud and acknowledge the freshness, originality, and power of his portraiture, but we do not regard him as a modernist artist, so little does he seem to strain against the limits of the painter's available resources, so relatively straightforward do his intentions seem. Straightforward in what sense? In the sense that he is not, or does not seem to be, principally interested in questions about his medium or troubled by the relation of his work to the standard high-modernist masterpieces that dominated the period in which he came of age. We expect genuine modernist works to entertain such preoccupations and to be, in some degree, "experimental," that is, to be asking themselves at every turn what they are doing and thinking about the limits and possibilities peculiar to their medium. When, in *Madame Bovary*, Flaubert briefly interrupts his narrative to reflect on the linguistic resources available to him as a novelist and complains of their inadequacy, he seems to us to be self-conscious in the way of the modernist, however much his work confirms in other respects his status as a realist writer. The preoccupation with form and medium will vary in emphasis and intensity from one modernist to another, but where it is entirely absent, the writer will inevitably belong to some other dispensation.

Is this kind of preoccupation a good thing? Obviously, the commitment to the experimental, like the habit of self-consciousness, is not bound to produce masterpieces. The annals of modernism are filled with tenth-rate "experiments" and pretentious, stultifyingly tedious, ostentatiously self-conscious works. But modernism was, at its best, a bracing idea. It seemed, for a time, the enemy of complacency in art and thought. It challenged the established canons of good taste and tested, by example, the belief that realism was, to a considerable degree, an exhausted idiom. It also made untenable the notion that success in art had much to do with popular acceptance or transparency of purpose, or proper sentiments, or verisimilitude. Though particular modernist works could seem unduly tendentious, or needlessly obscure, or obstinately resistant to the elementary satisfactions offered by more accessible works of art, the modernist revolution did surely inspire several generations of artists and their audiences to think seriously about the values to be found only in art and to try not to confuse them with values to be found elsewhere.

When modernism was first discussed as a more or less identifiable if not quite coherent phenomenon, interest was fueled by the outrage and incomprehension that often greeted the appearance of a new work. The howls of dismay sounded at the initial performance of Stravinsky's *Rite of Spring* became at once a signal feature of the legend of modernism. Joyce's *Ulysses* was early celebrated in part because it was felt to be "too much," and many were inclined to think well of its successor, *Finnegan's Wake*, in spite of the fact that they had no desire to wrestle with it. In fact, the frequent, loudly sounded expressions of outrage and incomprehension allowed modernist artists and their celebrants to mock the philistine, stiff-necked middle classes who early disdained Joyce and Picasso and others who seemed to "ordinary" people needlessly committed to difficulty. The success of modernism, its growing command of an era and of the artistic protocols that defined that era for sophisticated people, had much to do with the perception that, in this case, the success was hard-won, the enemies of modernism entrenched and unwilling to embrace the new. When Randall Jarrell wrote about "the obscurity of the poet," he reminded his readers that earlier poets and critics, long before the advent of modernism, who had come to seem anything but difficult, had once inspired cries of incomprehension from their first audiences.

But the modernists often made a virtue of their "obscurity" and declared, in effect, that they were decidedly not in the business of providing pleasure or edification. In fact, they wished—many of them, at any rate—to provoke and displease and to make art for an advanced minority uniquely equipped, and disposed, to struggle with unfamiliar, even offensive or off-putting works of art. And of course the audience for modernist art grew as more and more people wished to think themselves advanced and open to the shock of the new.

In 1961 Lionel Trilling published an essay on "The Teaching of Modern Literature" in which he considered problems generated by the widespread acceptance of modernism. It had been accepted, after all, as a source of accredited masterpieces and as an ethos that had renewed a culture otherwise unfortunately invested in the conventional, the safe, the traditional. That, at least, had more and more come to be the accepted wisdom on modernism. In the university, teachers were eager to share their passion for the difficult and the dangerous, and students were primed to submit to a canon recently enlarged to accommodate not only cubism and abstract expressionism but the varieties of decadence and nihilism to be found in the work of artists as various as Céline and Beckett. Peter Gay identifies at the root of the modernist sensibility what he calls "the lure of heresy," and Trilling, too, believed that it was the extraordinary seductiveness of the subversive that chiefly accounted for the sometimes frightening intensity of modernist writing.

What, then, was the problem? If readers, teachers, and students were primed to embrace the new and challenging, where would there be ground for complaint? Trilling argued that students were in no way inclined to resist the destabilizing insights they encountered in modernist literature. Asked by their instructors to follow Mann or Kafka or Gide to the lip of the abyss, students would gaily look down and feel duly edified by their enlarging encounter with the creatures of the night. What had been outrageous, inassimilable, disturbing had gradually become safe, so that Trilling could refer quite pointedly to "the acculturation of the anticultural . . . the legitimation of the subversive." The consequence was, in pedagogic terms, an invitation to students to collude, as it were, in the domestication of modern literature, which had rapidly became a standard academic subject, no more unsettling than any other object of study.

It is possible, of course, that Trilling exaggerated something that was, all the same, in the process of coming to pass. There is, in many recent tributes to the modernist imagination, a nostalgia for a time when an exhibition of surrealist paintings or the mere sight of a urinal mounted on a pedestal might inspire heartfelt revulsion or incomprehension. Anyone who has spent a weekend in New York City strolling from one gallery to another in the Chelsea art district will attest to the fact that those who belong to what Harold Rosenberg once called "the herd of independent minds" are today turned off by nothing. What passes for appreciation in the wake of modernism is a bland receptivity. In the present climate, perfectly forecast by Trilling in an essay that has not dated at all, authentic responses to original art are hard to come by, and few are inclined to differentiate between the genuine and the specious in works that aim to be "provocative." Ezra Pound's classic injunction, "Make it new," has been taken on as the primary criterion of value by persons for whom an inspiring emblem of audacity and newness is a shark suspended in a room-size tank of formaldehyde. For such a museum-goer, neither Gregor Samsa nor *Les Demoiselles d'Avignon* is apt to seem thrilling or appalling.

Few observers of the current scene are apt to be at all troubled by these developments in a culture for which Marcel Duchamp has long been the central iconic figure. Robert Motherwell called him "the great 'Saboteur,'" a verdict that now seems to most of us indisputable. Though he produced little first-rate work of his own, he did nevertheless exert enormous influence on the art of the past hundred years, and it is clear that much of the brashness we associate with the term "avant-garde" is owed to his example. Duchamp was a rigorous thinker. Those who have followed in his wake are, with few exceptions, neither rigorous nor original. Many of the complaints leveled at Duchamp are philistine, the expression of a disdain for anything that says no to conventional standards of beauty or decorum. But the refusal of most people associated with the visual arts in the past half-century to say "no" to the sophomoric nose-thumbing and posturing that today pass for avant-garde is the expression of a fear to be thought traditionalist or philistine. There is nothing wrong with efforts to distinguish between Duchamp's generally negligible achievement as a maker and his efforts to subvert the whole idea of art as a special or exalted realm. But it is something else to underrate the audacity and brilliance of Duchamp's critical enterprise simply because he has inspired several generations of untalented hacks.

Duchamp's example surely reminds us—insofar as we need reminding—that the destructive modernism he championed was far removed from the efforts of artists like T. S. Eliot, Wallace Stevens, and Georges Braque, artists who were committed to an aesthetic ideal of perfection and were by no means turned off by the notion that art made legitimate and decidedly special claims on our attention. The term "art-for-art's sake" was always more than a bit misleading, but the derisory modernism that led Duchamp to draw a moustache on the face of the *Mona Lisa* was hardly a typical aspect of a phenomenon that gave us Eliot's "Four Quartets" and the Mark Rothko Chapel in Houston, Texas. George Orwell, who had little use for the avant-garde, saw in James Joyce not merely an unusually "daring" writer and "elephantine pedant" but "a kind of poet": "When you read certain passages in *Ulysses*," Orwell wrote, "you feel that Joyce's mind and your mind are one . . . , that there exists some world outside time and space in which you and he are together." At its best, Orwell understood, the modernism of Joyce and other great artists was not a matter of posturing or of "mere verbiage" or "technique" but a way of getting at things never quite captured before: "States of consciousness, dream, reverie," in fact, "a special vision of life."

To be sure, as Orwell also noted, in many of the best works of modernism, "There is no attention to the urgent problems of the moment, above all no politics in the narrower sense." Sartre famously and acerbically noticed that during the Nazi occupation of his country Pierre Bonnard continued to paint as he had painted before, as if nothing remarkable or alarming had occurred. At the same time, critics of modernism often noted that a great many of the leading figures were "reactionaries," if not outright fascists, anti-Semites, racists. The controversy that erupted with the awarding of the 1947 Bollingen Prize for poetry to Ezra Pound had much do with the "scandal" that a leading modernist writer who had—in his Pisan Cantos—actually bothered to pay attention to the politics of his moment and to throw in his lot with the Fascists could nevertheless win the approval of a jury of his peers.

In truth, though we know that there are grounds for regarding Pound as a Fascist, and Céline as a virulent anti-Semite, and Neruda as an unrepentant Stalinist, and Yeats as a sometimes besotted Irish nationalist, and Wyndham Lewis as a reactionary, we do correctly think of modernism as a tendency in the arts that has no necessary or predictable relation to politics. Modernism, after all, took shape principally as an interrogation or repudiation of entrenched artistic values. As a current of feeling, it had little patience for merely prudential considerations. But politics, even radical politics, has much to do with calculation, with problems and alliances and mobilizations. It is not typically an occupation for loners and underground men, people for whom political activity will seem a prospect more suited to credulous partisans. The political allegiances of leading modernist artists rarely made it into their best work, which was neither hortatory nor, in any narrow sense, useful. We do not celebrate Picasso because for a time he took himself to be a committed Communist, and there is nothing in Yeats's greatest poems that is strident or didactic or programmatic.

Most modernist artists ridiculed those who supposed that art existed to change the world. Stevens asserted that the artist has no "sociological or political obligation." Wilde declared all art "quite useless," and Nabokov scornfully dismissed the notion that fiction existed to promote or even discuss ideas. In an essay on "Art and Ethics," Joyce Carol Oates notes: "'If I had a message,' Ernest Hemingway is said to have said, 'I would send a telegram.'" She also cites the Stephen Dedalus of *A Portrait of the Artist*, who declared, "I will not serve." Gay notes that for Baudelaire, beauty was not to be found "in the glamour of politics and war."

In fact, the modernists were a motley crew whose views ranged from the reactionary hatred of the masses exemplified by Arnold Schoenberg to the left-wing radicalism of Sartre and others associated with the influential French journal *Les Temps Modernes*. The critic Serge Guilbaut and others have studied what they call the "cold war politics" of the American artists associated with abstract expressionism in the 1940s and '50s, but even among the artists of that period there was no clear consensus and no desire to use works of art to promote political views. The primary threat for these artists lay in academicism or kitsch. Clement Greenberg warned painters against "subject matter" and "content," while others identified the desire to please as the worst of the dangers to be avoided. Artists and

critics associated with the avant-garde routinely promoted a revolutionary consciousness divorced from practical politics.

Because there was no dominant tendency—political or otherwise—
among the leading modernist artists and writers, observers have looked
for other commonalities. Peter Gay, for example, argues that, however
improbably, portraiture dominated modernist painting. To make this
case, he selects for special attention an artist like Max Beckmann, who
indeed painted a great many self-portraits and, as Gay notes, "characterized himself as immersed in the problem of the individual." From this Gay
asks us to accept that modernist painters in general were in the business
of making "a great confession," and that this "was true even, indeed especially, of major modernists who turned their back on representation altogether." No doubt such a sweeping claim can be supported by invoking
the work of artists who, like Beckmann, were drawn to self-portraiture,
or very different kinds of artists whose work may be said to have been
records of the inner life and thus, in a way impossible to define, implicit
self-representations. But to read the works of action painters or geometric
abstractionists in this way is, finally, neither helpful nor accurate. It is even
misleading as a reading of Beckmann. To be sure, Picasso's protean drive,
his need to master a whole succession of styles and to be constantly on the
move from one mode to another, may be said to express him. Picasso did,
indeed, suggest, as Gay reminds us, "that he wanted to leave to posterity
as complete a documentation of his life as he could muster." But Picasso's
work is not in an essential way illuminated by regarding it as somehow a
part of a modernist "great confession"—not unless the word "confession"
is taken to refer to everything that may conceivably be observed and felt
in an artist's work. By that token, every work of art, of every style and
period, might be said to belong to that same enterprise, to be the expression of interests, drives, reluctances, tastes that taken together constitute a
portrait of the individual maker. Such a perspective would then serve not
at all to differentiate modernist art from any other kind of art.

No doubt there will always be people around to tell us that, at bottom,
one thing is much like another, and that the reason it is so hard to come
up with a satisfactory, comprehensive definition of modernism is that
there is no such thing as a modernism distinct from every other dispensation. Critics studying Wallace Stevens will rightly note that, for all his

singularity, his project often resembled, at bottom, the project of William Wordsworth. This modern figure or that will sometimes be distinguished as a "belated" romantic or as "at heart" a neoclassicist. But the effort to understand a distinctive phenomenon known as modernism will by no means succeed if it dwells largely on its resemblance to other movements in the arts. Of course, the epithet "modern" has long been used simply to designate works or ideas that seemed unconventional, to break unmistakably from the dominant tradition. Thus the poet-critic J. V. Cunningham long ago noted that "the modern poets in Roman antiquity were Calvus and Catullus, who wrote in new and untraditional poetic forms . . . borrowed from another language and regarded by the traditionalists of the times as effete and decadent; whose subjects were novel and daring; and whose attitudes were in conscious distinction from those of the old morality."

From this and other examples, Cunningham is inclined to conclude that "to be modern depends on a tradition to be different from, upon the firm existence of customary expectations to be disappointed." In time, of course, everything loses "its quality of newness," as Cunningham says, and it is often the case that what had seemed dangerous or decadent or impossibly difficult will come to seem dominant, established, even traditional. Modernism was, for a long time, "in secure possession of the field," and if the great modernists now no longer "represent to the young writer" or artist what they did fifty years ago, that is, "the new, the adventurous, the advance-guard," that is a fact of cultural history that should not at all seem surprising.

And yet there are in modernism certain qualities—let us call them spiritual qualities—that would seem, in their way, to persist, even to prevail, if only as a reminder to us of all that art can be and mean. Something of an oppositional posture characteristically informs the modernist imagination. But Cunningham, in a brief essay, is more precise in getting at the heart of the matter. "For it is the condition of modernity in art," he writes, "that it appeal to the initiate, that it provoke the opposition of the ordinary reader. . . . Hence it has . . . its private ritual and its air of priesthood—odi profanum vulgus et arceo, 'I despise the uninitiated crowd, and I keep them at a distance.' It is obscure, and its obscurities are largely calculated; it is intended to be impenetrable to the vulgar . . . to exasperate them."

Lest we suppose, moreover, that the phenomenon Cunningham describes is merely an expression of a presumptuous disdain for the multitude characteristic of a relative handful of artists, he goes on to note that "there is something of this in all art that is genuine. For the genuine in art is that which attains distinction, and the distinguished is uncommon and not accessible to the many." When a species of art that had seemed difficult and disturbing starts to seem easy, when distinction is lost in commonness and the audience "becomes satisfied with a customary response" to works that look or sound advanced without at all seeming impenetrable or exasperating, then artists will have to look for new ways to create a genuine newness. Thus the need for the modern in art will always, presumably, be with us, even if we are bound much of the time to mistake "difference for distinction."

Conceived in this way, modernism was an expression of a recurring tendency in the arts, but it was also unique in its ability to make of the oppositional, the difficult, the excessively *outré*, a dominant force in the culture of the West. No other movement in the arts made the disdain for the accessible, the useful, the popular, the politically correct or commercially viable, a signal feature of its high ambition and its quest for distinction. Modernist artists could be narrow or omnivorous, abstract or representational, playful or sober, apparently detached and impersonal or openly emotional to the point of violence. But authentically modernist works can never be slack or lazy, can never aim merely to excite visual or literary bliss or to satisfy formulaic appetites for prepackaged, safely "advanced" experiences that confirm viewers or readers in nothing but the sense that they are in the know. The modernists were, of course, in varying degrees, irreverent and avidly committed to newness, but artists who now claim to be their successors, those who take themselves to be advanced, are in the main shallow and proceed with full confidence that their audience will always be eager to be pleasured by whatever mild shocks or puerile outrages they can provide for them. To think about the fate of what looks like, but is by no means to be confused with, the modernist imagination, one need only study the works and the fabulously successful career of a contemporary, hard-working, art-world entrepreneur like the painter Richard Prince. There we see how the brashness and irreverence and difficulty of authentically modernist art has by now given way to the work of a quintessentially "new," ostensibly advanced artist aptly described by the current *New Yorker* art critic Peter Schjeldahl as "an adept of juvenile sarcasm." If nothing else, such works should serve to remind us of what was lost when modernism ceased to seem vital to aspiring artists, whose ambitions were, as a result, more and more circumscribed by their reading of the market and the popular appetite for novelty.

Of course I can hear the cries of the standard issue apologists for change in the arts. They will say, or want to say, that modernism ran its course and that it is foolish to wax nostalgic about what is no more. They will affirm that the central, informing ideas of modernism have been transformed but are not in fact entirely lost to us. Do we not now believe that the art that matters necessarily reflects "a superior consciousness of history," as Clement Greenberg put it? Are we not alert to the fact that the "situation" of art largely determines what a work is and what it intends? Are we not more or less comfortable with the notion, early articulated by Harold Rosenberg, that new art will be largely "removed from the realm of habit, manual dexterity, and traditional taste into that of philosophy"? We may not be happy with the art produced under the sign of these ideas—so our most recent apologists for the new will contend—but we must concede that those ideas, still very much with us, originated in modernism.

To be sure, the modernists did insist that ideas were essential to an appreciation of the new art. They believed that their work would require nothing less than a redefinition of art itself. In refusing any necessary identification with traditional aesthetic principles, they emphasized the effort to create values never before embraced or acknowledged. Primary among these values was newness itself. "In our era," Rosenberg wrote, "art that ceases to seek the new becomes at once intellectually insignificant, a species of homecraft." No doubt, Rosenberg contended, "the dedication of art to novelty complicates the problem of values [and of originality] and exposes art to sensationalism and the influence of fashion and publicity." But that was a price, apparently, eminently worth paying for anyone convinced that in modernism lay our best hope. Though Rosenberg bravely confronted the results of this tendency in modernism, and of his own efforts to promote it, he remained committed to the idea that, in risking encounter with "the unknown," modernist artists were true in the only way possible to the culture of change they inherited. The strenuous effort to create work that was new, however puerile or shabby or expressive of "short-lived impulses," at least had the virtue of "displacing works from which vitality [had] departed."

In many respects the most bizarre feature of the theorizing we find in Rosenberg and other such critics is the status accorded to the work of art itself as an autonomous object. In literary circles, the "new criticism" was largely built around the notion that "society" or "environment" was of negligible importance. Works of art dictated the terms in which they were to be read and discussed, and this was true especially of the new art associated with modernism. Writers were, obviously, more or less responsive to the world in which they lived, more or less alert to changes in outlook and value in their culture, and more or less invested in ideas that seemed, to some of their contemporaries, appealing or dangerous. But the new critics believed that a good reader would draw what was relevant about a particular poem or novel from the text itself, from the signs deliberately or casually deposited within the text. Those signs were, inevitably, not always easy to identify. Influential textbooks were intended to instruct students in the discipline of a close reading that would regard a literary text as an independent organism with a life of its own, with laws and conventions and an informing logic and a tonal range that together constituted what it was and determined what a reader might legitimately infer.

This is an old story, of course, and the subject of the so-called new criticism has itself been often enough debated. But it is important here as an indication that, in the domain of modernism, strenuous efforts were made to establish, in a convincing way, the status of the artwork as an autonomous entity. The efforts of theorists to embed the products of modernism in a context and to make the situation of art essential for understanding and assessing new work was in many ways at odds with the other tendency to pay strict attention to the individual work without regarding it as a mere reflection of its cultural moment. The conflict, or contradiction, is apparent even within the work of so fiercely definite a writer as Rosenberg, who was at pains—even while insisting on the artist's "consciousness of standing in the midst of developing events"—to remind himself that everything in the end depended on "the particular instance." You couldn't know how to think about this work or that work armed primarily with ideas about the situation of art. You had to look, really look, at the paintings of Barnett Newman to see in them that it was a good idea "to dwell upon the quality of his taste" and "the rigor of his logic, his humor, his metaphysics of the sublime." Of course you wouldn't be in a position to dwell on those features of his work if you came to it completely ignorant of the situation. But then the same would be true of works of art created outside the framework of modernism, and in fact anything less than primary absorption in the particular works, conceived as independent objects with a life of their own, would result not in genuine comprehension but in something else entirely.

Rosenberg knew this all too well, as evidenced by reminders, liberally sprinkled throughout his criticism, that there are many bad ways of thinking about modernist art. What bad ways? Ways shaped, determined, by what he called "theoretical air bubbles," "gossip and far-fetched associations of ideas," "set phrases," "ritually repeated nonsense." Rosenberg wanted the new art to be considered within "the framework of humanly serious concerns," but those concerns were typically misrepresented in the promotional copy turned out by art journalists and others who, in the name of "human interest," were inclined to see works of art as nothing more than a reflection of their scene or moment.

Rosenberg's vacillations and misgivings, so characteristic of efforts to come to terms with the nature of modernism, are also on display in his efforts to differentiate himself from critics and educators who would function "as a kind of policeman on the lookout for misdemeanors," whose primary business was the reporting of "delinquencies" on the part of modernist artists. But he was himself more than occasionally forced to assume that role, to note where the works of esteemed figures, much favored in the present climate, had seemed to become pointless, self-indulgent. It was Rosenberg, not one of the policeman-hacks he despised, who told us that Joseph Beuys and others associated with his example had "dissipated art by translating it into social ideas." Rosenberg it was who noted that the public that rallied to Warhol and other pop artists at the tail end of the modernist era, late in the 1950s, "had little taste for the enigmas" that had made the work of Pollock and de Kooning so commanding and fertile. Whatever modernism had been, however brave and unpredictable its avant-garde, there was, Rosenberg rightly argued, a new "avant-garde audience" for which "art was not something to look at; it had become, in the newly popular phrase, an 'environment,' [and for such an audience] it was not necessary to scrutinize an exhibition; one needed only to know that it was there; one apprehended it with one's back." As Warhol's dealer, Leo Castelli, told Rosenberg about an exhibition about to open, there was "no need to see it . . . the pictures are the same as the announcement I sent you."

This was, to be sure, an extreme version of what happened to modernism. The desire to call everything into question had led to the notion that everything already accorded respect as an accredited work of art was thus in the process of becoming a cliché. From there it was but a short step to the view that art itself is a cliché, and that the bravest, most advanced artists are those willing to call the thing by its rightful name, to represent it as a cliché and to promote and sell it as such. Thus, in the wake of high modernism, did Rosenberg—who had such contempt for scolds and police—declare that with the inheritors of the avant-garde, "greatness in an artist [has become nothing more than] his high worth as a label." Early on, Rosenberg argued, "Warhol declared to a friend that he wanted 'to be Matisse' but there is no evidence that he was ever interested in Matisse's paintings." Rosenberg's modernism was a dispensation that entailed close and careful attention to actual works as well as to the "situation" that might help us to account for their novelty. He was an enthusiast for an avant-garde that he took to be serious about the deepest human concerns, however flamboyant or mocking the expression worn by particular works. But he never supposed that an art worthy of our sustained admiration could possess "no intrinsic qualities that invite devotion." The new avant-garde represented by Warhol of course regarded that very language—"intrinsic qualities," "devotion"—as absurd, inflated, even comical. And yet modernism did in fact, at its best, offer a wide range of works—often difficult to understand or appreciate—that clearly possessed "intrinsic qualities that invite devotion." That was what made it worth fighting for.

To speak of qualities intrinsic to a work is, of course, to speak of a work presumed to have a shape, a character, an idiom, and even some semblance of a discernible intention, qualities that set it apart from everything else. No doubt there is a logic associated with a Warhol Brillo box, but that logic is not properly described as intrinsic. It is a logic ascribed to it by the culture, or art establishment, into which it has cleverly inserted itself. Just so, the intention of such a work is not something that we can learn by studying it. Its intention is decidedly not intrinsic. Theory alone can make sense of such a work by ascribing to it a meaning the work itself cannot earn. Likewise, it is clearly ridiculous to speak of the character of a Warhol Brillo box, which has no intrinsic or expressive dimension. In fact, its sole reason for being resides in its emptiness, so that it can thus take on only the meaning attached to it by a viewer sophisticated enough—well enough conditioned—not to want character or indeed anything like intrinsic quality.

By contrast, with the high modernist artifact—with the work of Picasso—we have another relation altogether. We rightly accept that historical context figures in our understanding of an art that took shape in response to previous works and wished to unsettle deeply engrained habits of perception. We understand that modernist artists operated with a peculiar sense of the past as a burden and an opportunity for renewal or defiant repudiation. Derivation was, for modernist artists, a factor to be acknowledged, if at all, in the spirit of the maker who will not be intimidated or diminished by a sense of what has come before. But modernist artists—in accepting the burden of history and, as well, the ideological status of a work made to effect a rupture with previously accredited aesthetic values, did not in the main regard their own works as negligible. They did not suppose that the idea under whose auspices they created would alone be important. Even an artist like Kazimir Malevich, a Russian suprematist who liked to describe his work as "a part of the human conceptual range on a level with religion and materialist philosophy," did not believe that the program, the idea, was all.

If we ask, again, what may differentiate modernism from the several movements that succeeded it, we may need to insist on the autonomous status of the artwork. This is, to be sure, a controversial notion, argued for several generations. It is, in addition, a notion for which the evidence would necessarily vary, as from one art form to another. Clement Greenberg usefully wrote that "the essence of Modernism lies . . . in the use of the characteristic methods of a discipline to criticize the discipline itself—not in order to subvert it but to entrench it more firmly in its area of competence." The emphasis there, on the particular discipline with its own peculiar "area of competence," is especially fruitful for our purposes. To think about the autonomy of the artwork will entail an effort to identify the peculiar area of competence in any given case. Greenberg suggested that the task was twofold: "what had to be exhibited and made explicit," he wrote, "was that which was unique and irreducible not only in art in general but also in each particular art." If "flatness, two-dimensionality, was the only condition painting shared with no other art," then one would expect a modernist painter to grapple with the challenges associated with that condition, that set of constraints. Just so, a modernist sculpture would need to acknowledge the fact of "three-dimensionality" and work with that as something "unique to the nature of its medium." To think about the autonomous status of a modernist artwork, one would then need to take into account its willingness to operate with a frank (or at least implicit) recognition of its "unique and irreducible" burden.

The task is further complicated, in Greenberg's sense of it, by the fact—he takes it to be a fact—that "modernism defines itself . . . not as a program . . . but rather as a kind of bias or tropism: towards aesthetic value . . . as such as an ultimate." Such a work will have, or strive to have, "aesthetic validity" only if it is, in its nature, neither "arbitrary nor accidental," that is to say, only if it can be seen to "stem from obedience to some worthy constraint." In the case of an abstract or nonrepresentational artwork, this "constraint" will not mandate faithful imitation of "reality" as ordinarily conceived or apprehended. The constraint, clearly, will rather have to do with the acknowledgment of the burdens "unique to the nature of [the relevant] medium." Our assessment of "validity" would then entail, among other things, a consideration of the character of that acknowledgment: whether it is easy, or frivolous, or deft, or profound, or so disorienting as to alter our sense of the medium. Like other critics of the modernist generation, Greenberg was deeply influenced by Flaubert, who spoke of his own ambition to write "a book about nothing, a book dependent on nothing external, which would be held together by the internal strength of its style." That would seem, in many respects, to be at the root of the modernist enterprise, the ambition to create work "which would be held together by the internal strength of its style," almost as if, as Flaubert said, the work would have "no subject, or at least where the subject would be invisible, if that is possible."

No doubt the emphasis on the autonomous status of the artwork has much to do precisely with this sense of the thing—if such a thing "is possible." Within modernism, the insistence on style operated as a check on the impulse to approve or accredit work that was merely pleasing, or consoling, or stirring, or confirming. How a work was held together, what worthy constraints it obeyed, and what it did to prevent easy appropriation by an audience conditioned to want only the standard elementary satisfactions: these were the considerations central to the modernist experience.

In obvious respects literature was not an especially promising medium in this regard. The novel—Henry James's "loose, baggy monster"—inevitably gathered its material from the "outside" world of ordinary human experience. Flaubert could not prevent the reader of *Madame Bovary* from associating his heroine with women in general, or with women of a certain class or period or disposition; he could not prevent his reader from believing, or suspecting, that the pharmacist Homais embodied elements in the provincial culture he inhabited, or that Emma's lover Rodolphe represented other features of his society and resembled libertines familiar to readers of popular novels of the period. Neither would such a reader find it easy to suppose that the novel was "about nothing" or that its "subject" could only be the negotiation of those worthy constraints that might alone confer validity upon the novel.

Modernist novels, like modernist paintings or films, came in so many variants as to make any single instance seem hopeless as a demonstration of the general proposition that the modernist novel is, and must take itself to be, an autonomous object. And yet there is a sense, I believe, in which this is felt to be true in the case of modernist novels that come most readily to mind. Of course literary criticism has often demonstrated the essentially literary character of great modernist fictions like Woolf's *To the Lighthouse* or Faulkner's *As I Lay Dying* or Joyce's *Ulysses*. And in fact a reader cannot but read these works as artifacts whose strength is substantially, if not exclusively, stylistic. We accept, as readers, that the characters of Woolf's novel *The Waves* exist, as one critic says, "almost entirely in terms of clusters of images and verbal patterns" that constitute the modernist authority of the work. The novels of Samuel Beckett are impressive for their disciplined refusal to employ ordinary referential language or to commit to what Frank Kermode calls "ordinary criteria of meaningfulness." We understand, as we read a story by Ernest Hemingway, that for all its directness of presentation, for all its apparent "imitation of casual vernacular speech," as David Lodge has it, the author applies to that vernacular "an elaborate and [largely] hidden verbal craft," which produces "the magical incantatory quality of Symbolist poetry." Lodge goes on: "certain words, grammatical structures and rhythmic patterns are repeated [in given passages throughout any characteristic Hemingway story] . . . keeping particular words and concepts echoing in our minds . . . [with] a finality and resonance not easy to account for logically." The result is that, however much our interest may be trained on aspects of story or character, we are comparably absorbed by, attentive to, the stylistic features of a work that would not exist for us in a distinctive way without our awareness of those features.

Does it make sense to insist, with such writers, on the autonomous character of their work? Perhaps it is best to fall back on the language of tendency or "tropism." Modernist fiction relies on style as an objective point of substantial interest in a degree that differentiates it from other kinds of fiction. The attention to style, if it is serious and sustained, must be more than casual, and the reader must feel that something other than "life," or LIFE, is at issue, however much the problems of life—as evoked or reflected in the work—may also seem interesting.

In short, modernist works, in their different ways, exhibit a common tendency to regard their own procedures as problematic and compelling. Though the modernist artist brings to the work of creation impulses and intentions drawn from experience, the modernist artifact bears within it the mark of a primary allegiance to the aesthetic as a principle subordinated to no other value. That is at the heart of what we intend when we say that such a work is autonomous. It is its own reason for being and need not be appreciated in terms drawn from any other domain. Though readers may describe their own attraction to individual works in psychological or political or "humanistic" terms, and the creators themselves—writers or poets or painters—may well have believed that they were in search of truths about the meaning of life or the condition of "society," the modernist work is intrinsically invested in some singular, sustained, sustaining formal element.

We repeat that the degree of the investment will vary from one work to another. That is obvious. Also obvious is the fact that the commitment to the autonomy of an artwork is no guarantee of quality. Efforts to distinguish between "modernism" and "the avant-garde" often turn on the question of quality. Some say, even now, that one decisive "achievement" of the avant-garde was to banish the question of quality from the precincts of art. This "achievement" was of a piece with the effort to dismiss from serious consideration the question of what is and is not entitled to be considered art. For the modernist artists who did not rally behind the banner of the avant-garde, such questions remained legitimate and important. For many self-consciously vanguard artists, judgment itself seemed a betrayal of the will to freedom, and there was no reason to go beyond the assertion that anything might be art so long as someone wished to call it that. The debate along these lines could seem bracing or trivial, depending on one's sense of what was at stake. Critics of a certain cast of mind, shaped by an allegiance to masterpieces—I am one such critic—continue to believe that art itself cannot but be important, and that questions bearing on its character are fully consequential. Frank Kermode reminds us that assumptions governing the creation of modernist art may merely serve to promote work that casually "deserts the plane of the feasible" or yields no more than an "idiot randomness" no more admirable than an "idiot consistency." To say that a work is primarily attentive to its own intrinsic qualities as art or as language is to say merely that it makes a certain kind of claim on us. A work may seem to us autonomous and yet seem only nominally compelling.

Odd, perhaps, to consider that "from the start," as Greenberg wrote, "avant-gardist art resorted extensively to effects depending on an extra-aesthetic context. Duchamp's first readymades . . . were not new at all in configuration; they startled when first seen only because they were presented in a fine art context, which is purely cultural and social, not an aesthetic or artistic context." Would it therefore, we wonder, be useful to think of autonomy as a concept with little relation to avant-garde work as such, whose essential character is inevitably social, or cultural, rather than aesthetic? And would it also be useful then to suggest that the avant-garde exists for us principally as a phenomenon of the past, with little intrinsic interest beyond the statements it made—or seemed to make—at a time when such statements could seem shocking or provocative?

If such suggestions seem plausible, then it may also be plausible to suggest that what continues to seem vital in modernism is only the work that did not depend exclusively for its effectiveness "on an extra-aesthetic context." Avant-garde culture was indisputably an aspect of the larger movement or tendency we call modernism. It imparted to modernism much of its energy and its conviction of newness. But the work consigned more or less exclusively to newness and sure only of its function—to effect a shocking rupture with everything previously valued as art—now mostly seems to us narrow, often overheated, shallow. It has designs on us that can now mainly seem literal, quaintly programmatic. Its aura is a thing of a past now ended. We may aim, as educators, to make undergraduate students feel the sense of newness and rupture that freely circulated in the air breathed by those who were young and susceptible to surprise at a time when the avant-garde itself was young. But the exercise will seem to all concerned mainly academic. The thrill is gone.

In the end, of course, we are moved by work that exhibits independence, that is not reducible to statement or function. We admire what will seem to us quality, assessed in terms of order, coherence, energy, range of ambition, and inner necessity. The peculiar "tropism" of modernist art toward style and medium and newness did not decisively eliminate a corresponding preoccupation—surely not for all of us—with the intrinsic, the autonomous. The difference between the masterwork and the curio remains for us a vital distinction. To *épater le bourgeois* may once have been a worthy ambition, but it cannot now be counted on to inspire work that will challenge and sustain us.

[12]

JUDGMENT

Whatever it is, I don't like it.

—HOWARD JACOBSON

My therapist says I'm too judgmental, but he's an idiot.

—A FRIEND

Harold Rosenberg was right. You can't distinguish good from bad unless you know what you're looking at. When I told Harold, the two of us fresh from an encounter with new work at a 1974 gallery exhibition, that I had no idea what we'd just seen, he launched into a characteristically muscular riff on everything under the sun. So what do you think? he asked, ten minutes later. I think I still don't get what we saw back there, I said. What it was, he concluded, wanting to be only a little bit helpful, "was some guy trying to impress the hoi polloi. Not, in any case, a big deal."

A judgment there, I thought. Some sort of judgment even in not really a big deal. Though Harold was rarely content with anything so terse, he did occasionally end up there, after going on, and on, the tenor of the relentlessly brilliant talk unstable, lurching from the theoretical to the brutal and impatient with no apparent transition. "By the way the entire face expanded when he spoke emphatically," Saul Bellow wrote of a Rosenberg-type figure in "What Kind of Day Did You Have?," "you recognized that he was a kind of tyrant in thought." A man who knew himself to be called to judgment rather more frequently than other people. When he was doing art criticism for the *New Yorker*, Rosenberg used to say that he didn't want to be a policeman, and yet he was one of those self-summoned to pass judgment. This was genuine, that was fake. This was slick, that was kitsch. This lacked tension, that was derivative. Clever artists invent, the deepest artists explore. Rosenberg took himself to be always on the side of experiment and insurrection and hated to be asking artists if their papers were in order, but he had a gift for spotting what looked to him phony or pandering and could never resist calling it out and putting it down. Passing judgment while deploring the judge in himself.

Of course there are always questions we are moved—some of us, at any rate—to ask about judgment, about what makes it useful, or extravagant, or legitimate. Often I wonder about judgments whose status has much to do with the fact that they are shared by others, like the "values" recently invoked in an essay by Timothy Garton Ash, "values we citizens of this liberal republic of letters embrace." And why, exactly, should such values, or judgments, have won our common consent? So we rightly continue to ask. Nietzsche was, for quite some time, in love with the writings of Emerson, but he feared that the very qualities he most admired were a reflection of some fundamental failing in Emerson's thought. Even at the moment of his greatest infatuation, Nietzsche could write: "I do not know how much I would give if only I could bring it about, *ex post facto*, that such a glorious, great nature, rich in soul and spirit, might have gone through some *strict* discipline, a really *scientific education*." For then Emerson would have proven himself not merely an inspiring "professor of the Joyous Science," as he called himself, but a rigorous thinker whose judgments would have seemed to Nietzsche of great and binding importance. Even to an ecstatic like Nietzsche, judgment required, at bottom, the kind of discipline alluded to in Emerson's essay "Experience," where he wrote that "The life of truth is cold," and that a "sympathetic person is placed in the dilemma of a swimmer among drowning men, who all catch at him, and if he give so much as a leg or a finger, they will drown him." Judgment, in the sense intimated here, is always at risk of being too soft, too tolerant of exceptions or conditionals, too genial and forgiving, too unscientific, too much a matter of intuitions and impressions.

For others—think Tolstoy, or Stendhal, or, nearer our own time, Sebald or Kundera—judgment has seemed reliable only when unsystematic, when the relevant formulations betray no science or method "except unconditional honesty with oneself," as Herbert Luethy once put it. From this perspective, the only valid criterion for judgment is truthfulness, which can be achieved only when the writer or speaker persistently considers what a given thing can honestly mean to the person confronting it. Judgment, in this sense, a matter of resisting every kind of "enchantment," including what Luethy calls "the danger of self-enchantment." And who would claim to have been utterly insusceptible to that danger? The danger, more precisely, of loving and clinging to the estimates and prejudices that have long informed your own appetites and aversions. I can never think of judgment without recalling the misgivings I encountered in the late writings of T. S. Eliot, who had seemed to me just the sort of thinker who would always refuse to yield ground on assessments and positions that were the ripe fruit of his own early struggles. And yet Eliot came to doubt the durability of a great many judgments that had seemed to him indisputable. His own taste came more and more to seem to him the expression of attitudes that were, in several respects, "narrow," and he speculated about the need to revise his own sense of things, allowing that, by the 1940s, "a new simplicity, even a relative crudity" might well be a beneficial alternative to the sophisticated language and literature he had championed in his essays from twenty-five years earlier. Were there, might there be, in the moral and political sphere, ideas that had seemed to him clearly beyond the pale, or pernicious, but which he might now conceivably entertain? So it would seem. Of many things that had seemed to him permanently valuable, Eliot came more and more to feel what he writes in "Little Gidding": "These things have served their purpose.: let them be."

To be sure, the judgment that rests on a determination to let things be, to acknowledge that your view of things may sooner or later change and so ought not to be insisted on, is itself a highly dubious way of regarding your own faculties and obligations. Ludwig Wittgenstein declared that philosophy "leaves everything as it is," that "explanation" is more or less irrelevant, and that "description alone must take its place." Description here understood as fundamentally distinct from the process of judgment that relies on explanation. But then Wittgenstein himself understood that this was not easy to accomplish, and that thought itself, like judgment, always entails exertion. In fact, the inclination to let things be was, as Wittgenstein had it, associated with a great "exertion," an exertion "to get to the bottom." Oddly, for one committed to "description" rather than "explanation," Wittgenstein appears to have accepted that judgment, when it is not merely a parroting of received opinions, relies on a sense, or conviction, that the intelligence is bewitched when it leaves things as they are, or as they appear to be. The skepticism that results from the recognition that things change, along with our view of them, or that language is itself entirely problematic, does not inevitably entail, as a consequence, the determination to renounce judgment altogether or to be content with mere description—however rigorous the theoretical process pointing to "description" as our primary objective.

Some of us, like Rosenberg, are drawn to judgment the way others are drawn to mischief, or hedonism, or indignation. Often the disposition to judge has nothing whatsoever to do with success or failure in persuading others to share your judgments. There is even, for some of us, special pleasure in arriving at and publishing judgments certain to be rejected by friends and colleagues. Satisfaction in an exertion not empty but futile. Judgment its own reward. As when attending a lecture deliciously funny or amusing, joining with others in the room convulsed with laughter, and declaring to your fond companions on the way out that the lecture was petty, the targets selected for mockery sitting ducks, the entire performance thus in the end heart sinking. Once, years ago, when I wrote an essay on Gore Vidal for an anthology devoted to him and his work, I knew that most readers would prefer not to believe that, to enjoy what he wrote, they were in effect required to overlook his distortions of elementary fact and his deliberately misleading formulations. Was Vidal a clever fellow? He was. But the cleverness was intended to distract readers from the fact that often he had little to say and that, more often, his primary object was to strike superior poses and to provide for his readers the sense that they too would never be tempted to anything like earnestness. When I quoted Vidal to the effect that "the serious novel is of no actual interest to anyone including the sort of people who write them," or that "Americans will never accept any literature that does not plainly support the prejudices and aspirations of a powerful and bigoted middle class," I knew that most of those who read those sentences would not be moved to hold them against Vidal, or to think them fatuous and silly, and that my judgment of those sentences and others like them as patently false and ridiculous would seem somehow ungrateful, given the pleasure he had taught us to expect and savor in everything he delivered.

When, in my early twenties, I started reviewing for the weeklies and quarterlies, I had a crisis of conscience every time I said NO to something. Nothing in my disposition to compare with Vidal's fabulous insouciance and cool elegance. Could this book of poems by Gary Snyder be as awful as I thought it was? So I asked myself. Was it possible that I demanded from a book by Arthur Koestler what its author never proposed to do? Alert to the fact that people I admired often disagreed with one another, I grew uneasy about my own rush to judgment, however much time I put into preparing to write my reviews. I wanted not only to be right but to be, so far as possible, unanswerably right, and I agonized over judgments that seemed to me sound and yet somehow disputable.

At the same time, I had no doubt that there was nothing for an intellectual, young or old, to do but to make judgments and put them into circulation. I hated the thought that people I liked would ever hold back for fear of being wrong or hurting someone's feelings. It was okay to be conscience-stricken about something you wrote or were about to write, as long as you didn't muffle your criticism for fear of contradiction or censure. When I first sent something for publication to Irving Howe at *Dissent* magazine—I was twenty-two, the year was 1964—the piece was a response to Lionel Abel's tin ear take-down of Peter Weiss's play *Marat/Sade*. Irving wrote me a postcard indicating that, though he liked what I had written and planned to publish it, he worried that Abel would "come back hard" at me, and he wanted me to know that Abel would have "the last word." But the prospect of a fight with an older New York intellectual suited me well, and within a year or two Abel was sending me things to publish in my own fledgling *Salmagundi* magazine. And it bothered me only a little that, on the cover of *Dissent*, my name was printed as "Richard" rather than "Robert" Boyers.

Of course there are countless ways of thinking about judgment, and anyone who regularly makes decisions requiring the exercise of discrimination will often beat himself up in the aftermath. I'll never forget the letter I received one day in the late 1960s from a poet named Richard Braun, whom I'd singled out for dispraise in a review of the then new *Norton Anthology of Modern Poetry* for *The New Republic* magazine. Why me? asked Braun. Why not others you might just as easily have named? And in truth Braun was right. There were others who, in my view, likewise did not deserve a place in an august anthology when far better poets had been left out. But then I had named one particular poet merely to say that any comparison of this fellow with the overlooked writers I had named would prove my case. Naming someone in particular was necessary. If it was perhaps unfair—or just plain lousy—to single out Mr. Braun, when he had received little attention from anyone in the course of a long career and thought he deserved his moment in the sun, I was obliged, I thought, not to let mere feelings get in the way of the assessment I had agreed to deliver. Earnest, painfully earnest, in this sense, about my obligations. Once when I went on about this Harold turned to me and said, don't be so goddamn bleak about it.

The worst thing you can say about judgment is that it is never reliable, that it is always an expression of taste, or ideological disposition, or conditioning, or other factors that constrain a fully dispassionate assessment of the thing before you. But so what if that is true? So what if no judgment is ever entirely fair or "objective"? Some judgments are clearly better than others because there is more available evidence to support them. Others are compelling because they emerge from what seems an air-tight argument and are informed by an unimpeachable logic. And yet who would now lay claim to a perfect rightness? Who would now suppose that a judgment can be worthy only if it appears perfectly disinterested? Nowadays, when I set out to criticize, I hope to see the thing before me as it is, in its own true nature, but I don't imagine that the conclusions I reach will seem to anyone the last word on the subject.

Once upon a time, in academic circles especially, the word "partisan" was felt to mark an unfortunate tendency, a low or vulgar inclination to promote a cause or a faction or a narrow idea, no matter what it might take to accomplish that end. And yet I've always thought the word "partisan" attractive, suggesting an activity of thought that is—or can be—both lively and responsible. No necessary connection between partisanship and sleazy pamphleteering or bomb throwing. Why think "Rush Limbaugh" when you say "partisan" when you might just as well think "Russell Banks" or "Nadine Gordimer"? How better to regard your own faculty of judgment than to think of it engaged, committed to telling the truth as you see it, in the best sense partisan? Of course it is "partisan" to make a case for something, to promote a view of a subject or claim that it has been disastrously misunderstood. And it is "partisan" to complain that an important prize has been awarded to a fifth-rate author like Elfrieda Jellinek, or to argue that the case for a preemptive strike on Iran's nuclear facilities has been drummed up by the same people who urged a war with Iraq on the grounds that Saddam Hussein had weapons of mass destruction. Oscar Wilde had it that the best kind of writing has "no definite object of any kind," which makes great sense when you read *The Importance of Being Earnest* but seems decidedly less compelling when you consider the work of people like George Orwell and James Baldwin. Even judgments that seem to have no practical application will promote, at the very least, a particular way of engaging with artworks or ideas.

My own faculty of judgment, such as it is, has mainly been exercised not in the hundreds of reviews and essays I've written over many years but in the countless decisions I've made as the editor of my own little magazine. No way not to be "a judge" when you run a magazine, picking these things to publish instead of those, asking this writer for an essay but not that one, avoiding the familiar voices here, soliciting a trusted contributor there, courting controversy in this precinct, avoiding it in another where it is all too easy to stir up trouble. When I received for the first issue of *Salmagundi* an essay on "The Positive Function of Hate-White," I thought it partisan only in the best sense, for it was alert to its own incendiary motives and determined to appeal to no settled consensus. It seemed to me to invite not merely disapproval but discussion. Sharply contentious, it was also oddly generous, frankly speaking to the relevant issues in what was felt to be a heated, ongoing conversation.

Though I am drawn to many different kinds of good writing, when it comes to essays and opinion pieces I have mainly favored writers who are fired up about something but determined not to be swept entirely off their feet. Writers not afraid to pass judgment but sensitive to the ground persistently shifting beneath their feet. In recent years—to cite but a single example—I've been moved by the writing of Siri Hustvedt, who had this to say in a recent essay on "ground rules": "Losing perspective," Hustvedt writes, "is an intellectual virtue because it requires mourning, confusion, reorientation, and new thoughts. . . . Doubt is the engine of ideas," and however "happy" we may be "among the few residents" of our own famil-iar intellectual community, our own "particular island, that little island is not the whole world."

Easy, I suppose, to credit such a view without actually trying to grasp how radical is the "reorientation" often entailed in "losing perspective." When we began to publish Christopher Hitchens in the nineties, he was beginning to make the political and intellectual turn that made him per-sona non grata in circles that had once adored him in the reliably left-wing pages of the *Nation*. Like many of those disillusioned fans, I regarded as nothing less than incredible his stubborn, even perverse championing of the Iraq War. And yet I continued to think of Hitchens as a great essay-ist and a radically independent thinker, and often the source of the very "confusion" and "doubt" I wanted *Salmagundi* to sponsor. Could the work of such a writer be not merely provocative but a repository of sound judg-ments? In a way, his cardinal virtue was to make the very notion of sound judgment seem dull, provincial, small.

Back in the 1920s, William Carlos Williams declared that what he liked in little magazines was their "absolute freedom of editorial policy," by which I supposed he meant that their editors might do whatever they damn well pleased. An editor of such a magazine would know himself to be "a fallible person, subject to devotions and accidents." At first blush this seemed exactly right to me. For one thing, it clearly distinguished the little magazines from journals with a "dominating policy" that would "dictate" what might be considered and what would not.

And yet Williams was rather more committed than I could ever be to a "democratic" arrangement. He argued that a magazine he could like would have to be "a miscellany, a true, even a realistic picture of the rather shabby spectacle America still makes from the writer's viewpoint." The only thing essential for the editor was that he avoid being "decent," which was to say timid, cautious, predictable. It was okay for some of the mate-rial in a little magazine to be "especially poor" or "punk stuff," and alright too for it to avoid taking up political or cultural issues, so long as it didn't presume to adopt an official or respectable posture.

Of course I know well enough what Williams intends when he warns against the merely decent. But it was always hard for me to imagine running a magazine genuinely miscellaneous in Williams's sense. What would it mean, after all, to aim for "a realistic picture of the rather shabby spectacle America still makes"? Wouldn't that entail an editorial openness to things tenth-rate or stupid or vicious, on the grounds that they realistically represent what is out there? To say NO to palpable nonsense or run of the mill fiction or ill-informed polemic would then amount to what, exactly? Censorship? An antidemocratic effort to promote the respectable or the difficult at the expense of "the real"?

In a half century as the editor of my own little magazine, I have often had reason to regret judgments I have made. Occasionally when a new issue comes out, I open it to a poem we accepted a year earlier and wonder how we could have made such a mistake. When in a 1967 issue I published my own deliriously favorable review of a book by Anne Sexton, I thought it apt and wonderful only to discover years later that it was an expression of my own youthful, largely misplaced enthusiasm for confessionalism. More recently I shook my head over a piece we published challenging the "myths" about global warming disseminated by "missionaries" in thrall to "ideology." Good, I had thought, to interrogate what has in fact become, among the enlightened of the earth, a carefully orchestrated consensus. But then no, I decided, not good to suggest that skepticism without knowledge is a virtue, not in precincts where there is plenty of hard evidence to support the newly enlightened consensus about the destruction of the environment.

But then second-guessing or despairing over your own fine judgments would seem an essential aspect of thinking itself. You discover, try as you may to deny it, that the harder you work to call things by their rightful names, to be at all costs lucid and precise and just in your estimations, the more the mystery of things is apt to elude you. Not invariably, but often enough to give you pause or heartache. I know how to read and judge a garden variety poem or essay, but my equipment will never routinely adapt itself to new work produced by the deepest and most original thinkers. I can think, confronted by a competent piece of work, this is merely competent, and I can think, confronted by a terribly disjointed story, this guy doesn't know what he's doing. But how to think about something whose defiance of ordinary decorums and assumptions leaves you staggered and reeling? Not so very astonishing, after all, that André Gide should have rejected Proust's enormous novel when it was first submitted to him—then the editor at a major French publishing house—for publication, or that Natalia Ginzburg, as a senior editor at Einaudi in Turin, should have rejected Primo Levi's *Survival in Auschwitz*. Not surprising that often the most audacious and original writers are overlooked at the mainstream magazines, which have eyes mainly for the tame and the plausible. When Peg Boyers first plucked Daniel Harris's zany essay "Baby Talk" from the *Salmagundi* slushpile in the late 1980s, she knew at once that we would have the work of this writer largely to ourselves for as long as we wanted, so indigestible would he seem to others accustomed to more conventional fare.

Of course you tell yourself to remember all the cautionary tales, repeat to yourself those stories about Gide and Ginzburg, try to be the one on whom nothing is lost. You remind yourself that difficulty is not always a "problem" but an opportunity or a strategy, and you vow to remain open even to things you find impossible or distasteful. And yet you find, more often than you'd like, that your instincts, the best thing you have going for you, some of the time betray you, whatever your determination. One day, at my office at the New School for Social Research, where I teach a graduate course each year in the spring semester, I was surprised to find at my door Slavoj Zizek, looking characteristically wild-eyed and bemused. We spoke for perhaps fifteen minutes, until he left with me a hefty "philosophical" manuscript he thought appropriate for the pages of *Salmagundi*. I had read a bit of Zizek's work and was mildly charmed by his incendiary posture and his fondness for paradox. But when I tried to read the new manuscript I found myself balked at every turn, unable to penetrate the thickets of theory-speak or to keep up with the willful swerves in what seemed to be an argument. My feeling that the piece was hopeless was confirmed by the Liberal Studies program director at the New School, who avowed that he too could make little of it. When I gave it back to Zizek with apologies a week later, he seemed not at all disappointed to learn that I was no match for such a work. Of course I was right to turn back something I couldn't understand, and I thought it odd that my judgment—on this count at least—didn't accord with the impression, shared in many quarters, that Zizek was always worth the trouble he gave. And only a few years later, when other work by Zizek came into my hands, I thought it strangely (if only intermittently) brilliant and wished that I had tried harder to find a way through the paper he'd handed me.

In 1966 I received in the mail an essay called "Beginnings" by a young writer named Edward Said. It was, he said in his cover letter, a "blueprint" for a book he had begun. Though I struggled with the essay—it sports sentences like "Husserl tries to seize the beginning proposing itself to the beginning *as* a beginning *in* the beginning"—I knew at once that it was an extraordinary work and that we would have to publish it in the magazine. What I could not have imagined was that a year later it would be awarded a $1,000 prize by the National Endowment for the Humanities as "one of the best essays of the year," and incidentally bring to the magazine what then seemed like the enormous sum of $500. The award announcement came in the form of a phone call from an officer of the endowment. It was late June, and of course I thought at once that I would have to track down Said himself, a man I'd then never met or seen. When I phoned his apartment I reached not Said but his wife, Maire Kurrik, who would soon become another *Salmagundi* contributor. To say that she was thrilled to learn of the thousand bucks is no exaggeration. But almost at once, when she'd told me that Edward was out of town and out of reach, and stopped the flow of her own excited chatter, she said, quietly, confidingly, but tell me, Bob—that's alright, isn't it, if I call you Bob?—you've read Edward's article, I imagine, yes? And so I want you to tell me, really, you didn't, did you, understand a word of it? I mean I'm a very well educated person myself, and I've read that piece, and I can tell you I understand nothing about it. And neither—I'm sure of this—neither did you.

Only a little shaken by this exchange, I continued to suppose that in fact I did understand what Said had written, and the fact that my head hurt when I read that early essay of his in no way suggested to me that it was anything but what it had to be. Pleased, even now, about having made the right judgment there, but also remembering that even the judgments of which I'm proudest have often been subjected—at least temporarily—to scorn. When in 2006 we announced a conference to be built around a book called *War, Evil and the End of History* by Bernard-Henri Levy and planned as well to build from the transcript of that conference an entire issue of the magazine, many of our friends and colleagues declared this a dreadful idea. Hadn't Levy come out with things that more sober French thinkers regarded as ridiculous and laughable? Hadn't his recent "Tocquevillean" book on America been pilloried in the *New York Times* by Garrison Keillor? Wasn't he one of those "Zionists" who never found anything done by Israelis in "self-defense" to be less than justifiable? And didn't he parade around in shirts open to the navel and often make pompous pronouncements about barbarism and civilization? It was one thing to give the guy a hearing, but something else to ask others to address themselves to his work in the course of an arduous three-day public meeting.

But then I felt that the shirt was an entirely forgivable flourish and a trademark colorful enough to mark so eccentric a thinker. And as for Garrison Keillor, well, his murderously funny put-down was no more than a series of cheap shots. Nor was Levy's Zionism at all one-dimensional. Though one of my conference speakers told me he couldn't bear to sit next to Levy—"not even for an hour"—the book we were to discuss was an uncommonly sobering account of some of the worst places on earth and by no means a display of unbridled egoism or histrionics. The man who said he couldn't stand someone who "carried himself" as Levy did ended up, after reading the book and spending three days jousting with Levy, declaring himself "a convert." In short, the judgments that routinely follow around eccentric thinkers like Levy grow out of an established wisdom that is mainly an expression of rank, uninformed prejudice or ressentiment.

Much of the time my own judgment is exercised on tiny things. Often as an editor I labor over questions of pacing, or diction, or punctuation. I spent a half hour one day talking on the phone with Robert Pinsky about a poem of his we'd accepted, in which punctuation marks were sometimes employed, elsewhere not. No consistency in the thing, no "system," so that I thought to "fix it," only to be told by my friend that he wanted it exactly as it was, thank you, and who cares if "your readers" hold you accountable for the failure to correct obvious "errors"? At another time years earlier I was taught a similar lesson by William Gass, who refused to let me break up paragraphs that seemed to me far too long. Such instances a mark, I suppose, of my own readiness to judge and yet also of a willingness to back off in a way that editors at commercial magazines, operating in accordance with fixed protocols, cannot entertain.

In the editing of interviews and conference transcripts, I've been rather more aggressive than some of my readers—let in on my "secrets"—may think legitimate. Once I sent a friend to conduct an interview in England with John Fowles for a special issue we were planning on "The Sense of the Past." But the transcript my friend brought back was thin stuff, Fowles himself clearly not sufficiently engaged, the answers curt, abrupt, ungenerous, as I wrote to Fowles, suggesting that he develop his answers in perhaps six or seven pages of text we might incorporate into the transcript. But no, he responded, that was one thing he wouldn't do, though he'd be happy to "leave it to you to develop the thing," "use what I've said elsewhere," "as you think fit." Which, in truth, I did, believing, one, that what was promising in the text should be preserved, and two, that I knew not only what Fowles thought about the sense of the past from reading his novels but what he'd said on the subject here and there in scattered reviews and lectures.

So that—forgive me—judging my own powers adequate to the task, and empowered by the go-ahead I'd received, I proceeded to cull from several far-flung sources, mainly British, vagrant passages of reflection and insight, all belonging to Fowles, which I cut, sculpted, and interpolated into the transcript, so that in the end it seemed no longer thin or withholding, and created a full and cogent document. When I sent the newly edited text to Fowles for his approval or correction, I received in return a postcard containing two words: Thank you.

I'll not pretend to engage here with the ethical questions that might well follow upon such a confession. But I will say that writers who submit to interviews designed for subsequent print publication do not think it at all wrong to revise, sometimes even to rewrite, what they have said. In the several interviews I did with Susan Sontag, and the several symposia in which she was featured, she never failed to rewrite much that she had said, and she often revised the very questions I had put to her so as to accommodate the answers she wished to give. Others I worked with over the years—from Richard Rorty and Robert Nozick to Mario

Vargas Llosa—asked me to revise things for them in accordance with one or another requirement. No respect was accorded to the pretty notion that what had actually been said was sacrosanct and not to be drastically altered by the editor. Saul Bellow told me, both times we ran an interview with him, to just make sure he didn't sound confused, or confusing, and "whatever you do, don't show me the thing until it's published in the magazine."

Of course there are no really good rules out there to cover every one of the quandaries that require the exercise of judgment. Writers know better than anyone else that apparently sound principles are often of no use to them, especially when they find themselves drawn to take a risk on behalf of an unfamiliar form or a fresh idea. Phillip Lopate has written of the "maddeningly self-perpetuating, open-ended style" of Montaigne, "the Jackson Pollock of essayists, employing an all-over style that covers every inch of the composition with equal emphasis, rather than obeying the laws of literary perspective" or worrying over "topic sentences, central themes," or "orderly development." Can a "serious" writer refuse "to take full responsibility" for his "cerebral meanderings"? Apparently so, and a judgment that rules out the very possibility of a work "with only an incidental relation to . . . consecutive logical argument"—as Leonard Michaels once put it—is a judgment ill-equipped to assess original work.

In some respects the judgments hardest for some of us to recommend are those most unsavory or most tendentious. And yet, if those judgments nonetheless accord closely with our own views, we may wonder why others find them so offensive or extravagant. When I read in the pages of a venerable conservative monthly a few years back that the "secret ambition" of many Republican politicians and operatives was to wreck the economy so that the programs brought to us by liberals would come to seem unsustainable, I found myself appalled, and only a little skeptical, and when I referred to this charge at a noisy public meeting as "completely believable," I wondered, given the hard evidence available to support the suspicion, why it seemed to some audience members bizarre and even unspeakable. If that's actually true, one fellow shouted at me from his front-row seat, why don't we hear it raised all the time by talking heads and editorial page writers? Because, I answered, it sounds "extreme" and therefore "irresponsible" and therefore "partisan" in a way that seems to discredit the idea all apart from whether or not it's true. It's more than partisan, the guy shouted back, it's outrageous. You mean the very idea is outrageous, I said, or you mean it's outrageous for me to say it? But this exchange ended when the man stood up and walked out of the room, marching in high exasperation up the central aisle and disappearing through the exit door at the rear.

Almost anything you say or publish on certain subjects, if it goes beyond the standard, widely accredited line, is bound to seem offensive or extravagant. One of those subjects is surely the Israeli-Palestinian conflict. The mail we received a few years ago when we published a piece on "Zionism and Apartheid" by a Canadian scholar named Derek Cohen was nasty and dismissive. I was most taken aback by a phone call I got from the parent of a Skidmore College student—one who had earlier written a check to the magazine in a fund-raising campaign—proposing that we issue a "retraction" right away. This was not the only time in my more than forty years at the college that a person who had admired our work was moved to accuse me of "poor judgment," though of course I stood by the Cohen piece as an entirely responsible piece of journalistic commentary and insisted that a magazine like ours existed at least in part to piss people off. So you're saying you won't even consider printing a retraction, the man asked. That's exactly what I'm saying, I replied, and anyway, there's no need to retract what is merely an opinion. To my surprise, that gambit seemed to have soothed the caller, as if it had actually settled something. Probably I should then have moved the conversation on to other issues, like the state of the lawns at the college, but I couldn't resist saying that other Jewish intellectuals were also openly worrying about the fate of Israel and the growing disaffection of young American Jews. Well, apartheid is only an analogy, the suddenly more amiable parent offered. Yes, I said, exactly, and like all analogies, it merely proposes a connection without insisting that the one thing is identical with the other.

Who knows why some people have a special fondness for judgments that rest on disputable analogies or just barely plausible arguments. My own long-tested affection for thinkers like Mill and Orwell has not made me insusceptible to the spice and charm of contrarians like Paul Goodman, Christopher Hitchens, and Hans Magnus Enzensberger. The savage attacks directed at Hannah Arendt's *Eichmann in Jerusalem* in the

1960s never shook my conviction that this "report on the banality of evil" would remain for me an essential document, that its association of evil with "thoughtlessness" had introduced into our thinking an indispensable idea. Was Arendt's thesis, as elaborated in her book, one of those just barely plausible arguments? I didn't think so, and I was astonished to find that many people I knew in the New York intellectual community thought the book scandalously deceitful and misleading. When in 1980 we were preparing a special issue of the magazine on Arendt, I wrote to Sir Isaiah Berlin—he had recently written for our pages a long essay revisiting the "two cultures" debate—proposing that he write again for us on "the banality of evil" and the debates it had engendered. Sorry, but no, Berlin replied, expressing "amazement" that I found anything "of value" in "such a thinker," whose "concept" he declared "of no interest whatsoever." No doubt, he speculated, the issue we were planning would "find a ready audience," but that could hardly be "sufficient reason" to bring out such an issue.

In truth I have known in myself the impatience and scorn informing Berlin's letter. Often I hate in a writer what is, unmistakably, a function of his or her peculiar virtue. Nowadays I hate in a journalist like Chris Hedges his tendency to wax hysterical over all sorts of things I too deplore, policies and positions he obscures with his unchecked incendiary rhetoric and his will to radical virtue. When he writes of his commitment not merely to "rebellion" but to "revolution," condemns "the liberal class" for its "cowardice" and "cynicism," and portrays the United States as living "under the darkest night of state repression," I recoil not only from the bullying and imprecise language but from everything else Hedges says, interested as he mainly is in fueling his fury and establishing his bona fides as the one and only righteous truth-teller around. Just so, Berlin recoiled from Arendt at least in part because he mistrusted a theory of evil that purported to account for a great deal when instead it might have been deployed more judiciously, with less of a claim to comprehensiveness. It was not Arendt's rhetoric that got under Berlin's skin; it was what he took to be her immoderate, overweening ambition that turned him off.

Berlin might well have objected as well to another notable flaw in Arendt's Eichmann book that was cited in numerous scholarly attacks, specifically her apparent unwillingness to take into account or contend scrupulously with other writers who had made major contributions to the study of "evil" in the Nazi period. My own sense is that this line of attack is by no means warranted in the case of Arendt, but it does point to one great resource available to writers of every kind. I speak here not of scholarship per se but of conversation. When I write an essay on the novels of W. G. Sebald, I feel that I am in conversation with others, like George Steiner and James Wood, who have written about him, as also with novelists, poets, and filmmakers who have shaped my thinking about the Shoah. When I read or write something about the American culture wars, I find myself talking at length with the historian Christopher Lasch, a friend and *Salmagundi* columnist who died twenty years ago but has known, for all those years, how to engage me in conversation and talk me through my delusions. The alternative to real conversation along these lines is what may rightly be called provinciality. You can hear the note of provinciality in those angry jeremiads of Chris Hedges, who cannot hear in his own sentences the accent of exaggeration and ostentatious, self-righteous breast beating that would be obvious to him if he were in regular conversation with his betters—with Orwell, say, or Virginia Woolf, or Richard Rorty, or Tzvetan Todorov.

Much the same imperative—I do see it as an imperative—obtains in writerly, or readerly, transactions with works of the imagination, as I have suggested. When I find myself absorbed in a newly published political novel, I set it alongside the earlier works of this kind I have admired, and I listen closely to the conversation these books and their authors conduct with one another. My judgment of the new work, my admiration or love or distaste, emerges more or less inevitably from the dialogue set in motion, almost as if I myself had little to do with its orchestration or its outcome. The tenor of that dialogue is not usually competitive. The judgments made are rarely definitive or permanent, and rarely of the either/ or variety, though now and then we know that something we have considered is not to be recommended, or countenanced, or loved.

As the editor of a magazine I am routinely putting together "conversations" and regard each issue as one such event, with each separate issue taking a part in a larger, ongoing "conversation" with other earlier issues and those to come. Often I think of an issue as a bringing together of disparate voices, with always some prospect of contention, even where the individual authors have no such sense of context or contention. A reader's judgment—as regards visceral immediacy, intellectual reach, or freshness of content—is a variable, constantly in motion, taking shape, losing shape, important, less important, the one essay a factor in the reader's sense of another, one poem or story implicitly declaring the primacy of one kind of precious thing only to be upstaged or confirmed by the assertion of another sort of primacy, the beautiful austerities of an oddly chaste yet lavishly emotional poem by Louise Glück in some sense the measure of (and the alternative to) the brutal, driven grandeur of a poem by Frank Bidart.

Of course our responses to things, like our judgments, will always have something to do with the cultural moment. I want the things we publish in the magazine to reflect or respond to their moment without being constrained by it or operating from a narrow or doctrinaire ideal of relevance. Is the novella we recently published by Andrea Barrett, about a mid-nineteenth-century scientific seminar-in-the-wild, in any way relevant or useful? Though there are ways of making it seem so—for example, by associating it with current debates about creationism—the very notion of relevance in this sense is a distraction from everything that makes the novella strange and affecting. Barrett's work is in fact relevant in the only ways that can matter, first by being so entirely committed to its own premises and its own distinctive voice, and then by participating as it does in a conversation with other first-rate works and thus declaring the very nature of the cultural moment, which is best marked by its variousness and unpredictability.

Sometimes, whatever our commitment to conversation, civilized contention and implicitness, we listen for a rather different species of judgment, something punishing and explicit. I wouldn't want my own love of "conversation" to suggest that I am less than exhilarated by this other kind of judgment. The kind that makes no apology or concession. I may have heard it first many years ago in the attacks on mid-cult and mass-cult launched by Dwight MacDonald, who never apologized but could also say, "My greatest vice is my easily aroused indignation—also, I suppose, one of my great strengths." I heard the accent—not always indignation but blunt, disdainful disparagement—more than occasionally on Leon Wieseltier's "Washington Diarist" page of *The New Republic*, as in a fall 2011 attack on President Obama: "Obama is reaping the harvest of his superiority to the sordidness of power," Wieseltier writes: "the revival of the American right in 2009–2010 was owed in part to his squandering of his early strength upon a prissy dream of bi-partisanship, or post-partisanship. . . . Obama came to lift us to a higher place, when a better place was all we needed. . . . The president's high-minded misreading of the Republicans will stand as one of the most consequential delusions of our time."

Do we detect at least the ghost of "conversation" there, in lines of such blunt, poignant disparagement? Not, perhaps, in the way we do in other comparably punishing attacks. I think of an essay by Irving Howe on the fascism of Ezra Pound, an essay that rightly touches on the Stalinism of Bertolt Brecht and the violent anti-Semitic rants of Louis-Ferdinand Céline—all of this orchestrated as a way of asking what we are to make of politics in works of art when the politics is clearly disgusting and impossible to set aside as if merely incidental to our experience of the artwork. The habit or instinct informing the essay an unmistakable commitment to conversation, the critic inviting each of the writers invoked to engage with one another and to participate, as it were, with each of us in establishing a context for addressing the issue. All this, in Howe's essay, a foundation for turning to a then more recent instance of the thing at issue, specifically, the poetry of Leroi Jones (later Amiri Baraka), an influential though far less consequential writer, whose work Howe has prepared himself to address, as follows: "When I read Leroi Jones calling for 'dagger poems in the slimy bellies of the owner-Jews' or urging black people to say 'the magic words . . . : Up against the wall mother fucker this is a stick up!' to 'Sears, Bambergers, Klein's, Hahnes', Chase and the smaller Joosh enterprises,' then I know I am in the presence of a racist hoodlum inciting people to blood. And I am not going to be deflected from that perception by talk about rhythm, metaphor and diction."

A cleansing judgment there. So I thought it many years ago and so it seems to me still. A judgment harsh and punishing but fully compatible with the civilized commitment to conversation, Howe willing, on his way to Jones, to stop patiently at Pound, Céline, and Brecht to consider the literary uses of ideology and hatred, the better to see and to say what differentiates one sort of thing from another related thing. Howe a notable example of a writer with strong views who arrived at them by immersing himself in the tradition and in the debates raging in every quarter of the culture, allowing a host of voices to speak to him and through him.

One day, on a walk we took through Central Park on an early spring afternoon, I asked Irving how he'd feel about doing with us a three-day symposium on "kitsch." Already, I told him, I'd invited "Susan" to partici-pate—knowing as I did that Sontag and Irving did not much care for one another. "Well, that will be fun," Irving said, and in truth, he welcomed the prospect of contention and knew that Susan would have more to say on the subject of kitsch than anyone else he or I could imagine, the con-versation certain to be throughout exhilarating, the shared judgments likely to be more frequent than the sharp disagreements, both Susan and Irving—like the others we assembled for the three days—fully alive only when engaged in real talk, by turns disputatious and amiable, aggressive and inquisitive, open and, where necessary, judgmental.

BIBLIOGRAPHY

Addison, Joseph. Cited in Martin Price, *To the Palace of Wisdom: Studies in Order and Energy From Dryden to Blake*. New York: Doubleday, 1964, 362.

Adorno, T. W. *Negative Dialectics*. Trans. E. B. Ashton. New York: Seabury Press, 1973, 48.

Amis, Martin. "When Amis Met Updike . . . Martin Amis's 1987 Interview with John Updike." *Observer*, January 31, 2009. http://www.theguardian.com / books/2009/feb/01/john-updike- interview-amis-martin.

Angier, Natalie. "The Anatomy of Joy." *New York Times Magazine*, April 26, 1992. http://www.nytimes.com/1992/04/26/magazine/the-anatomy-og-joy.html.

Applebaum, Anne. "Yesterday's Man." *New York Review of Books*, February 11, 2010. http://www.nybooks.com/articles/archives/2010/feb/11/yesterdays-man/.

Arendt, Hannah. *Eichmann in Jerusalem: A Report on the Banality of Evil*. New York: Viking, 1963.

Arnold, Matthew. *Culture and Anarchy*. Oxford: Oxford University Press, 2006, 100.

Ascherson, Neil. Cited in Ryzsard Kapuscincki, *The Other*. Trans. Antonia Lloyd-Jones. New York: Verso, 2008, 8.

Ash, Timothy Garton. "Freedom and Diversity: A Liberal Pentagram for Living Together." *New York Review of Books*, November 22, 2012. http://www.nybooks .com/articles/archives/2012/nov/22/freedom-diversity-liberal-pentagram/.

Auden, W. H. "In Memory of Sigmund Freud." In *Selected Poetry of W. H. Auden*. New York: Modern Library, 1959, 55.

——. "In Memory of W. B. Yeats." In *Selected Poetry of W. H. Auden*. New York: Modern Library, 1959, 53.

Auden, W. H., and Louis Kronenberger, eds. *The Viking Book of Aphorisms*. New York: Viking, 1962, vii.

Badiou, Alain. *The Communist Hypothesis*. Trans. David Macey and Steven Corcoran. New York: Verso, 2010. Cited by Leon Wieseltier, "Non-Event," *New Republic*, June 30, 2010. http://www.newrepublic.com/article/politics / 75954/non-event.

Banville, John. "Homage to Philip Larkin." *New York Review of Books*, February 23, 2006. http://www.nybooks.com/articles/archives.2006/feb/23/ homage-to-philip-larkin.

Barrett, Andrea. "The Island." *Salmagundi* 166–67 (Spring–Summer 2010).

Barthes, Roland. "The Great Family of Man." In *Mythologies*. Trans. Richard Howard. New York: Hill and Wang, 1957, 198.

Bayley, John. "Canetti and Power." In *Selected Essays*. Cambridge: Cambridge University Press, 1984, 179.

Bellow, Saul. *Herzog*. New York: Viking, 1964, 75.

——. *Mr. Sammler's Planet*. London: Penguin, 1972, 215, 236, 286.

——. "What Kind of Day Did You Have?" In *Him with His Foot in His Mouth and Other Stories*. New York: Harper and Row, 1974, 96.

Benjamin, Walter. "On Some Motifs in Baudelaire." In *Illuminations*. New York: Houghton Mifflin Harcourt, 1968, 155.

Berlin, Isaiah. Cited in Seyla Benhabib, *The Reluctant Modernism of Hannah Arendt*. Lanham, Md.: Rowman and Littlefield, 2003, li.

Boyers, Robert. "An Excitable Woman." In *Excitable Women, Damaged Men*. New York: Turtle Point Press, 2005.

——. "Paintings of Voislav Stanic." In *Vojo Stanic: Sailing on Dreams*. Ed. Robert Boyers, Valeri S. Turchin, and Emir Kusturica. London: Philip Wilson, 2008.

Browning, Robert. "Andrea del Sarto." In *Selected Poetry of Robert Browning*. Ed. Kenneth L. Knickerbocker. New York: Modern Library, 1951, 345.

Burke, Kenneth. Cited in Denis Donoghue, *On Eloquence*. New Haven: Yale University Press, 2008, 1.

Canetti, Elias. *The Torch in My Ear*. Trans. Joachim Neugroschel. New York: Farrar, Straus and Giroux, 1982, 159.

Castle, Terry. "Desperately Seeking Susan." *London Review of Books*, March 17, 2005.

Cioran, E. M. In *The Viking Book of Aphorisms*. Ed. W. H. Auden and Louis Kronenberger. New York: Viking, 1962, 336.

Coetzee, J. M. *Disgrace*. London: Secker & Warburg, 1999, 4, 5, 32.

——. *Elizabeth Costello*. New York: Vintage, 2004, 22, 152–55, 167, 172, 224, 229.

Cohen, Derek. "Zionism and Apartheid." *Salmagundi* 157 (Winter 2008).

Cunningham, J. V. *Tradition and Poetic Structure*. Denver: Alan Swallow, 1960, 106–8.

Danto, Arthur. Cited in Alexander Nehamas, *Only a Promise of Happiness*. Princeton: Princeton University Press, 2007, 97.

Diski, Jenny. "Not a Pretty Sight." *London Review of Books*, January 24, 2008, 7.

Donoghue, Denis. *On Eloquence*. New Haven: Yale University Press, 2008, 2, 3, 45, 151.

Dostoyevsky, Fyodor. *The Possessed*. New York: Heritage Press, 1959.

Duchamp, Marcel. Cited in Arthur Danto, *Andy Warhol*. New Haven: Yale University Press, 2009, 56.

Eagleton, Terry. *Reason, Faith, and Revolution: Reflections on the God Debate*. New Haven: Yale University Press, 2009, 37, 111.

Eisenberg, Deborah. "Introduction." In *Memoirs of an Anti-Semite*, by Gregor von Rezzori. New York: New York Review of Books, 2008, xvi, xvii.

Eliot, T. S. "Little Gidding." In *Collected Poems; 1909–1962*. Boston: Houghton Mifflin Harcourt, 2014, 204.

——. *The Use of Poetry and the Use of Criticism*. London: Faber and Faber, 1933, 35.

——. "What Is a Classic?" In *Selected Prose of T. S. Eliot*. Ed. Frank Kermode. New York: Mariner Books, 1975, 120, 121.

Emerson, Ralph Waldo. In *The Viking Book of Aphorisms*. Ed. W. H. Auden and Louis Kronenberger. New York: Viking, 1962, 100.

Enzensberger, Hans Magnus. "The Industrialization of the Mind." In *Critical Essays*. New York: Continuum, 1982, 9, 10.

Farber, Leslie H. *The Ways of the Will*. New York: Basic Books, 2000, 17, 79.

Fardy, Jonathan. "Eye Candy / Food for Thought: Gonzales-Torres at Williams College." *Big RED & Shiny* 1, 80 (April 13, 2008). http://www.bigredandshiny.com/cgi-bin/BRS.cgi?section=review&issue=80&article=EYE_CANDYFOOD_FOR_10102054.

Flaubert, Gustave. Cited in Michael Fried, *Courbet's Realism*. Chicago: University of Chicago Press, 1992, 358.

——. *Madame Bovary*. Cambridge: Cambridge University Press, 1992.

Ford, Ford Madox. *The Good Soldier*. New York: Vintage, 1957, 12.

Foucault, Michel. "Sexual Choice, Sexual Act: Foucault and Homosexuality." In *Politics, Philosophy, Culture: Interviews and Other Writings 1977–1984*. Ed. Lawrence D. Kritzman. New York: Routledge, 1988, 298–99.

Fowles, John. Interview with Robert Foulke. "The Sense of the Past." *Salmagundi* 68–69 (Fall 1985–Winter 1986).

Freud, Sigmund. *Dora: An Analysis of a Case of Hysteria*. Ed. Philip Rieff. New York: Simon and Schuster, 1997.

——. *The Future of an Illusion*. New York: Classic House Books, 2009.

Gay, Peter. *Modernism*. New York: Norton, 2008, 4, 37, 129, 152.

Ginzburg, Natalia. *All Our Yesterdays*. Trans. Angus Davidson. New York: Arcade, 1952, 149.

Gombrich, E. H. *The Story of Art*. New York: Phaidon, 1950, 270–72.

Gordimer, Nadine. *Burger's Daughter*. New York: Viking, 1979.

Gray, John. *Gray's Anatomy: Selected Writings*. London: Penguin, 2010, 65–66, 263.

Greenberg, Clement. *Art and Culture*. Boston: Beacon Press, 1961, 205, 4.

——. Cited in Thierry de Duve, *Clement Greenberg Between the Lines*. Trans. Brian Holmes. Chicago: University of Chicago Press, 2010, 51, 52.

——. "Counter-Avant-Garde." In *Marcel Duchamp in Perspective*. Ed. J. Mashek. Englewood Cliffs, N.J.: Prentice-Hall, 1975, 103.

Guilbaut, Serge. *How New York Stole the Idea of Modern Art*. Trans. Arthur Goldhammer. Chicago: University of Chicago Press, 1985.

Hazlitt, William. "On the Want of Money." *Monthly Magazine* (January 1827).

Hedges, Chris. *Death of the Liberal Class*. New York: Nation Books, 2011, 205.

Hirsch, Edward. Cited on dust-jacket of Adam Zagajewski, *Mysticism for Beginners*. New York: Farrar, Straus and Giroux, 1997.

Hitchens, Christopher. "Mind the Gap." *Atlantic*, October 1, 2004. http://www.theatlantic .com/magazine/archive/2004/10/mind-the-gap/303487121.

Hollington, Michael. "Svevo, Joyce, and Modernist Time." In *Modernism: A Guide to European Literature 1890–1930*. Ed. Malcolm Bradbury and James Walter McFarlane. Harmondsworth; New York: Penguin, 1976, 433, 434, 436, 437.

Howe, Irving. "The Case of Ezra Pound." In *The Critical Point: On Literature and Culture*. New York: Horizon Press, 1973, 117.

——. *Politics and the Novel*. New York: Horizon Press, 1957, 11, 23.

Hustvedt, Siri. "The Islands of the Happy Few." *Salmagundi* 168–69 (Fall 2010–Winter 2011): 29.

James, Henry. *The Princess Casamassima*. New York: Harper & Row, 1959.

James, William. *The Varieties of Religious Experience*. London: Routledge, 2008, 388, 309–10.

Jardine, Lisa. Cited in John Banville, "Homage to Philip Larkin." *New York Review of Books*, February 23, 2006. http://www.nybooks.com/articles/archives/2006/feb/23 /homage-to-philip-larkin/.

Jarrell, Randall. "An Introduction to the Selected Poems of Williams Carlos Williams." In *Poetry and the Age*. New York: Vintage, 1959, 217, 218, 224.

——. "The Obscurity of the Poet." In *Poetry and the Age*. New York: Vintage, 1959.

——. "On Preparing to Read Kipling." In *Kipling, Auden, and Co.: Essays and Reviews 1935–1964*. New York: Farrar, Straus and Giroux, 1980, 332, 335.

Kael, Pauline. *The Age of Movies: Selected Writings of Pauline Kael*. New York: Library of America, 2011, 723.

Kandinsky, Wassily. *Complete Writings on Art 1 (1901–1921)*. Ed. Kenneth C. Lindsay and Peter Vergo. Boston: G. K. Hall, 1982, 360.

——. *Concerning the Spiritual in Art*. New York: Courier Dover, 1914. 19.

Kapuscinski, Ryszard. *The Other*. London: Verso, 2008, 37, 57, 88.

——. *The Shadow of the Sun*. Trans. Klara Glowczewska. London, Penguin, 2007, 188, 252, 253.

——. *Travels with Herodotus*. New York: Vintage, 2008, 131, 146.

Kermode, Frank. "Beckett Country." *New York Review of Books*, March 19, 1984.

——. *Concerning E. M. Forster*. New York: Farrar, Straus and Giroux, 2010, 128.

Kincaid, Jamaica. *A Small Place*. New York: Farrar, Straus and Giroux, 1988, 4, 8, 14, 16, 17, 53–55.

Koestler, Arthur. *Darkness at Noon*. New York: Bantam, 1986.

Kolakowski, Leszek. *Main Currents of Marxism: The Breakdown*. London: Oxford University Press, 1981, 523, 530.

——. "Utopianism Redux." *American Interest*, June 1, 2006. http://www.the-american -interest.com/articles/2006/06/0/utopianism-redux/.

Kraus, Karl. Cited in Roberto Calasso, *The Forty-Nine Steps*. Minneapolis: University of Minnesota Press, 1973, 48.

——. In *The Viking Book of Aphorisms*. Ed. W. H. Auden and Louis Kronenberger. New York: Viking, 1962, 356.

Kundera, Milan. *The Book of Laughter and Forgetting*. Trans. Michael Henry Heim. New York: Penguin, 1980, 37.

Larkin, Philip. *The Complete Poems*. New York: Farrar, Straus and Giroux, 2012, 115.

——. Cited in Martin Amis, "Don Juan in Hull." *New Yorker*, July 12, 1993, 77, 79.

La Rouchefoucauld. Cited in Tzvetan Todorov, "Exposures." *New Republic*, April 21, 2003. http://www.newrepublic.com/article/exposures.

Leavis, F. R. *The Great Tradition*. New York: New York University Press, 1963, 63.

Lessing, Doris. "Against Utopia: An Interview with Doris Lessing." *Salmagundi* 130–31 (Spring–Summer 2001): 59–74.

Lévinas, Emmanuel. Cited in Ryzsard Kapuscinski, *The Other*. London: Verso, 2008, 34, 35.

Levy, Bernard-Henri. *War, Evil and the End of History*. Trans. Charlotte Mandell. Hoboken, N.J.: Melville House, 2009.

Lodge, David. "The Language of Modernist Fiction: Metaphor and Metonymy." In *Modernism: A Guide to European Literature 1890–1930*. Ed. Malcolm Bradbury and James Walter McFarlane. Harmondsworth: Penguin, 1976, 490.

Lopate, Phillip. "How to End an Essay." *Salmagundi* 168–69 (Fall 2010–Winter 2011): 136, 137.

——. "The Movies and Spiritual Life." In *Portrait of My Body*. New York: Doubleday, 1996, 79–81.

Lucretius. Cited in "Of the Useful and the Honorable." In *The Complete Essays of Montaigne*, by Michel de Montaigne. Stanford: Stanford University Press, 1958, 60.

Lukács, George. "Tolstoy and the Development of Realism." In *Studies in European Realism*. New York: Grosset and Dunlap, 1964, 190.

Luethy, Herbert. "Montaigne, on the Art of Being Truthful." In *Encounters: An Anthology from the First Ten Years of Encounter Magazine*. Ed. Stephen Spender, Irving Kristol, and Melvin Lasky. New York: Basic Books, 1963, 209, 210.

MacDonald, Dwight. Cited in Franklin Foer, "The Browbeater." *New Republic*, December 15, 2011. http://www.newrepublic.com/article/books-and-arts/magazine/97782/dwight-macdonald-midcult-masscult.

MacIntyre, Alasdair. *After Virtue: A Study in Moral Theory*. London: Bloomsbury Academic, 2013, 147.

Malevich, Kazimir. Cited in Hilton Kramer, "Art, Revolution, and Kazimir Malevich." *New Criterion* (November 1990).

Mann, Thomas. *Death in Venice*. Trans. Michael Henry Heim. New York: Harper Collins, 2004.

——. "Goethe and Tolstoy." In *Essays*. Trans. H. T. Lowe-Porter. New York: Vintage, 1977, 177.

——. Cited in Harold Rosenberg, *Tradition of the New*. New York: Da Capo Press, 1994, 130.

Marcuse, Herbert. *One-Dimensional Man*. Boston: Beacon Press, 1964, 6.

Marinetti, F. T. "The Futurist Manifesto." In *On Ugliness*, by Umberto Eco. London: Harvill Secker, 2007, 370.

McEwan, Ian. *Saturday*. New York: Anchor Books, 2006, 39–41.

Melville, Herman. *Bartleby the Scrivener*. London: Hesperus Press, 2007.

Mill, John Stuart. "The Subjection of Women." In *Three Essays*. London: Oxford University Press, 1975.

Montaigne, Michel de. Cited in David Quint, *Montaigne and the Quality of Mercy: Ethical and Political Themes in the Essais*. Princeton: Princeton University Press, 1998, 54.

Motherwell, Robert. Cited in Peter Gay, *Modernism*. New York: Norton, 2008, 167.

Musil, Robert. *The Man Without Qualities*. New York: Capricorn Books, 1965, xii, 2, 12, 24, 80, 139.

Naipaul, V. S. *Among the Believers: An Islamic Journey*. New York: Knopf, 1981.

——. *A Bend in the River*. New York: Vintage, 1989, 91.

——. *Guerrillas*. New York: Vintage, 1980.

——. *Half a Life*. New York: Knopf, 2001, 163.

——. *A House for Mr. Biswas*. New York: Knopf, 1983.

——. Cited in Elizabeth Hardwick, "Meeting V. S. Naipaul." *New York Times Book Review*, May 13, 1979, 5.

Nehamas, Alexander. *Only a Promise of Happiness*. Princeton: Princeton University Press, 2007, 124, 132.

Neu, Jerome. "Pride and Identity." In *A Tear Is an Intellectual Thing*. London: Oxford University Press, 2000, 108.

Newman, Barnett. *Selected Writings and Interviews*. Berkeley: University of California Press, 1992, 240.

Newman, Charles. *The Post-Modern Aura: The Act of Fiction in an Age of Inflation*. Evanston: Northwestern University Press, 1985.

Newman, John Henry. "An Essay in Aid of a Grammar of Assent." In *Victorian Literature*. Ed. G. B. Tennyson and Donald J. Gray. New York: Macmillan, 1976, 445.

Nietzsche, Friedrich. *The Antichrist*. New York: Knopf, 1920, 148.

——. Cited in Patrick J. Keane, *Emerson, Romanticism, and Intuitive Reason*. Columbia: University of Missouri Press, 2005, 170, 171.

——. *The Gay Science*. New York: Vintage, 1974, 266.

——. In *The Viking Book of Aphorisms*. Ed. W. H. Auden and Louis Kronenberger. New York: Viking, 1962, 321.

Oates, Joyce Carol. "Art and Ethics." *Salmagundi* 111 (Summer 1996): 76, 77.

Ondaatje, Michael. *Anil's Ghost*. New York: Knopf, 2000, 43, 203.

O'Neill, Joseph. *Netherland*. New York: Vintage, 2008, 5, 6, 212, 248, 249.

Orwell, George. "Inside the Whale." In *The Collected Essays, Journalism, and Letters of George Orwell: An Age Like This*, vol. 1. Ed. Sonia Orwell and Ian Angus. New York: Harcourt, Brace and World, 1968, 495, 498, 508.

——. "Review: The Heart of the Matter by Graham Greene." In *The Collected Essays, Journalism, and Letters of George Orwell: In Front of Your Nose 1945–1950*, vol. 4. Ed. Sonia Orwell and Ian Angus. New York: Harcourt, Brace and World, 1968, 441.

Pamuk, Orhan. Quoted in Robert Boyers, "Between the Lines." *Lapham's Quarterly* (Fall 2012).

——. *Snow*. Trans. Maureen Freely. New York: Knopf, 2011, 46, 71, 76, 170. http://www.laphamsquarterly.org/essays/between-the-lines.php?page=all.

Pater, Walter. *Selected Writings of Walter Pater*. Ed. Harold Bloom. New York: Columbia University Press, 1974, 60.

Paulin, Tom. Cited in John Banville, "Homage to Philip Larkin." *New York Review of Books*, February 23, 2006. http://www.nybooks.com/articles/archives/2006/feb/23/homage-to-philip-larkin/.

Paz, Octavio. *The Labyrinth of Solitude*. New York: Grove Press, 1961, 52.

Perl, Jed. "Laissez-Faire Aesthetics." *New Republic*, February 5, 2007. http://www.newrepublic.com/article/laissez-faire-aesthetics-what-money-doing-or-how-the-artworld-lost-its-mind.

——. "Postcards from Nowhere." *New Republic*, June 25, 2008. http://www.new-republic.com/article/postcards-nowhere.

Pettingell, Phoebe. "Philip Larkin: A Writer's Life." *New Leader*, November 15, 1993. http://www.highbeam.com/doc/1G1-14714630.html.

Phillips, Adam. *Monogamy*. New York: Vintage, 1996, 30, 46, 53, 56, 107, 121.

——. *Promises, Promises: Essays on Psychoanalysis and Literature*. New York: Basic Books, 2001, 20–24, 27, 31, 32.

Pinsky, Robert. "At Pleasure Bay." In *The Figured Wheel: New and Collected Poems 1966–1996*. New York: Farrar, Straus and Giroux, 1996, 98.

——. "Exit." In *The Figured Wheel: New and Collected Poems 1966–1996*. New York: Farrar, Straus and Giroux, 1996, 74.

——. "Immortal Longings." In *The Figured Wheel: New and Collected Poems 1966–1996*. New York: Farrar, Straus and Giroux, 1996, 73.

——. "The Refinery." In *The Figured Wheel: New and Collected Poems 1966–1996*. New York: Farrar, Straus and Giroux, 1996, 91.

——. "Work Song." *Salmagundi* 148–49 (Fall 2005–Winter 2006): 197, 198.

Plato. *Phaedrus*. In *Plato: Complete Works*. Ed. John M. Cooper. Trans. Alexander Nehamas and Paul Woodruff. Cambridge, Mass.; Hackett, 1995, 238–39.

Pritchard, William. "The Bleakest Poet." *New York Times Book Review*, August 1, 1993. http://www.nytimes.com/1993/08/01/books/the-bleakest-poet.html.

Proust, Marcel. Cited in Joseph Epstein, *Snobbery: The American Version*. Boston: Houghton Mifflin, 2002, 251.

Rezzori, Gregor von. *Memoirs of an Anti-Semite*. New York: New York Review of Books, 2008, 223.

Richter, Gerhard. "Notes." In *Beauty*. Ed. Dave Beech. London: Whitechapel Gallery; Cambridge, Mass.: MIT Press, 2009, 181.

Rieff, Philip. *Charisma: The Gift of Grace and How It Has Been Taken Away from Us*. New York: Pantheon Books, 2007, 5, 29, 90, 134, 140, 171, 220, 222, 225.

——. *Fellow Teachers*. New York: Harper and Row, 1972, "Prefatory Note," 12, 24, 36.

——. "From: 'Fellow Teachers.'" In *A Salmagundi Reader*. Ed. Robert Boyers and Peggy Boyers. Bloomington: Indiana University Press, 1983, 28, 39.

——. *The Triumph of the Therapeutic: Uses of Faith After Freud*. Chicago: University of Chicago Press, 1987, 6, 8, 11, 12.

Rivers, Larry, and David Hockney. *Theories and Documents of Contemporary Art: A Sourcebook of Artists' Writings*. Ed. Kristine Stiles and Peter Selz. Berkeley: University of California Press, 1996, 224, 225.

Rorty, Richard. *Philosophy as Cultural Politics*, vol. 4: *Philosophical Papers*. Cambridge: Cambridge University Press, 2007, 38, 60.

Rosenberg, Harold. "The American Action Painters." In *The Tradition of the New*. New York: McGraw Hill, 1965, 34, 37.

——. "Criticism and Its Premises." In *Art on the Edge*. Chicago: University of Chicago Press, 1983, 136, 138, 140, 141.

——. "The Herd of Independent Minds." In *The Tradition of the New*. New York: McGraw Hill, 1965, 207.

——. "Warhol: Art's Other Self." In *Art on the Edge*. Chicago: University of Chicago Press, 1983, 99, 101.

Roth, Philip. *American Pastoral*. Boston: Houghton Mifflin, 1997, 86.

Rougemont, Denis de. *Love in the Western World*. Trans. Montgomery Belgion. New York: Harcourt, Brace, 1940, 321.

Rubin, Alissa J. "How Baida Wanted to Die." *New York Times Magazine*, August 12, 2009.

Rushdie, Salmon. On dust-jacket of Jamaica Kincaid, *A Small Place*. New York: Farrar, Straus and Giroux, 1988.

Ruskin, John. *Sesame and Lilies, Lecture 2*. New Haven: Yale University Press, 2002, 77.

Said, Edward. "Beginnings." *Salmagundi* 8 (Fall 1968): 44, 45.

——. "Intellectuals in the Post-Colonial World." *Salmagundi* 70–71 (Spring–Summer 1986): 53.

Santayana, George. "The Poetry of Barbarism." In *Interpretations of Poetry and Religion*. Cambridge, Mass.: MIT Press, 1989, 194, 107, 108, 113–16, 126.

Santayana, George. In *The Viking Book of Aphorisms*. Ed. W. H. Auden and Louis Kronenberger. New York: Viking, 1962, 289.

Sartre, Jean. *What Is Literature?* New York: Harper & Row, 1947.

Scarry, Elaine. *On Beauty and Being Just*. Princeton: Princeton University Press, 2013, 87.

Schjeldahl, Peter. "The Joker: Richard Prince at the Guggenheim." *New Yorker*, October 15, 2007.

Smith, Zadie. "Two Directions for the Novel." In *Changing My Mind: Occasional Essays*. New York: Penguin, 2009, 77.

Sontag, Susan. *Against Interpretation*. New York: Farrar, Straus and Giroux, 1966, 6, 7.

——. "Mind as Passion." In *Under the Sign of Saturn: Essays*. New York: Farrar, Straus and Giroux, 1980, 191, 192, 203.

——. "On Beauty." In *At the Same Time: Essays and Speeches*. New York: Farrar, Straus and Giroux, 2007, 4, 5, 8–10, 12.

——. "The Salmagundi Interview." In *A Susan Sontag Reader*. New York: Farrar, Straus and Giroux, 1982, 343.

——. "Susan Sontag and Philip Fisher: A Conversation." *Salmagundi* 139–40 (Summer–Fall 2003): 183, 184.

Stein, Gertrude. Cited in Donald Sutherland, "The Pleasures of Gertrude Stein." *New York Review of Books*, May 30, 1974.

Steiner, George. *The Portage to San Cristobal of A. H.* New York: Simon and Schuster, 1981.

Steiner, Wendy. *Venus in Exile: The Rejection of Beauty in Twentieth-Century Art*. Chicago: University of Chicago Press, 2002, xv, xxi.

Stella, Frank. Cited in Carl André, "Preface." In *Sixteen Americans*. New York: Museum of Modern Art, 1959.

Stendhal (Marie-Henri Beyle). *The Charterhouse of Parma*. Trans. Richard Howard. New York: Modern Library, 1999.

——. "The Duchess of Palliano." In *The Abbess of Castro and Other Tales*. Trans. C. K. Scott Moncrieff. New York: Boni & Liveright, 1926, 208.

Stevens, Wallace. "The Noble Rider and the Sound of Words." In *The Necessary Angel: Essays on Reality and the Imagination*. New York: Knopf, 1951, 27.

Svevo, Italo. *Zeno's Conscience*. Trans. Beryl de Zoete. New York: Vintage, 1989, vii, 74, 138.

Tischner, Józef. Cited in Ryzsard Kapuscinski, *The Other*. Trans. Antonia Lloyd-Jones. New York: Verso, 2008, 67.

Todorov, Tzvetan. *Eloge du quotidien: Essai sur le pienture hollandaise du XVIIe siècle*. Paris: Seuil, 1993.

——. "Exposures." *New Republic*, April 21, 2003, 29, 30.

Tolstoy, Leo. *Anna Karenina*. New York: Norton, 1970, 32, 33.

Trilling, Lionel. "The Fate of Pleasure." In *Beyond Culture*. New York: Viking, 1965, 58–60, 65, 68, 71–73, 79, 81, 85, 86.

——. "On the Teaching of Modern Literature." In *Beyond Culture*. New York: Viking, 1965.

——. *Sincerity and Authenticity*. Cambridge, Mass.: Harvard University Press, 1972, 166.

Turgenev, Ivan. *Fathers and Sons*. New York: Norton, 1996.

Vargas Llosa, Mario. *The Real Life of Alejandro Mayta*. Trans. Alfred MacAdam. New York: Farrar, Straus and Giroux, 1986.

Vendler, Helen. "I. A. Richards at Harvard." *Boston Review* (April 1981). http://www.boston review.net/BR06.2/vendler.html.

Vidal, Gore. Cited in Robert Boyers, "Gore Vidal: Wit and the Work of Criticism." In *Gore Vidal: Writer Against the Grain*. Ed. Jay Parini. New York: Columbia University Press, 1992, 165.

Wieseltier, Leon. "Washington Diarist: After Nobility." *New Republic*, October 6, 2011. http://www.newrepublic.com/article/politics/magazine/94966/protests-politics -egypt-israel-spain-india.

Wilde, Oscar. *The Picture of Dorian Gray*. New York: Simon and Schuster, 2014, 4, 26.

Williams, William Carlos. Cited in Robert Boyers, "The Little Magazine in Its Place: Literary Culture and Anarchy." *Triquarterly* 43 (Fall 1978): 53.

Wittgenstein, Ludwig. *Tractatus*. London: Routledge & Kegan Paul, 1955, episode 7.

Woolf, Virginia. "Mr. Bennett and Mrs. Brown." In *Essential Theories of Fiction*. Ed. Michael J. Hoffman and Patrick D. Murphy. Durham: Duke University Press, 2005, 33.

Wordsworth, William. *The Prelude*. New York: Norton, 1977, 217.

Zagajewski, Adam. "December Wind." In *Mysticism for Beginners*. Trans. Clare Cavanagh. New York: Farrar, Straus and Giroux, 1997, 37.

——. *A Defense of Ardor*. Trans. Clare Cavanagh. New York: Farrar, Straus and Giroux, 2004, 26, 32, 33, 39.

——. "Holy Saturday in Paris." In *Mysticism for Beginners*. Trans. Clare Cavanagh. New York: Farrar, Straus and Giroux, 1997, 67.

——. "On Swimming." In *Mysticism for Beginners*. Trans. Clare Cavanagh. New York: Farrar, Straus and Giroux, 1997, 66.

——. "Self-Portrait." In *Mysticism for Beginners*. Trans. Clare Cavanagh. New York: Farrar, Straus and Giroux, 1997, 36.

Žižek, Slavoj. *Violence*. New York: Picador, 2008.

INDEX